MW01485321

# THE
# BLUE FOOD
# COOKBOOK

FROM THE PRODUCERS OF

*Hope* IN THE WATER

THE

# BLUE FOOD
# COOKBOOK

HARVEST

*An Imprint of* WILLIAM MORROW

# Delicious Seafood Recipes
for a Sustainable Future

## Andrew Zimmern and Barton Seaver

Photographs by Eric Wolfinger • Illustrations by Yulia Shevchenko
Project management by Kathryn Kennedy Rivera

Without limiting the exclusive rights of any author, contributor or the publisher of this publication, any unauthorized use of this publication to train generative artificial intelligence (AI) technologies is expressly prohibited. HarperCollins also exercise their rights under Article 4(3) of the Digital Single Market Directive 2019/790 and expressly reserve this publication from the text and data mining exception.

The material on linked sites referenced in this book is the author's own. HarperCollins disclaims all liability that may result from the use of the material contained at those sites. All such material is supplemental and not part of the book. The author reserves the right to close the website in their sole discretion following October 2025.

THE BLUE FOOD COOKBOOK. Copyright © 2025 by Fed By Blue, a project of Multiplier. Foreword © 2025 by Shailene Woodley. All rights reserved. No part of this book may be used or reproduced in any manner whatsoever without written permission except in the case of brief quotations embodied in critical articles and reviews. For information, address HarperCollins Publishers, 195 Broadway, New York, NY 10007. In Europe, HarperCollins Publishers, Macken House, 39/40 Mayor Street Upper, Dublin 1, D01 C9W8, Ireland.

HarperCollins books may be purchased for educational, business, or sales promotional use. For information, please email the Special Markets Department at SPsales@harpercollins.com.

hc.com

FIRST EDITION

Designed by Tai Blanche with Shawn Scott
Photography by Eric Wolfinger
Project Manager: Kathryn Kennedy Rivera
Culinary Assistant: Michelle Minori
Prop Styling by Alison Attenborough
Illustrations on pages i, vi, 1, 2, 11, 20, 21, 24, 26, 27, 30, 33, 41, 47, 57, 58, 119, 123, 135, 193, 209, 259, and 291 by Yulia Shevchenko; halibut line art on pages 23 and 24 from the Archives of Pearson Scott Foresman; all others © stock.adobe.com.

_____

Library of Congress Cataloging-in-Publication Data

Names: Zimmern, Andrew author | Seaver, Barton author | Wolfinger, Eric
   photographer | Shevcenko, Yulia illustrator
Title: The blue food cookbook : delicious seafood recipes for a sustainable
 future / Andrew Zimmern and Barton Seaver ;
  photographs by Eric Wolfinger ; illustrations by Yulia Shevcenko.
Other titles: Blue food cookbook
Description: First edition. | New York, NY : Harvest, an imprint of William
  Morrow, [2025] | Includes index.
Identifiers: LCCN 2025009183 (print) | LCCN 2025009184 (ebook) | ISBN
  9780063379770 hardcover | ISBN 9780063379794 ebook
Subjects: LCSH: Cooking (Seafood) | LCGFT: Cookbooks
Classification: LCC TX747 .Z566 2025 (print) | LCC TX747 (ebook) | DDC
  641.6/92--dc23/eng/20250327
LC record available at https://lccn.loc.gov/2025009183
LC ebook record available at https://lccn.loc.gov/2025009184

_____

ISBN 978-0-06-337977-0

Printed in Malaysia

25 26 27 28 29 IMG 10 9 8 7 6 5 4 3 2 1

*Dedicated to the fishers, water farmers, and innovators
whose commitment to nurturing our blue food system
ensures a sustainable future for us all*

# Contents

## Part 1
## A Guide to Responsible Blue Foods

## Part 2
## The Seafood Cook's Provisions

# Foreword

**By Shailene Woodley, activist and actor**

As I grew up in Los Angeles, the ocean played a massive role in my childhood. Whether I was camping along the coast and waking up to the sunrise over the water, or spending hours chasing waves with a boogie board, the ocean always brought an abundance of awe and excitement. I was fortunate to grow up with a mom who had an extraordinary respect for the power of the sea but had no fear when it came to knowing it with adventurous intimacy. I watched her free dive along vibrant reefs, snorkel alongside sharks and technicolor coral, and body surf in towering waves— her freedom gave me permission to find my own.

In my late teens, I moved to Hawai'i on my own for a couple of years. I was fortunate to know and live with Indigenous Hawaiians and other locals devoted to living symbiotically within the ecosystem around them. I watched my local friends rely on the abundance of the ocean for their food—spearfishing, collecting seaweed, working in the business of salt . . . I was blown away. (I should note: The state of Hawai'i as a whole still has a long way to go in terms of establishing a holistic exchange with the land and waters they govern.)

Since then, I have spent years on shorelines and weeks on various sailboats and vessels hundreds of nautical miles from land. I have watched communities across the world rely on their relationship with the ocean for food and survival. The ocean has always been humanity's largest food bank, and wherever people have access to clean water, they should be able to harvest food to nourish their families.

* * *

It is no secret that our oceans are undergoing immense transformations right now. What used to be is no longer, and what could be is truly up to the active choices we make in our individual lives today.

Before working on the series *Hope in the Water*, I wasn't well educated on how sustainably harvested blue foods could play a significant role in aiding the future of our planet. I learned so much working alongside Andrew Zimmern and PBS. Off the coast of Southern California, I dove with local sea urchin divers and witnessed firsthand how creativity and care could not only restore the ecosystem of our local coral reefs but also improve human nutrition. The divers collect overpopulated purple "zombie" urchins from the seabed floor and bring them to a local abalone farmer, who, through careful and passionate technique, turns them into a delectable delicacy for people to enjoy.

I was deeply moved by how easily and efficiently this process worked. Our native reefs benefit from losing some of the invasive urchins, while our bellies are nourished by them. A light bulb went off for me: by employing practices focused on blue food, both our oceans and our people can thrive.

The destruction of our waters affects not only the environment but also humanity, leading to malnutrition, human trafficking, and forced migration. Blue foods like shellfish, seaweed, and salmon can nourish vulnerable populations and offer sustainable solutions. Ensuring healthy food accessibility is crucial for both thriving communities and a safer future for our oceans and ecosystems.

Global food systems currently use three-quarters of the planet's fresh water, occupy half of the ice-free land, and emit a quarter of greenhouse gas emissions. In order to feed the future without overwhelming planetary boundaries, this environmental footprint must be reduced. Blue foods offer an opportunity to contribute to more sustainable diets and a flourishing future. It's a complicated puzzle, but we can solve it together by understanding the enormous potential of our individual choices and lives.

I often hear, "I'm overwhelmed. How can I help the oceans?" The answer may not be glamorous, but it starts with us—each of us and our communities. By exploring new ways to experience seafood and learning more about blue foods, we can all contribute to safeguarding the health of the oceans and future generations.

In these pages, you'll learn how getting to know your local fishmonger or fisherman can have a significant impact. You'll also discover how expanding your palate beyond salmon, tuna, and shrimp not only benefits the natural world but also impresses your taste buds and boosts the nutrition your body receives. Supporting marine-protected areas, enjoying seaweed chips, and expanding your knowledge of blue foods will help restore abundance to our oceans.

*I am grateful to be on this journey with you!*

# Introduction

**Hope in the Water**

We have traveled far and wide, seen places where the sea serves sustenance and survival. We've stood shoulder to shoulder with those who have dedicated their lives to harvesting the bounty of our waters. The stories of those people and the deep connection they have with their environment are the cornerstone of what this book represents. This is not just a collection of recipes—it's a narrative about why seafood matters, how it has sustained cultures for millennia, and why we need to protect and enhance it for generations to come.

Many of the stories we hear about seafood are of the deprivations and degradations we've caused. In New England, where the fabled cod, truly the first heritage food of our colonial nation, is no longer found in the abundance described by early settlers as competing with water for space. And the cod are not coming back. Such stories of depletion, opportunism, and ignorance of the impact of our actions are a too-true fish tale told the world over. These stories need to be remembered as part of our heritage. The plundered abundance must be mourned as a warning for what's within our power to cause. But our oceans are resilient. As are we. The riches-to-rags path can be reversed. And from these stories we author a new chapter about how we can and will do better. We place our hope in the water because we are doing better. And that's why this book. That's why now is the time to tell the stories of hope we find in our waters. *Blue food*, a term we use to describe this next chapter of seafood, is the banner under which this conversation will move forward.

## Seafood That Matters

There is yet much to do to improve our relationship with our oceans, lakes, and rivers. We are fully aware of the threats to our oceans from overfishing, pollution, habitat destruction, and climate change as well as the threats to the people who ply them. While there is much to fix about seafood, we know that we can use seafood to fix much about so much else. With human population rising, agriculture reaching dangerous limitations and massively contributing to the climate crisis, and the global health crisis we face due to modern diets: to do more of what we've been doing won't work. Food systems are broken. Blue food systems are a fix. And blue will feed ourselves and our global neighbors food that helps us thrive in an environment that is stable, resilient, and abundant. As we acknowledge the ever-increasing importance of blue foods in our future, it's wise to look back and think that our past began along the water. Some of the earliest evidence of human presence is found along our coasts. And we humans have done so much to conquer the planet since those first days of piling oyster shells and fish bones in middens and caves. And now as we face the hard limits of what our lands can provide, it's time we smart humans evolve our food systems to return to the tides where it all began.

This book is a delicious manifestation of our journeys, our learning, our cooking, our hope. In these pages we will show why blue foods matter and acknowledge innovations in both the ancient industries of wild fisheries and aquaculture. There is ample cause for celebration, and what better way to do this than by cooking up a meal?

Hope is the foundation upon which sustainability takes form. This book is intended to inspire and marshal a community of cooks who know what a relationship with our oceans can and should be. Our mission, as manifested in these pages, is that this generation of sentinel stewards will care, cook, consume, communicate, and vote.

This book revels in all that is good about seafood, but more than that, it's a call to action. We believe that by embracing seafood as a central part of our diets, we can create a more sustainable, more delicious future. We hope that the stories, recipes, and ideas in these pages inspire you to cook more seafood, to think about where it comes from, and to share it with your family and friends.

## Cooking with Purpose

We've designed this cookbook to be accessible, practical, and, most importantly, purposeful. You'll find that our inspirations are global, taken from our vast experiences as travelers, cooks, anthropologists, and neighbors. Many of the recipes you'll find here are perfect for busy weeknights—simple, quick, and delicious. We often say that "less is more," and that's certainly true when it comes to cooking seafood. Gentle heat, short cooking times, and the right combination of ingredients can transform even the simplest effort into a culinary masterpiece.

In this book, we've organized the recipes around the idea that many species of fish can be used interchangeably, depending on what's freshest and most sustainable where you live. If snapper isn't available, why not try tautog or barramundi? By diversifying the seafood we consume, we not only support better fishing practices, we also increase our chances of getting the highest quality product. But beyond the simplicity, there's a deeper message here. These recipes are an invitation to use your choices in the kitchen to make a difference.

Sustainability as a concept, and its metrics, can be overly complex and confusing. But the action of sustainability is really quite simple: It is that of being a good neighbor. And what better way to be a good neighbor than to feed others. Food is love for both the people we serve and the planet that sustains us.

## Why Now?

With the mounting threats to our oceans, it's easy to feel overwhelmed. But there is hope. We've seen it in the protected waters of Toubakouta in the Gambia, where life in abundance is returning to areas once made barren by fishing efforts. We've seen it in the evolution of aquaculture, where best-in-class producers are pioneering innovations to meet the growing demand for seafood without further depleting wild stocks. We see it in the work of organizations such as Minorities in Aquaculture and the Native Conservancy helping to rematriate people to their rightful place in our coastal waters. In Bangladesh, hatcheries are producing mud crabs for the first time; this graces local fishers with a safe, reliable income, one that isn't tied to coastal erosion or stock preservation. The list goes on and on.

In the face of climate change, overfishing, and pollution, we need to do more than just talk about sustainability. We need to act. And that's where you come in. By choosing blue foods and learning how to cook them and appreciate their nuances, you become part of the solution. This book charts a course, filled with recipes, stories, and insights, that will help you build a deeper connection with our waters, the people who ply them, and the food they provide. All the good that this way swims are but ideas—community, health, sustainability— until a reader picks up this book and cooks these recipes. At that point these ideas become actions. We give you permission to fall in love with blue foods. To embrace our blue bounty to achieve our health, a healthy relationship with our environment, and stronger ties to our community. Hope is abundant in our waters. So, let's dive in, deliciously.

**—Andrew Zimmern and Barton Seaver**

# Part 1
# A Guide to Responsible Blue Foods

# How to Buy and Store Sustainable Seafood

COOKING GREAT SEAFOOD DISHES starts with buying great quality seafood. There is no trick, tip, or technique that can make up for poor quality product. Buying great quality seafood is ultimately easy, and it's available to everyone in a range of product forms, and can be found in any grocery store, specialty shop, or big box market. Hey, we'd argue the only sustainable food you can find in the gas station is sustainable seafood (in the form of canned seafood).

There are a few fundamental aspects of buying great quality product that will help you ensure that you are always spending dollars wisely. Before we get into the details, let's first talk about some overarching things you should be looking for.

First up, is the store inviting, clean, well-lit? Does it smell like fish? (If it does, turn around and walk out.) Or does it smell good, like a pleasant sea breeze? Yes? Then take a look at the people behind the counter. Are they wearing clean aprons and gloves? Are they smiling? If all of these details inspire confidence in you, awesome, you're more than halfway there. While these points apply to the fresh counter, don't forget that great quality and sustainable seafood is found in three places in the store. So be sure to check out the canned foods and the frozen aisles as well!

Additionally, before you even start looking at the seafood, introduce yourself to the person behind the counter. When you are on a first name basis with the expert, you've harnessed the power of a personal relationship and created a dynamic of responsibility. Bottom line is, people are a lot more likely to steer you in the right direction if they know you appreciate them. Ask that person, what's freshest and best? And then understand that you have a responsibility to heed that advice.

Now onto the details of the product itself. Seafood is sold in many forms, given the great diversity of species available. Each category has its own parameters for quality. As most seafood in America is bought in fillet form, let's start there.

# Fillets

- The counter and its immediate environment and the fish itself smell right. (What does right smell like? It gives no sense of doubt!)

- The fillets have been arranged in an orderly way, at least not haphazardly heaped on top of each other. Some stores take great pride in artful displays, assuredly a good sign.

- The fillets are not in contact with any liquid, but are sitting above the ice in pans or sitting on cold blocks such as marble. Contact with water hastens spoilage and leeches flavor.

- There is no gaping or torn flesh in the fillets, which is a sign of age and/or mishandling.

- The flesh and the skin (if present) are lustrous, having a slight sheen.

- The flesh is uniform and consistent in color, showing no sign of age or oxidation, such as a slight browning along the edges or bleaching due to contact with water. Nor should there be any green spotting indicative of poor handling during the gutting process.

- When fresh, the fillets are still taut and firm. They should be resilient to gentle pressure, bouncing back after a slight press of the thumb. Age leads to flabby texture, and if you can see your thumbprint in the fillet, it is not a good sign. (Maybe ask the person behind the counter to do this so you aren't touching all the food.)

- If the placard indicates that the fillets were previously frozen, ask when they were thawed. And don't be afraid to ask for still-frozen if it works for your schedule, as the freshness clock has not yet been started.

# Whole Fish

Whenever you have the opportunity to buy whole fish, we highly recommend you do so. One of the most exciting aspects of seafood is discovering the range of tastes, textures, and aromas offered by myriad species. And that excitement is not just between species but within an individual fish. For example, the top and bottom fillets of flatfish, such as flounder, can have subtle nuances to their flavor. But there's also more to a fish than just a fillet. And there are several recipes in this book to help you take advantage of whole fish cookery. When appraising the quality of whole fish, many of the same cues as above apply, but there are a few additional ways to evaluate quality:

The fish smells right.

- The fish smells right. (Right equals no doubt.)

- The eyes are vibrant. (Though not always clear, as in some species the eyes can cloud even when pristine.)

- The gills are moist and bright in color (ask the attendant to show you).

- The scales firmly adhere to the skin.

- The outside of the fish has a lustrous sheen.

- The fins are mostly intact and pliable.

- If gutted, the belly cavity is clean and free of blood and green bile stains (in most markets whole fish is gutted before it is sold).

- The flesh is resilient to pressure and bounces back after a light touch (ask the attendant to do this for you).

# Shellfish and Bivalves

Many of the same cues that apply to fillets and whole fish equally apply to shellfish, such as shrimp and scallops (most often sold out of their shell). When it comes to whole bivalves, you're almost always buying live creatures, such as mussels, clams, and oysters. These species can maintain their quality even for weeks out of water if properly stored. They do so by keeping their shells tightly closed, a sign of remaining vigor. If there are any that are slightly open, if they are still worth eating, a gentle tap will prompt the shells to close quickly. Because you're buying multiple creatures, not all of them will always make the journey from store to plate. It's important to check all bivalves again just before cooking and discard any that do not close. These are the primary ways to evaluate quality:

- The shells are moist and don't look dried out and brittle.

- They are sitting proud above any ice, not resting in any liquid. (This won't always be true for scallops, as they do exude a bit of moisture, but this should not be excessive.)

- Scallops, being sold as shucked meats, will exude a bit of moisture, especially because many scallops are treated with water retention agents. This is perfectly legal, though we don't recommend these from a culinary perspective. Look for scallops that are marked "untreated."

# Shrimp

Shrimp come in a vast variety of market forms, from whole animal, head-on/shell-on, and in every step of potential processing, such as meat or even just the shells. All the same environmental and general quality characteristics as above apply here. Given that shrimp are particularly perishable, it is entirely likely that what is on offer was previously frozen. Fresh shrimp are an absolute delicacy and worth seeking out. But generally, when frozen properly, they don't lose much of their charisma, and there is greater assurance of ultimate quality. Given that shrimp come frozen and they're often individually quick-frozen, meaning you could pick out just three shrimp from the bag they came in, you might as well opt for the still-frozen product. This is not an inconvenience, as they will thaw very quickly and not delay your dinner. These are the primary ways to evaluate quality:

- If the head is present, it is consistent in color.

- Any black spotting you notice in the head is a sure sign of degradation. This doesn't necessarily mean it's bad, but it's a sign to use them right away if you so choose.

- Eyes and tentacles are mostly intact.

- If the head is missing but the shell is present on the tail, the swimmerets (legs) underneath are generally intact, a sign of proper handling.

- The shell (if intact) does not look dried out or brittle.

- If buying shelled meat of any form, it is somewhat tacky to the touch and not sitting in any liquid.

# Frozen Seafood

We wholeheartedly recommend frozen seafood. Yep, you read it right. We know it has earned a bad reputation, but the tide is changing. See page 14 for more.

Given that frozen seafood mostly comes in packaging, many quality markers can be hidden. Generally, it doesn't give off much aroma, good or bad. And sometimes you can't even see it through the cardboard box. But there are some general environmental markers to look for, as well as some visual cues.

- The case is relatively well organized. This will speak to general attention to detail and product rotation.

- The door, shelves, and any packages show no signs of ice crystal buildup. Ice crystal buildup is a sign of temperature variation, not a good thing.

- The packages are intact and not dented or broken.

- If it is packaged in a vacuum pack (as is increasingly the case), check that the seal is tight.

- If you can see the seafood, look for any ice crystallization on it. Any spots of uneven color can indicate frost burn and slight browning can indicate oxidation.

---

**NOTE:** Individually frozen pieces of fillet or shrimp are often coated in a micro-mist sheath of ice on purpose. This creates a protective barrier that helps to preserve quality. This is different from ice crystallization that forms naturally. These sheathings should be mostly intact, a sure way to tell that the coating is intentional.

# How to Store Seafood

You've done the work to get great quality seafood home. It's important that you then store it properly. It's imperative to keep seafood as cold as possible, getting it from the cold of the store to the cold of your refrigerator ASAP. Quality seafood will keep for several days if stored as cold as possible. Some seafood will stay "fresh" (in this case meaning edible and still desirable) for up to two weeks. This is especially true with some farm-raised products, such as trout, tilapia, and mussels. But just because this is true doesn't mean we recommend delaying your enjoyment of said seafood for that long.

Just like all seafood, keep shellfish as cold as possible, preferably away from the refrigerator door to avoid temperature swings. With bivalves, it's important to keep them in a damp environment. A good way to do this is to put a damp, clean dish towel or paper towels over the top. Make sure that there is some airflow to the shellfish and periodically drain away any liquid that they exude. Mussels, clams, and oysters that are in good condition can last a week or more if stored properly. That said, we recommend using them as quickly as is convenient.

*A lot of books will tell you* to keep seafood in its wrapper on ice in the refrigerator. I find this to be inconvenient and burdensome. In my kitchen, I make sure that I put the seafood in its wrapper in the coldest part of the refrigerator, meaning away from the door and best if in a drawer, as this will help avoid temperature swings every time the refrigerator is opened.

# Where to Shop

Many retailers, large and small, do an incredible job offering seafood that inspires. It used to be in America that the vast majority of seafood was bought at specialty seafood markets. These were almost entirely small mom-and-pop shops, and often legacy businesses within a family. In recent decades, seafood purchases have mostly shifted to large grocery stores. While we certainly recommend buying seafood from any trustworthy source, just as we recommend shopping at farmers markets, we also recommend supporting smaller, independent stores. Yes, it might mean an extra trip in your already busy day, but it can be worth it for the increased variety, expertise, and quality you might find. Also, fishmongers tend to be fun people. Get to know them.

# Alphabet Chowder

Acronyms abound in the sustainable seafood world, representing the many organizations and entities swimming in this pool. What to make of all this "alphabet chowder"? Well, it's a rich mix of tools, each useful in its own way toward understanding provenance and production and the importance of, when it comes to seafood. Whether it's NOAA, MBAY, MSC, BAP, GSA, or ASC, each of these can serve a role in helping us to navigate what sustainability means in an ever-changing environment. None of these tools in and of itself addresses or encompasses the entire scope of issues related to our relationship to our waters. But together they form a very rigorous and full complement by which we can direct our purchases toward the good we want to see.

The most obvious value of any of these tools is that they offer us a quick snapshot at the point of decision in order to inform and empower us to make responsible purchases. Many retailers, most really, are engaged with one or more of these programs to various extents and communicate to customers how these tools serve their commitment to sustainable seafood. For each tool, there is a deeper dive to do online to learn about how they conduct assessments and the parameters they use to define sustainability. Importantly, these tools are not just for consumers but also provide producers an opportunity to gain recognition and additional market share as they move toward sustainability. This economic carrot is an important mechanism to incentivize improvements. So, let's make some chowder!

**ASC (Aquaculture Stewardship Council)** is a program that sets standards for responsible water farming practices, including requirements for environment, animal health, and labor conditions. Part of this program is a chain of custody auditing process that ensures authenticity of product and practice from farm to plate. Producers that achieve these standards earn the right for their product to carry the ASC checkmark.

**BAP (Best Aquaculture Practices)** is another certification for farmed seafood, assessing everything from fish feed mills, hatcheries, environment, and processing. BAP, a program of the Global Seafood Alliance (GSA), uses a star rating system, helpful for understanding which aspects of the production are exemplary and where there is room for improvement. One star, up to four, is awarded per pillar of assessment.

**MBAY (Monterey Bay Aquarium's Seafood Watch Program)** is a well-known seafood guide, not certification. It offers a rigorous assessment of both wild and farmed seafoods using multiple metrics. This results in a traffic light system: red means avoid, yellow means consume with caution, and green means go for it. Their consumer app is particularly useful and convenient.

**MSC (Marine Stewardship Council)** is a global nonprofit with a standard and certification for environmentally sustainable, wild fisheries. Their mission is to restore global fish stocks and safeguard seafood supplies for future generations. When you see their MSC blue fish ecolabel on seafood packaging and menus, it means your seafood is wild, third-party certified, and harvested from healthy populations with minimal environmental impact.

**NOAA Fisheries** is the US agency responsible for the stewardship of the country's seafood resources. It manages fisheries to promote sustainability and for economic opportunity within fishing communities by using the best available science. FishWatch.gov contains a particularly interesting collection of species profiles. This is not a certification or recommendation, but their work is best-in-class. As such, if it's domestic, it's well managed and worthy of our support.

**Ocean Wise**, long the leader in sustainable seafood recommendations in Canada, is now an emerging part of the conversation in the United States. They work with fishers, restauranteurs, and retailers to make it easy for all of us to support healthy oceans. Look for their "happy fish" logo, a symbol recognizing their role in ensuring the sustainability of products offered.

# Busting Seafood Myths

There are a few myths surrounding seafood that we'd like to debunk, or maybe just lend some context to so you can better understand how to consider this delicious and healthful ingredient category.

**Seafood makes my house smell!** Well, duh, of course it does. Cooking anything makes your house smell. Have you ever cooked a hamburger in your house? Bacon? What does your house smell like afterward? Yummy aromas that linger for a long time. Yes, cooking seafood in your house can make your house smell like seafood. In our minds, this is not necessarily a bad thing. And if the quality of seafood you're using is tip-top, those smells are subtle and pleasant. It's poor-quality seafood that doesn't smell good. Methods such as sautéing that vaporize some of the oils in the seafood erupt those smells from the pan into the air. But methods like deep or shallow poaching, roasting, or braising/ stewing minimize the amount of particulate thrown into the air.

**Seafood is toxic.** You've heard it's risky to eat seafood. And this information has likely found you through a reputable source, like your doctor or a trusted news outlet. And there is truth to this. Yes, some seafoods have levels of toxicity such as methylmercury, dioxins, or PCBs that should give us pause. As much as we consider those seafoods risky, we must also consider our behaviors that caused these issues in the first place, such as burning fossil fuels, which is how methylmercury ends up in the ocean. But the vast majority of seafood does not carry toxicity levels of concern. And for the vast majority of our population, the potential risks associated with eating seafood are far outweighed by the known benefits of including it as a regular part of our diet. Studies from Harvard, Tufts, and the University of Texas, among others, have shown that one of the riskiest things Americans do every day is that they do not eat enough seafood. See more about the health impacts of seafood on page 18.

Pregnant and nursing mothers need to be aware of toxicity concerns. But they should be most encouraged to eat a lot of seafoods we know to be low in methylmercury and high in omega-3s. The benefits to mama and baby are astounding, from development of cognition to mental well-being, to overall development of a healthy child and a healthy postpartum experience. Fish like sardines, anchovies, mackerel, herring, salmon, and some species of tuna all bring an incredible upside, not only to the maternal couple but to all populations.

While it's smart for all people to be aware of toxicity, think of it more as a cost-benefit ratio. The benefits of omega-3s in our diet far outweigh the potential toxicity concerns for most people. Large charismatic species and those we know to be higher in toxicity like tilefish from certain areas or freshwater fish from polluted lakes—well, we should be eating those less often and with more celebration than we do anyway (see Marine Food Chain, page 16). The bottom line is seafood should be what's for dinner.

**Seafood is too expensive!** This is a very real consideration. For the working family, any additional expense is a burden. We're not going to preach that you should be spending more money on food. That's just not realistic for many people. But we'll offer some context to the price of seafood, especially given the health benefits we know flow through it. Ultimately, we think, in the long term, it's cheaper for all of us to eat more seafood than it is to continue with the standard Western diet. We typically consume large quantities of red meat and processed foods, making many of us sick and contributing to the number one cost in the United States economy: healthcare.

Perhaps a better way to understand the price of seafood is not that it is expensive, but rather that it is rationally priced.

In sum, when we buy meat, we're paying far more than we realize: once with our taxes for agricultural subsidies, again at the store, then again in the healthcare system when our Western diet results in ill health, and yet again with climate change. But these costs are hidden behind that $2.99 hamburger meat on sale this week. Admittedly, this might not be actionable information to the single parent working three jobs struggling to get food on the table. But for those of us who can afford to consider and act upon this knowledge, it's a good idea to invest our dinner dollars in seafood.

Small-scale, well-managed meat production can absolutely be a positive force, supporting communities and ecosystems. That said, the most sustainable and healthful choice we can make remains clear: prioritize plants on our plates and see meat as an occasional complement, not the center of the plate protein.

And, of course, portion size plays a role in this too. We only need so much protein per meal. Anything more than that, in our physiology, becomes waste. So, mitigating any increased immediate costs to seafood, the fact is that we really don't need to be eating much of it at a time to enjoy it and to gain the healthful benefits from it. (Caveat: Our dinner plates should feature mostly plants.)

Frozen and canned options also help to lower the cost of seafood because of decreased perishability of the product and slower transport times to market.

**Farmed is better than wild. / Wild is better than farmed.** Whether sustainably fished, or sustainably farmed, seafood is seafood. There is a common misperception that farm-raised seafood is somehow of lower quality than wild-caught or vice versa. This simply isn't true. You may prefer wild salmon, say the robust flavor and deeply red hue of sockeye caught in Alaska. You may find farmed white shrimp more to your taste than the iodine-rich flavor of Texas wild-caught brown shrimp. But let's not allow personal preferences to obscure broader truth: that great quality seafood deserving of our culinary attention comes from sustainable producers, both fishing and farming. And while there can be appreciable differences in the nutritional profile of the same/similar species, seafood is still great-for-you-to-be-eating-more-of-it.

There are some areas of the world where a particular form of seafood, say wild-caught fisheries in Alaska, largely culturally preclude the adoption or acceptance of farmed seafood. It is entirely the right of those communities to decide. So, we are speaking here in broad terms about the category of seafood more so than provenance. Categorically, seafood is seafood and quality is quality. Once it breaks the surface of the water, it is the same thing for us in the way that we consider it, order it, prepare it, and serve it. When choosing what we serve, we should decide by virtue of the quality and sustainability of the ingredient, not whether it is farmed or wild.

# How Sustainable Seafood Is Produced: Fishing and Farming

Since the dawn of humankind, we've been drawn to coasts, rivers, and lakes for their abundance, and one would think an appreciation of their beauty. In evolutionary biology, there's evidence to suggest that the omega-3s in seafood we consumed was one of the primary factors that allowed the human brain to increase in size and for us to become the dominant species we are today. In many coastal areas, if you were hungry, all you had to do was wait for low tide. There's a Native American saying that when the tide goes out the table is set. Clams, mussels, oysters, crabs, lobsters, seaweeds, all available for gathering. Of course, we also hunted, and methods evolved, ranging from spears to simple hooks and nets employed from the shore or small boats.

Today, fishing vessels can be technological marvels, plying the global oceans and able to catch, process, and freeze all aboard. With the explosion of our human population, and the ever-more-efficient modern methods, we have certainly wrought damage upon our marine ecosystems as we have taken more than the sea can afford to give. But this is not a one-way narrative. Through regulation, as well as sustainable adaptations to fishing gear, we know and have proof that we can fish sustainably. The long-term abundance of our oceans requires that we be constantly vigilant, responding to best available science and changing behaviors in accordance with natural fluctuations and human impacts.

To be clear, the story of seafood is one of good and bad. It's crucial to understand there are best actors, who are examples and innovators, showing us how we can responsibly capture seafood. And of course there are worst actors, whose intentions and methods hurt all of us. The abuses are not just upon the environment, as there are also major issues with forced and slave labor, truly among the worst of human sins. This is not to throw shade or doubt at the industry at large—in fact, the purpose of this book is to show that despite a commonly negative narrative about seafood, there is indeed hope in the water and there are producers worth celebrating.

After eons of hunting and gathering, humans began dabbling in the farming of seafood. There are records of various fish farming methods being employed throughout the world, some dating back thousands of years. These were always small, localized efforts, as was everything before globalization. As a large-scale production model, aquaculture, the farming of fish, shellfish, and seaweeds, has only gained market traction within the past sixty or so years. And we've seen an incredibly steep learning curve in the decades since. Despite its long history, aquaculture is really the first "new food system" that we've created in ten thousand years, since we first furrowed the soil and planted the seeds of modern society.

As with anything new, there have been growing pains. And the result has not always been sustainable. Done poorly, aquaculture can damage sensitive ecosystems, disrupt communities, and pose a threat to human health. But the technology, understanding, and economy of fish farming has evolved rapidly and is now in many ways inclusive of sustainable principles. Again, this is not always the case, as there are best and worst actors. But the evidence is clear: All outcomes are better, for the fish, the economy, and the end consumers, when sustainability is built into the framework of a farm. There's a lot of work still to be done, but there is great reason to pursue it: so we can ensure that we can meet growing demand, global food security challenges, and human nutritional needs and improve environmental resilience.

As for public perception, we need to build a frame of reference for what aquaculture is. Because it is new and because it happens, more often than not, out of sight, we simply lack cultural context through which to view and come to understand what this industry is. Think of it this way: There are some people who farm on land. There are some people who farm on water. These are not different from each other in their purpose or in their general undertakings. To sustainably produce food for a community is always a noble effort.

Given the diversity within both wild capture and aquaculture, species, regions, and waters (some aquaculture happens on land, within water of course), it would take an entire master class to teach all of the ways that aquatic life becomes seafood. We'll not take the space here to elucidate these methods, especially as there are great resources available online. In general, most methods can be done sustainably. There are some, such as fishing with dynamite, or even lacing waters with cyanide, that will never be sustainable. It's also important to note that the method must also fit into the larger paradigm of a resilient ecosystem in which it is practiced. If removed from a broader environmental process, it's possible to miss that acutely sustainable practices are not sustainable on a broader level. For instance, you can do everything right in the farming of shrimp, but if an essential habitat of mangroves is decimated in order to make room for that farm, it doesn't pass muster. Just as we wouldn't consider it sustainable to organically farm a section of slash-and-burned rainforest. Method and context must also be viewed in light of surrounding culture. Not all forms of fishing or aquaculture belong in all places. For example, in Alaska, where wild salmon and Indigenous people are one and the same, the advent of the farmed salmon industry is of existential contention. We have to respect that. But one culture's approach to their relationship with the sea should not be imposed on another culture. Food systems at their best are a function of democracy, of the community, by the community.

Learn more about the methods at NOAA's Fishwatch.gov.

# What Your Food Ate

Aquaculture is a very young industry, relatively. As we advance our techniques and understanding of how to farm various species, we further our understanding of what we can feed them. At the outset of farming on a global scale, species such as salmon were often fed a diet of fish meal and fish oil derived from forage fish, such as anchovies, that had been caught specifically for this purpose. That put pressure on the sustainability of those small fish and also had a cascading impact on the ecosystems in which they were caught. As veterinary science of farming seafood has evolved, there has been rapid movement toward reducing and replacing wild capture feed ingredients. We now see feed from novel ingredients such as fermented algae, insect meal, and sugarcane by-product and a greater capture and upcycling of fish waste (heads, skin) that was for a long time discarded in the processing of wild capture fish for our tables. While there will certainly be continued evolution of our understanding of fish nutrition and welfare of these farmed species, we are witness to some very exciting innovations now. This makes farmed seafood an opportunity to go from a net loss of nutrients to becoming part of circular economies based on full utilization of available nutrients, thus giving us the opportunity to create healthful, delicious seafood in ways that promote a resilient food-system-wide relationship with our planet.

# How to Behave Sustainably

Sustainability is often considered the responsibility of the producer. After all, that is where the direct impact on our environment happens. And it's absolutely upon producers to act responsibly within their ecosystem and beyond. But it's not enough that we as consumers, ultimately investors in and enablers of those producers, demand sustainably produced ingredients. We also have to behave sustainably. Our responsibility is above the surface of the water. And there is much that we must do to sustain our delicious and resilient world.

## Eat Your Vegetables

This is a book about cooking seafood. It's about sustainability. It's about delicious cuisines from all over the world and the people who make the products that make this possible. But sustainability, both that of the natural world and that of our own health, is impossible without diets made up of mostly plants.

The intention of this book is to help you fall in love with seafood, or to deepen your relationship with it if you've already joined our ranks. And so the dishes in these pages focus on that. In writing these recipes, we challenged ourselves to add vegetables wherever possible. You'll see, for instance, we use herbs like a vegetable, calling for many tablespoons of them at a time, not just as a fluttery garnish. Some classic dishes, such as Shrimp al Ajillo–Style (page 349), again include lots of herbs but also almonds to bolster the nutrition and to bring something new to a classic dish. While seafood certainly takes center of the plate in most of the recipes that follow, the vast majority of dietary advice suggests we eat mostly plants, greens, legumes, pulses, and all the delicious vegetables and fruits that we are so blessed to have access to. And this is what makes eating really fun. It's also what keeps us healthy and minimizes our impact on the environment.

## Frozen Seafood

Frozen seafood has earned a bad reputation. Since the advent of the freezing machine, invented by Clarence Birdseye in the 1920s, seafood has been subjected to the fate of being poorly frozen. Seafood mostly has been frozen as a means to stop spoilage, a last effort to prevent it from going into the trash can. Oftentimes it's been frozen inexpertly in freezers that are made to keep things frozen. Yes, the process of freezing and keeping frozen are different—the temperatures needed to achieve best results differ. Think of that bluefish in the back of your uncle's freezer from that derby trip he took last summer. It was caught, then it might have sat on a deck in a beat-up cooler over ice for hours and later filleted, thrown in some zip-top bags, and placed in the home freezer among the ice cream and nuggets. But this once glorious bluefish no longer retains any of its former grace. Seafood, fresh from the water at the height of pristine quality, frozen expertly in machines designed to freeze very rapidly at very low temperature, is a recipe for success. With such a process, we can arrest freshness at its peak, virtually stopping time. And when we reach for that product for dinner, the clock starts ticking. But we're still just off the boat.

A quick science lesson: When water freezes, it expands. The faster water freezes, the less it expands; the slower it freezes, the more it expands. The volume of that expansion is in the form of rather sharp little ice crystals. Seafood is made up of cells that are made up mostly of water. Cell walls can rupture during a slow freezing process, as those pointy little crystals can stab through. Once ruptured, when the seafood is thawed and cooked, the water (read moisture, flavor, succulence) leeches or is forced out of those cells, reducing the quality of the eating experience as well as the yield. If a piece of seafood is frozen very quickly at very low temperatures such as –80°F, the resulting ice crystals are much smaller and less damaging to the cell walls. This gives us greater retention of moisture, flavor, and succulence. There is always going to be some damage to cell walls, no matter how deep the temperature, and thus there is an inherent difference between fresh and frozen. But think about it this way: Once frozen, that seafood is locked in a steady state of quality. That's not true of the "fresh" product that might have taken two weeks or more to get to your table, degrading that entire time. Y'all remember that book-turned-movie *The Perfect Storm*? Recall how they steamed for several days to reach fishing grounds, fished for a couple days, then went out farther. They caught a lot of fish over those many days before taking several more days to steam back to port, ill-fated as this story may have been. And God bless fishermen for the risks they take in order to feed us. We're not saying there's anything wrong with those fish. In fact, that's simply how the process works. We just use this as an example to make the case that the first fish caught on that trip will be weeks old before hitting the market.

Fresh frozen, signifying seafood frozen within a day (if not hours) of capture, may well be a better-quality product by the time Tuesday night rolls around and you're looking for an option for dinner. In fact, some fish, like Alaska pollock, caught on very large, efficient factory trawler-processor boats, can be processed so quickly after the point of harvest that they don't have time to go through rigor mortis, and rigor mortis greatly adds to the flavor profile of fish. Yes, we're saying that sometimes fish can be "too fresh."

In Alaska, through great sustainability measures over decades, there is now an incredible abundance within their fisheries. But they are so far isolated from major population centers that the expense and carbon of flying fish to the Lower 48 and beyond is simply not feasible in all cases given the extreme volume of product caught there. (About 60 percent of all seafood landed in the United States is landed in Alaska!) Lower waste, consistent availability, and more transportation options all lead to lower price for you, the consumer.

Now that we've talked about the quality benefits of freezing, let's talk about the environmental benefits. When the salmon season is on in Alaska, and literally tens of millions of fish are flowing back into the rivers and streams, there's an intense red-gold rush. It's not possible for the market to consume all of that fish all at once, so if not frozen, the glut would cause prices to drop. Fishermen benefit from freezing because it stabilizes the value of the fish by making it available throughout the year.

From a carbon perspective, it takes a reasonable amount of energy to get something frozen. But once it has been frozen, it doesn't take a lot of energy to keep it frozen. Plus, frozen fish doesn't need to race to market, so it can take slower, more efficient means than air transportation, such as shipping via boat, train, and truck.

Another huge benefit of freezing seafood well is that the high perishability of the product is greatly diminished. It's estimated that about 50 percent of all seafood that is bought in America is thrown away. This is an absolutely horrid circumstance. There is no such thing as sustainable seafood if it ends up in the trash.

Frozen makes seafood a convenience food that is available on hand. Rather than requiring a trip to a store, it can be bought whenever you do your shopping. Plus, the way many Americans shop is once a week, with large carts, so if you buy your seafood on a Saturday (or whenever you do your shopping), that "fresh" product might not make it until Friday night. But the frozen will. And then you just pull it out of the freezer the day before (or even just before) you need it. All in all, with frozen seafood, we don't waste it, we don't lose our money, and we gain convenience.

As much as it's important that seafood is frozen properly, it's also important that it's thawed properly. Most packages of frozen seafood will have instructions for the optimal way to thaw it: Follow those. In a pinch, you can thaw it under cold running water. Or you can cook seafood such as salmon or cod directly from frozen to be slow-roasted or sautéed. This will take a little longer but will ultimately have great results. See Slow-Roast (page 62) for more information about cooking from frozen.

# Marine Food Chain: Why Eating Small Matters

Sustainability in seafood is often considered to be just about how the species at hand was caught or the health of its status in the ecosystem. But there's also a more fundamental aspect of sustainability, and that is looking at how ecosystems function and acting more sustainably within them. In addition to eating more diverse seafood (see page 17), it's also a great idea to eat smaller fish. Now we're not suggesting eating baby or juvenile fish but rather choosing seafoods that are lower on the marine food chain, as these can be inherently more sustainable. All marine life is ultimately based on sunlight, the contemporary energy that enables all life. This, in combination with nutrients in the water, allows for phytoplankton, microscopic plants, and algae to grow. There's a biblical passage that says all flesh is grass. Well, in the ocean, all flesh is microscopic plants. The next steps in the marine food chain are microscopic animals called zooplankton. Up from there we find filter feeders, bivalves like oysters, mussels, and clams, and fish like anchovies and sardines, that sieve their microscopic dinner from the water. These species breed in prolific numbers and swim in vast schools. Their place in the ecosystem is so important that they are often referred to as keystone species—species upon which the entire health of the ecosystem depends.

Like all life, marine species have evolved to eat and to be eaten. And as we move up the marine food chain, the nutrients and sunlight become more and more aggregated in generally larger and larger species. These larger species tend to breed less prolifically than their smaller brethren. A herring, for example, may have several thousand offspring in a year, whereas a shark, a species at the top of the chain, gives birth to only a few pups, sometimes only every few years.

There's something called the marine trophic efficiency scale, which states that for each step in the food chain, there is a tenfold increase in the amount of food needed for that level. An anchovy eats ten pounds of phytoplankton and zooplankton per pound of its flesh. A fish that feeds on anchovies will in turn eat ten pounds of them for each pound of its flesh. And so on. That means that the larger the species of fish we choose to eat, the higher up the food chain it is, which means it is ultimately a less efficient use of marine resources. Why should we eat one pound of tuna all the time when, from an ecosystem perspective, that represents one hundred pounds of anchovies we could have consumed? But we don't need one hundred pounds of anchovies per meal, do we? A pound of tuna and a pound of anchovies are equally good at satiating us, but their overall impact on the environment is radically different.

Think of our choice for dinner as a diving board, with the large, charismatic, admittedly delicious species (tuna, halibut, swordfish) out there as the end of the board. Oysters, anchovies, and so on are located more toward the base of the diving board. When we tiptoe out to the end, tense our muscles, and jump into the air, we use the board to create the biggest reaction to throw us into the deep. Now consider walking just a foot or two out onto the board, tensing our muscles, jumping onto that board, only to have the system absorb our efforts and we remain where we started. All action begets an equal and opposite reaction. If we are trying to have the smallest impact on our ecosystems, then let's not exert such leverage upon those systems.

In this book, you'll find plenty of recipes for those larger, tasty species. You'll also find a whole lot of recipes for the smaller ones. And we urge you to incorporate more of these than is currently common in the American diet into your routine. Oh, and those smaller species are often very high in omega-3s, so it's a win-win all the way around.

# Diversity

Diversity is the cornerstone of sustainability. This is true for a stock portfolio, society, biological systems, you name it. Nothing uniform exists for long. When we talk about sustainable seafood, we consider how this or that fish is or is not sustainable. Additionally, we need to consider how we engage with an ecosystem on a broader scale, not just species by species. Fishing is inherently a treasure-hunting effort—we're never quite certain what's going to haul up, if anything. And when we run a net through the water, what comes to the surface is a snapshot of the world in which we have trespassed. In that world swims an abundance of species. And yet, due to relatively narrow consumer preferences, only a few of those are profitable, and thus they are the ones fishermen target. Those fish are profitable because we are willing to pay for them. We are willing to pay for them because we know and like them. It's a bit of a chicken-and-egg scenario in that our appreciation of one species acts as an obstacle to discovering an appreciation of others.

Cod sure is delicious. And it was the founding bedrock of the early American economy. With cod has always swum haddock and hake and cusk and ling and wolffish and dogfish and eels and pout and rays and flounders and dabs and halibut and soles and plaice (all flaky white-fleshed fish that cook in very similar ways) . . . But consumption patterns show that we've never favored these, not because they lack quality but because we've just never invited them to dinner. But when we think about seafood in terms of culinary categories—the organizing concept of this book—it's easy to take advantage of such diversity. This provides a strategy to make the most of the culinary opportunities made available to us, if only we ask for them. This way of thinking about how we interact with ecosystems must also be an operating principle of sustainability. When we tell the oceans only what we're willing to eat, we create an inherently unsustainable system based on demand, rather than on supply. No one wins in this situation. But if we're willing to ask of the ocean what it can sustainably offer and are willing to accept the answer—also known as the catch-of-the-day—whatever it may be, then we rationalize our relationship with the ecosystems and economies of fisheries. And we as cooks benefit, because whatever is most abundant and seasonal is likely going to be higher quality than whatever cod the fishmonger is able to find, from wherever it may have come. If we get it out of our head that quality is related to species, and instead see quality as a function of season, region, intent of producer, and care of handling, perhaps we'll find that the much-maligned dogfish takes best in show today.

## Top Ten Species

America does not eat seafood diversely. Over the last decade the list of top ten species consumed has changed very little, and these species together account for roughly 75 percent of total seafood consumption in this country. Shrimp, salmon, and canned tuna together account for over 60 percent of total consumption. Tilapia, Alaska pollock, pangasius, cod, crab, catfish, and clams round out the list.

# Seasonality

We are seasonal cooks. And so much seafood, especially coming from regional/local fisheries, has a time and a season of its own where it is freshest and the best quality. Lush, lusty flavors of summer-fat fish as a mackerel is perfectly flattered by a brightly acidic Sungold tomato, doused with spicy olive oil, perhaps adorned with fresh herbs and a grating of freshly harvested garlic. That's it, that's all you need. And anyway, we want to spend more of our time outside in the summer splendor. Why labor in the kitchen any longer than need be? Come cooler times, we might like to dally for hours in the kitchen with the mindful labor of menial tasks, perhaps with a bottle of wine to slowly savor, as we layer together the flavors of root vegetables and spices as the base of a chowder or stew of taut, meaty monkfish.

But we live in a global economy, where bounty is always available somewhere, for better or worse in terms of flavor and quality. That sungold mackerel dish with the insipid flavors of long-refrigerated cherry tomatoes from the grocery store is just not going to be the same as it will be directly after a trip to the farmers market or garden. So, while the recipes in this book are tasty year-round, think about them in terms of seasonal bounty, when most of their ingredients are going to be at their best.

# Portion Size

This is perhaps the simplest part of sustainability. Take only what you need. Leave the rest. Our bodies only need so much, and more is often too much. When it comes to protein, what we most often consider seafood's contribution to our diet, our bodies variously need only as much protein as is in a few ounces of meat or seafood. When we eat more than what our bodies variously require, that overage is simply extra. When you go to the gas station, you fill up your gas tank. Would you then spray extra gas over the car just for fun? No. Food is fuel for your body. And your gas tank is only so big. This is not a castigation; we certainly understand the entertainment and satisfying aspects of sitting down to a large steak. Feeding people and eating for oneself is an act of generosity and kindness. It feels good to serve and receive abundance. But sustainability itself is a form of love, and when we give ourselves and our guests what we need—deliciously, thoughtfully, and respectfully—that love for people and place comes together. This doesn't mean that your plates need to be sparse—they should be full of vegetables.

The recipes in this book have been written with modest portion sizes of seafood, and we encourage you to consider this to be a fundamental act of sustainability. That said, there are some seafoods like farmed clams, mussels, and oysters that we actually encourage overconsumption of, as their presence in the economy and ecosystem is wholly beneficial. For every dollar we spend on these products, we encourage more to be planted in our waters, a win-win for everyone.

# Omega-3 Fatty Acids

In addition to the culinary and cultural reasons to celebrate seafood, the positive impact that increased seafood consumption has on the American diet is so great that we consider it a moral imperative that more Americans consume more sustainable seafood more often. Seafood offers lean protein packed with vitamins and minerals that are important for our health. A key aspect of good health is high levels of omega-3 fatty acids, and seafood is the very best dietary source. Fatty fish, such as mackerel, sardines, herring, sablefish, and salmon, have levels often well above the recommended daily allowance. Even leaner, lower-omega-3 species such as cod and tilapia still have overall positive health impacts.

Why omegas? Studies have shown that by replacing two servings of red meat a week with omega-3-rich fish results in an over 30 percent reduction in cardiac mortality incidences and a 17 percent reduction in overall mortality incidents.

Further studies show how essential omega-3s

are for cognitive development in babies and youth as well as postpartum maternal health. Omega-3s help in the retention of cognitive abilities, support mental health and well-being, help in the management of diabetes and obesity, and protect macular health as we age. With all of these benefits so deliciously available to us, it's certainly an act of love for ourselves, those we feed, and our environment to serve sustainable seafood more often.

For the most up-to-date information on the science, as well as resources on how to include more seafood in your diet, check out our dear friends at Seafood Nutrition Partnership (seafoodnutrition.org).

# The Whole Animal

When we take a fish from the water, it's only right and sustainable that we use as much of that bounty as possible. There's so much more to a fish than the fillet. And throughout history, humans have always made best possible use of all they could. As hunger has been a motivating context of life for the vast majority of human history, it has never been a good idea to waste anything that can nourish and sustain. In modern times, with the advent of global food systems capable of providing for our needs, we've developed not only a deeply embedded preference for the fillet but also distaste for the "off bits," or the rest of the fish, that now goes into cat food, fish food, fertilizer, and landfills. If we are going to take the life of a creature, truly the highest and best use of that life is to feed a person. There's been a huge recent growth of interest in both the sustainability prospects of more complete utilization of seafood and the culinary opportunities inherent in it. Sure, making stock from bones has long been part of our repertoire. But how about sauces mounted with a puree of delicious rich liver, soups thickened by the proteins in eyeballs, or fish skin crisped into a deliciously salty crunchy snack or garnish?

There is a deep culinary history of methods and dishes to preserve and enjoy everything-but-the-fillet. And chefs are diving deep to rediscover and invent new means to appreciate the whole fish.

The undisputed champion of this rising tide is a chef named Josh Niland in Australia. We can't recommend enough that you pick up any of his incredible books to learn more about this ideology and how to incorporate more of it into your cooking. He is also among the pioneers of aging fish, just as we age beef, for maturing flavor and texture. Aging fish inherently adds cost, and it is not easily done at a massive scale. So, it's likely to remain a relatively niche category, but certainly a compelling one. While in our cooking we include some off-cuts and aged fish, for this book, we decided to meet people mostly where they are, which is at a traditional fish counter buying fillets, while hoping they become more curious about the source of their fish and the sustainability thereof. But if you see something interesting on a menu or in a store, we greatly encourage you to give it a go.

Another example of seafood sustainability is the development of entirely new products and economies based on fish waste, such as in Iceland. Here a collaborative of entrepreneurs is discovering all sorts of new uses, from skin care to fashion and nutraceuticals to industrial products and beyond. As a result of this work, a cod that in years past fetched only a few dollars can now be worth thousands.

Aging fish? Yep, you read that correctly. Chefs are beginning to discover that the texture and flavor of fish can be greatly evolved or enhanced by aging in controlled conditions. This requires the fish to be handled with particular care from the moment it comes out of the water in order to take every step possible to prevent bacteria buildup and reduce moisture. There's some fun stuff happening, and people like @The_Dry_Aged_Fish_Guy and Josh Niland have digital content that we encourage you to check out to learn more.

# Culinary Categories and Species Profiles

OUR OCEANS OFFER US a huge diversity of seafood, each species unique and wonderful in its character and qualities. And while this bounty is diverse—literally thousands of different species that are eaten all over the planet—it doesn't need to be daunting. By and large, most seafoods can be put into culinary categories based on the general attributes of texture, flavor, fat content, color, and how they are most often cooked (i.e., skin-on or skin-off).

These culinary categories help us to see what is similar among them and how their shared qualities can be used to our advantage. Populating these culinary categories are a range of species that are largely interchangeable, which helps us to take best advantage of whatever our waters can sustainably offer.

Note that some species can be listed in multiple culinary categories. For example, catfish is at once both flaky and white but can also be meaty and dense depending on the cooking method. There is nothing precise about these categories, but they offer a reference by which the quality of raw product is paramount in any recipe, regardless of the species called for.

While the recipes in this book often call for a specific kind of seafood, the success of that recipe wholly depends on the quality of fish you use. So, if the cod fails to impress, but the pollock gleams today, go ahead and make that substitution. If the snapper is lackluster, but the black bass screams for your attention, go with it. Rare is the case that such substitution will call for a big shift in the process or other ingredients in the recipe.

The seafood in the lists below does not factor in current sustainability status or provenance. As these details can change rapidly, we encourage using any of the programs detailed in Alphabet Chowder (see page 7) for the most up-to-date recommendations.

Some seafood is singular, such as lobster, clams, and octopus. Though the recipes for bivalves, shellfish, and cephalopods have been organized into these sections in the pages that follow, these species do not have equal or proper substitutes. Lobster is lobster. Octopus, there's nothing else like it. And an oyster is an oyster.

These lists represent seafoods that we've seen with some regularity at market on both the regional and national levels but are by no means exhaustive. For a truly deep dive on availability of species, we recommend Barton's book *American Seafood*.

# Small Silver Fish

These fish, which are rich in flavor, healthy fats, and edible bones and skin, are most often found in the canned and preserved sections. The flavor of canned or preserved fish is assertive and robust—not a bad thing at all. But in their fresh form, species such as anchovies, herring, and sardines are gregarious in their flavor and when grilled or broiled offer a wonderful balance. These methods work so well because of the contrast between the rich flesh and the charred skin they create. It's always a joy to see people's surprised reactions when they are first exposed to the clean, bright, and briny the flavors of fresh small fish. These species can range greatly in size: some, such as smelt, as small as a pinky, others as long as a foot (herring or mackerel). So read small as context, not necessarily measure. A quirk of this category is that herring, sardines, and anchovies are both the names of species and categories into which many unrelated species fall. For the purposes of the list below, we treat herring—Atlantic, Pacific, southern, alewife, etc.—as one. The same is true for sardines: pilchards, capelin, etc. In continuing the complexity, herring can be sold as sardines. This is why we're keeping it simple.

**Anchovies:** There are dozens of species legally called anchovies—they share the same culinary characteristics with their larger brethren. This category is largely defined by size. When fresh their flesh can be bright in color (think boquerones, the Spanish pickled preparation). We are used to seeing them preserved in a manner called a red cure, months under salt, which makes their flesh deep ruddy brown and their flavor robust. When freshly headed and gutted and popped into a fryer, their flavor is far milder than most people would expect.

**Herring:** These small fish offer dynamic culinary possibilities. With their high fat content, they can range from mild and clean in taste to very full-flavored when coaxed by curing or pickling. They can be filleted or prepared whole.

**Mackerel:** See Fillet Fish (page 29).

**Sardines:** Often sold as herring, and vice versa (which they resemble), these offer plenty of culinary possibilities. They can be filleted or prepared whole and, depending on the seasoning, range from full-flavored to very mild and clean despite their high fat content.

**Smelts:** These small silverside fish are commonly sold dressed and frozen, though they can be found fresh in the early spring. They have a wonderful, delicate flavor and an incredible cucumber-melon-like aroma. Smelts are almost always served bone-in; they are very small and delicate and wholly edible.

**Whiting:** See Flaky White Fish (page 23).

Less common (fresh) species: eulachon, whitebait

# Flaky White Fish

This broad category features fish that are generally lean in texture and have a delicate convex flake when cooked. And while, say, pollock is certainly more flavorful than flounder, the range of intensity of flavor within these species remains quite mild. Gentle heat is best to retain moisture in the flesh. When fully cooked, species in this category flake easily under gentle pressure. Nearly any technique can be used to cook these, though grilling is usually avoided due to the delicate/fragile structure and flakiness of the fish. Feed your family; don't feed the fire. Most often, these are served skin-off as your classic slab of good old white fish. But the skin of these species generally is delicious and cooks/crisps well. It also helps to support structural integrity and retain moisture. Because this category is so large, a lot of fish here overlap into other categories.

**Acadian redfish:** Though this fish also fits in the fillet fish category, its pearly white flesh and mild flavor make very good stand-ins for flatfish, especially flounder dishes, when served skin-off.

**Alaska pollock:** This is the most common white fish variety found in many packaged products, such as fish sticks and breaded fillets. Its clean, mild flavor is a great canvas for many flavors, though it can be overpowered by too strong of a pairing. It has a benchmark flaky texture with a sweet, moderate flavor.

**Carp:** This fish has a pearly white and mildly flavored flesh, though directly under its skin is a layer of fat and a sinewy band of red tissue that are best removed before cooking. As carp is flaky and white, it is included here, but it can also be treated as a meaty, dense fish, great for braising and pairing best with robust flavors, such as hard herbs, smoke, and red wine.

**Catfish:** The many market varieties of catfish all have similar eating characteristics. Flavors range from sweet and clean to slightly muddy depending on the environment in which the fish were caught or farmed. We are particularly fond of fish harvested from brackish or salt waters.

**Cheeks:** This cut from the head of any fish, most often available from the cod family, skate, halibut, and monkfish, can all be cooked the same way. When sautéed in butter or olive oil, parsley, and sherry, they render a very gelatinous sauce. They also are fantastic when added to stews. The texture is a bit more resilient, with a band-like structure, rather than the flake of the fillet, a quality that also lends them well to braising.

**Cod:** Atlantic and Pacific cod cook in much the same way. They are meaty, white-fleshed fish with a large convex flake. Cod can range in size from small and thin fillets to large and meaty-thick portions. They often exhibit a pleasing flavor and aroma of butter and mashed potatoes.

**Dogfish, spiny:** This small shark has a firm, snappy/elastic texture, though it flakes delicately. It has a very sweet, briny flavor, but freshness and quality of care after catch is of the utmost importance, as this fish can develop off flavors if mishandled.

**Flat fish:** The fish in this category tend to have a smaller flake and more delicate structure than cod and its relatives. This is due largely to their size and the thickness of their fillets, though they are otherwise similar in flavor and recommended preparations.

# Flaky White Fish

**Flat Fish (*continued*):**

**Dab**: This small flatfish has characteristics of sole: a delicate texture, small flake, and sweet taste. It is best prepared whole.

**Flounder:** This group encompasses a large variety of species, all with very similar culinary characteristics. The mild-flavored, thin, white to off-gray fillets are best served with the skin off.

**Sole:** The most delicate of the flatfish, sole is very similar to and interchangeable with flounder. Its smooth, delicate white meat has a mild and elegant flavor.

**Haddock:** This staple of New England cuisine, in particular in Maine, is very similar to cod, with a mild taste, firm texture, and small, dense flake.

**Hake:** This relative of cod has a very sweet flavor, mild brininess, and a thin flake that requires delicate handling when cooking.

**Halibut:** The largest of the flatfish, this snow-white-fleshed fish is often very large in size with a pleasantly mild, blank canvas-like flavor.

**Pacific rockfish:** There are dozens of species that fall into this category; many are commonly referred to as rock cod. They generally share a few common characteristics: a dense yet flaky structure and a moderate, briny flavor that plays well with most other ingredients. Nearly all of these species can also be classified as fillet fish.

**Perch:** See Fillet Fish (page 29).

**Pollock (Atlantic):** This is the firmest-textured northern white fish with the most assertive flavor. The light, pinkish-gray fillets have great integrity of texture, a toothsome bite, and a briny sweet finish.

**Sablefish:** This incredibly svelte queen of the northern Pacific is about as elegant as seafood gets. It's also known as black cod, though its silken texture has led to the unofficial nickname *butterfish*, which describes its character rather well. An elastic texture when raw yields to a beautiful flake. Its mild but broad flavor pairs well with acidic ingredients and herbs.

**Skate:** Skate, like sharks, don't have bones but a skeletal structure of cartilage. Wholly unique in its texture, skate's ribbons of flesh are delicately strung together in a fanlike shape. Its flavor is very sweet with a hint of brine. It is best cooked and served on the cartilage.

**Tilapia:** A great gateway fish, tilapia has a very mild flavor and toothsome texture that make it a good canvas for the ingredients it's paired with. It is very lean and is almost always sold skin-off.

**Whiting:** Very similar to hake in its fine texture and very small flake (though not as sweet), whiting pairs well with smoke and acidic flavors. Given the thin fillets and low yield of this fish, it's best cooked with the skin on, though it can be easily removed before serving. This fish can also be considered a small silver fish, though it is at the lowest fat end of that category.

Less common species: barrelfish, black driftfish, bowfin, cusk, grenadier, lingcod, lionfish, lizardfish, remora, skate, snakehead, wolffish

# Salmon Family

This category could also be called orange-fleshed fish, as the distinctive color represents to most eaters a familiar flavor profile that is broadly shared among the species. They have a medium-firm texture but also a delicate flake. They can be cooked either skin-on or skin-off and by every method we can think of. It's not necessary to remove the scales, as they disintegrate with heat. However, the scales have moisture trapped under them, and if you're trying to get a good crunchy sear, that moisture is your enemy, and the scales should be removed. When fully cooked, the flesh will change from the brilliant hue of raw to a more opaque and lighter coloration and will flake easily under gentle pressure. Species in this category are often good for raw preparations. Their fat content imparts a lusciousness. Even the leanest among this category, pink salmon and rainbow trout, are still considered rich, especially compared to flaky white fish. We include opah, sablefish (black cod), and wolffish in this category, none related to salmon and having white(ish) flesh, but otherwise sharing culinary qualities

**Arctic char:** This is a pale orange-fleshed fish with a delightfully yielding texture and slightly milder flavor than that of salmon. Sometimes referred to as "salmon lite."

**Sablefish:** See Flaky White Fish (page 23).

## Salmon

**Coho:** Of the salmon family, this has the most structured flavor, meaning balanced between gamey flavor, fatty richness, and acidity of the flesh. On the lighter side of fatty, it has a firm texture when cooked and easily pairs with a wide range of ingredients.

**Farmed:** This darling of the culinary world because of its consistent availability and affable personality is an easy fish to prepare. It's often considered a "gateway" because it is a great vehicle for learning common cooking methods that can be applied to lesser available species. There is a wide spectrum of quality in farmed salmon: Some are incredibly rich and flavorful, while others are leaner and milder in flavor.

Note: Most farmed salmon is the Atlantic species, but other species are increasingly being produced in regions all over the world.

**Keta:** Light in flavor, this wild salmon has a nuanced character. It is a less common food species than other salmons simply because of cultural preferences and the greater popularity of other types of wild salmon. Its character is quite appealing thanks to its balance of "salmon-ness" with a leaner fat content.

**King:** The richest and by far most expensive of all types of salmon. It has a very distinguished flavor and very high fat content and is worth every penny. King salmon can sometimes be white due to a genetic variation.

**Pink:** This salmon has the lightest color, mildest flavor, and leanest texture of them all. Its relatively lower fat content means it must be treated more delicately. Canned pink salmon, the most common form of this fish, is great for fish cakes and pasta preparations.

**Sockeye:** This darkly hued red fillet has a delightful gamey/wild flavor. Its assertive nature allows for more robust flavor pairings and makes it a near perfect pairing with light red wines.

## Trout

**Rainbow/Brown:** Often sold head-on and butterflied, these fish make for great stuffed preparations. The delicate, thin fillets benefit from cooking skin-on. Its broad flavor and lack of brininess pair very well with butter-based sauces that have a slight acidity. Only farmed trout is sold in any appreciable quantity and the color of the flesh can range from beautiful beige to the familiar reddish ochre of salmon depending on what they're fed.

**Steelhead:** Similar to farmed salmon in appearance, it has a slightly more angular and acute flavor and denser texture.

Less common species: opah, wolffish

# Meaty Dense Fish

Meaty dense fish are exactly that: dense and taut, in contrast to flaky and delicate white fish. Some species are part of this category at any size while others are species from other culinary categories that grow past a certain size and develop different culinary qualities.

When raw, these fish have a meat-like texture that cooks up springy and chewy—hence the name. These fish tend to have a confident flavor and can stand up to stronger pairings than most other seafood. They are particularly good for braises and stew dishes, as slow, low gentle heat coaxes and develops subtleties not often present in quicker cooked preparations. Some of these species, like monkfish, can take a real beating—as in a literal beating (see Monkfish Piccata, page 272).

**Carp:** See Flaky White Fish (page 23).

**Catfish:** See Flaky White Fish (page 23).

**Cobia:** See Fillet Fish (page 29).

**Monkfish:** This fish is charming in its ugliness. It is most often sold in loins, of which there are two per fish, but it can also come to market in the form of tail, with a thin purplish skin and a single cartilaginous spine running down its center. It has a very snappy, elastic texture with a meat-like density and chew. Loins can be sliced into medallions or, when small, cooked whole as a single portion. When served on the spine it can mimic meat in the form of an osso buco, and the cartilage lends great richness and structure to any liquid in which it's cooked.

**Striped bass:** When small, these are better suited to fillet preparations, but when large, they develop a texture that benefits from slow braising. Their flavor too becomes more intense and pairs well with hearty ingredients.

**Sturgeon:** Once plentiful in the wild, this species is enjoying a culinary resurgence due to successful farming operations. It has very dense meat streaked with thick bands of fat and a texture similar to swordfish. It is as good for kebabs as it is in scaloppini preparations.

Less common species: amberjack, barrelfish, sea robin, wreckfish

# Steak Fish

Steak fish are too large to be sold whole to the home cook. There aren't many people who would have the ability to handle a whole swordfish, say, or even enough friends to serve it to. When we find such species in the market, they almost always have been cut into loins from which slabs or steaks are then sliced. All steak fish are highly active fish and share a sturdy muscle structure defined by concentric rings rather than by flake. They all exhibit a rich, full flavor. Their texture is more steak-like, not in the way of having sinuous chew, but not quite tender enough to flake apart with a fork. They also mimic meat in the way they are cut, cooked, and presented. The fat content of species in this category can range quite a bit—between species, between individuals of that species, and within an individual of a species. Some of this depends on the individual's genetics, but it is also greatly influenced by seasonality and what the fish has been eating. The skin of these species is quite leathery and is almost never served, and when it is, it is with the expectation that the diner will remove it.

**Albacore tuna:** Among the lightest in color of all the tunas, these gorgeous light pink loins are charming in flavor. Though fatty compared to most fish, albacore can dry out easily. To prevent this, keep the doneness to medium or below.

**Bonito tuna:** The lightest and leanest of the tunas is also among the smallest. It is similar to albacore. Bonito is mostly caught as a sport fish and is not often found at market. This fish can dry out easily, so don't cook it beyond medium.

**Mahi mahi:** Mahi is a staple from the Carolinas to the Gulf and in and around Hawai'i. Its pinkish white meat has an almost chicken-like texture. In keeping with its more tropical origins, its balanced briny flavor is well partnered with fruit. Frozen mahi is a great option, though when it ages and oxidizes it can take on a tin-like metallic flavor.

**Sturgeon:** See Meaty Dense Fish (page 27).

**Swordfish:** Despite its richness and massive size, swordfish, with its buttery, steak-like texture, can have a mild flavor. It makes great kebabs. It is as well suited for braise and confit preparations as well as grilling and broiling.

**Tuna, red-fleshed varieties:** While there are a number of species in this category, they all cook in a similar way, the difference being fat content and flavor. The smallest, blackfin tuna, has an iron-rich/mineral flavor. Yellowfin and bigeye, the most commonly seen at the market, offer a benchmark flavor and texture that many know well through sushi preparations. And bluefin, the largest of all the tunas, have the highest level of fat and a gamey-yet-elegant, meaty flavor.

**Wahoo:** The largest member of the mackerel family, wahoo eats like a cross between mahi and tuna. Its texture is like larger tunas, with concentric rings defining its flake. Its white and lean flesh and light and charismatic flavor offers a clean eating experience.

Less common species: marlin, sharks

# Fillet Fish

Taking a step up in fat content from generally lean white fish, this category contains species typically served with their skin on and whose size sometimes allows for whole fish preparations. (Think: snapper, black bass.) These modestly sized fish are often cut and cooked as whole fillets, though larger individuals will be divided into portions. The skin-on approach to cooking them helps to retain moisture in the flesh, but where the technique calls for it, the skin can be crisped to add a textural contrast. The color of the flesh can range from creamy white to rich beige, and the fat content is generally in the middle of the spectrum. Fish in this category are fully cooked when their flesh is uniformly opaque. Their texture is initially snappy but with a yielding flake. The intensity of flavor in this category ranges from medium (such as snapper) to full-flavored (such as bluefish). Many fish in this group are great for raw preparations, such as crudo or ceviche.

**Acadian redfish:** This deepwater northern species, also known as ocean perch, has beautiful pinkish-red skin, mild to moderate flavor, a lean fillet, and snapper-like qualities.

**Barramundi:** With a sweet buttery character, the larger this fish gets, the stronger its flavor profile becomes. Its thin skin crisps easily from a layer of fat just beneath it.

**Black bass:** A nice fish for whole presentations, black bass has an exceptionally elegant flavor and a beautiful thin-skinned fillet.

**Bluefish:** This fish is mild when small and fuller-flavored when larger. The bloodline—the highly flavored, dark-colored flesh just under the skin—can easily be removed after cooking.

**Branzino:** Also known as European sea bass, this is often seen as a whole roasted fish, but its fillets are equally delicious when pan-seared or grilled. Its delicate mild flesh is versatile in the range of flavors it pairs with.

**Butterfish:** These small silver fish have very cute fillets usually no more than four inches long. It's very hard to remove the skin without taking too much of the fillet, but luckily the skin eats very well. It is most often served pan-dressed (head and fins removed).

**Cobia:** Also known as lemonfish, this is a firm, flaky, grayish-white fillet. It has a moderate flavor and is usually served with the skin off. This fish is perfect for tacos.

**Croaker:** These relatively small fish have a mild, sweet flavor, thin skin, and a slightly elastic bite. They can either be pan-dressed or filleted.

**Drum, black:** This cousin to the red drum (redfish) is a wonderful eating fish. The textured flake is snappy and slightly meaty and carries a moderate but clean, briny flavor.

**Drum, red:** Also commonly known as redfish, this fish was made exceedingly popular in Cajun cuisine by the legendary Paul Prudhomme. Popularly presented under a thick layer of blackening spice, the fillet has a quite delicate flavor that is worth coaxing out with mild accompaniments, such as fresh herbs.

# Fillet Fish

**Grouper:** Encompassing many species, these fish all have charismatic flavor and meaty fillets, ranging from hand size to far larger. It is a staple of Southern cuisine and is highly regarded for its firm texture. The larger the fish, the more steak-like and braise-worthy it gets.

**John Dory:** This unique-looking fish is not commonly available in markets. Always served in fillet form, it is distinguished by having three separate pieces to each fillet that naturally separate when cooking. It has a moderate, sweet flavor, good briny finish, and firm yet smooth texture.

**Mackerel, Boston:** These sleek, bullet-shaped fish yield small, smooth, fine-grained fillets. They are highly flavored and best served with the skin on, as the meat can fall apart.

**Mackerel, Spanish:** This gorgeous silver fish with yellow spots has varying flavors, depending on where it comes from. Fish caught in northern regions can have clean, bright flavors. A more southerly catch tends to be larger and have a finer texture and slightly more robust flavor.

**Mullet:** People don't think fish anymore when they hear mullet, and there's some speculation that the fish and the haircut bear some relation in origin. This once very common food fish has largely fallen out of favor, but its medium flake and soft, charismatic flavor recommend it to our tables.

**Pacific rockfish:** While many of these species are similar to the flaky white category, they can be treated as you would a snapper, either roasted whole or pan-seared skin-on fillets.

**Perch:** These small pan-sized fish, frequently caught in the Great Lakes and the Chesapeake, though commonly distributed, have a mild flavor, thin skin, and a delicate texture that can be served pan-dressed.

**Pike:** This freshwater game fish is popular in European cuisine and in the Midwestern United States. Fillets have a delicate, small flake but good structural integrity, a snappy bite, and a moderate but charismatic flavor.

**Pompano:** A matte-silver fish with a very thick skin, pompano has a fine-grained meaty texture with a small flake. Its flavor is buttery with a sweet, mild aftertaste.

**Porgy:** This category, which includes scup and sheepshead, has snapper-like qualities. These medium-flavored, flaky, sweet fish are thin-skinned and great for fillet or whole preparations.

**Shad/roe:** This cult favorite food floods into US rivers every spring. It's a bony, difficult-to-cut fish that is worth the effort, as the reddish-gray meat has a delicate character with a mild brininess. Fortunately, it is most often sold already filleted. Its roe, prepared separately, is a delicacy and, like shad fillets, tastes best sautéed in butter.

# Fillet Fish

**Snapper:** These universally loved fish, which include many different species, such as red, lane, mutton, vermillion, and so on, all share a beautiful, elegant flavor. Small and firm with a delicate flake and a thin skin, all of these fish pair well with a wide range of seasonings. Though snapper is most common in Southern cuisine, you will find it in stores and on menus almost everywhere.

**Striped bass:** Also known as rockfish on the East Coast, this "king of fish" has a very dense, meaty flesh and a very clean yet robust flavor. It's one of the few fish that really benefits from a crisp skin and hard sear. Due to their active nature, these fish have a lot of highly developed muscle tissue, which breaks down in high-heat cooking but makes them unsuitable for methods such as poaching or slow-roasting. When large they fit into the meaty dense category, and when small—in particular the farm-raised hybrid variety—they are firmly within the fillet category.

**Tautog:** Also known as blackfish, this species has a unique sweetness with a texture similar to grouper, for which it is a great stand-in. Their diet of barnacles, crabs, mussels, and other such tasty things gives it a very similar flavor. The skin has a seam of scales running down its lateral line that are very hard to remove, so it is often best to cook this fish with its skin on. Remove the skin before serving.

**Tilapia:** See Flaky White Fish (page 23).

**Tilefish:** This opaque, pinkish-white fish is akin to mahi and striped bass in culinary quality. Its very large flake gives it a steak-like texture. It has a firm but sweet flavor, which shows best when paired with a rich sauce or accompaniment to counteract the somewhat prevalent tinny flavor.

**Triggerfish:** This dense fish is a textural cross between snapper and grouper with meaty fillets, a mild sweetness, and a briny finish.

**Tripletail:** Very similar to grouper, this fish has dense but flaky flesh and broad, mild, yet charismatic flavors.

**Trout:** Though it has orange flesh, trout fillets can equally be treated as fillet fish. Their rich fat content and thick skin helps keep the flesh moist.

**Weakfish and spotted sea trout:** These two distinct fish are commonly used interchangeably, as they have very similar culinary characteristics. Both are highly prized for their briny, sweet flesh, which is delicately textured and rich.

**Yellowtail:** This is a complicated category when it comes to species, but from a culinary perspective, multiple species fit the bill and are sold as such. This includes relatives within the jack family, also known as Hiramasa or seriola, jack, kampachi, kanpachi, and yellowtail. These have an incredibly rich, luxurious fillet, their fat content sometimes reaching 25 percent or more. These are fabulous fish for serving raw (see notes on serving raw fish, page 214). Because their defining characteristic is their richness, they are best suited to cooking methods in which some of the fat is allowed to cook out, self-basting the fish.

Less common species: barracuda, bigeye, bluegill, boxfish, cutlassfish, flying fish, grouper, grunt, shad, splendid alfonsino, spot, walleye, wolffish, wrasse, wreckfish

# Bivalves, Shellfish, and Cephalopods

This category is a bit different from the others, as the culinary category concept is about interchangeability and empowering the cook to use whatever is best in the situation. For the most part, the species in this category stand somewhat alone (for example, lobster is not much a stand-in for squid, nor are mussels and oysters quite analog). Yet this is a category that we feel cooks should be very confident in, as bivalves are among the world's most sustainable foods and most prized shellfish.

## Clams

Clams are for happy people, so writes the great cookbook author and chef Howard Mitcham. Harvested from the wild as well as extensively farmed, clams come in a range of shapes, sizes, and forms.

**Softshell/steamer clams**, known by many different monikers, are often shucked, the meats then breaded and fried, or simply steamed in the shell and served alongside their broth and drawn butter, in the dish accurately named *steamers*. Their shells are considered soft, as they are far more brittle and they don't fully close the way hardshell clams do.

**Hard clams (butter, cockle, mahogany, Manila, quahogs)** This range of species all have slightly different flavors, mostly due to the area of farming/ harvest, but are largely interchangeable. The major difference within this category is the size of the clam, which determines how it's used. All are equally delicious, in our opinion. The chowder clam, the largest size designate of a quahog, is great for chowder because it has a huge meat-to-shell ratio and can be chopped and integrated into a dish, but it wouldn't be great in Andrew's Linguine with Clam Sauce (page 134), which features clams in their shells. For that, a cherrystone-size or countneck-size is appropriate, as is the diminutive Manila and cockle, different species with very similar characteristics.

**Razor clams** are an outlier in their shape—their name reflects their somewhat brittle shells that are shaped like a straight razor. These are best seared on a griddle or dry sauté pan, perhaps with a splash of wine to help them steam open. We like to serve them in their shell with a scattering of garlic-herb oil or finely diced salsa.

## Mussels

The multiple species of mussels we commonly find in market, mostly produced on farms, are interchangeable in their culinary use.

**Blue, Pacific, and Mediterranean mussels** are mostly farmed all along both coasts in colder waters. While the species certainly have nuances between them, it's their origin that is the principal determinant of their character. Size is also a factor, though that's more to the discretion of the farmer than inherent to the species.

**New Zealand green lipped mussel** is an outlier here. While the other species are most often sold live, these are available cooked, frozen on the half-shell, and are significantly larger than their domestic counterparts. A simple reheat in a flavorful broth or soup is enough to bloom their flavor. Or try tossing them in a marinade and placing them back in the shell for an easy and elegant canapé/tapa.

# Bivalves, Shellfish, and Cephalopods

## Oysters

There are five species of oyster, and the vast majority that you might find in your local market are farmed. They are most commonly sold live in their shells, but also shucked and jarred with their liquor, and they are increasingly available raw, frozen on the half shell, which is a wonderful, convenient and perfectly delicious product. The range of flavors you'll find in oysters is so vast that it would require more space to discuss than we can commit to here. There are, in fact, entire books on the subject, including two from our dear friends, *A Geography of Oysters* by our friend Rowan Jacobsen and *Oysters: A Celebration in the Raw* by Jeremy Sewall. All oysters can exhibit a range of flavors and textures to reflect their origin. All five are grown on the Pacific coast of the United States, while the Atlantic is home almost exclusively to European flat and Eastern oysters.

**Kumamoto** are deep-cupped oysters, rich and creamy with hints of green melon.

**Olympia** are tiny oysters with a bright metallic tang and smoky flavor.

**Pacific** have a soft texture, sweet flavor, and cucumber aroma.

**European flat (Belon)** are intensely briny, with coppery notes and a nutty, rich finish.

**Eastern** vary depending on their provenance, ranging from the firm, briny acidic oysters of the Northeast, to the medium-textured briny sweet oysters of the mid-Atlantic, and the plump, medium-textured, buttery sweet oysters of the Southern and Gulf coasts.

## Scallops

Sea scallops are prized for their rich, sweet flavor, typically harvested using dredges towed by boats. A niche market exists for ultra-high-end diver scallops, hand-selected by scuba divers from December to February, which command higher prices. The term *diver scallop* now often refers to any large scallop (generally under ten per pound, written as U10), suitable for searing or raw dishes like carpaccio. Medium-sized U20s work well in kebabs or stews, while smaller bay scallops (seventy-plus per pound) find a great home in pasta or ceviche. Only the adductor muscle of the animal is typically consumed. Treated scallops include an added water-retaining agent, a legal market practice but one that we reject, as it diminishes quality. Seek out untreated, dry-packed scallops for their superior flavor and texture.

## Shrimp

At the market shrimp are most often sold by size—medium is usually our go-to, but don't hesitate to adjust for small or large with slight tweaks in cooking times if that's what is available. Frozen and fresh are both good options, as are canned and dried (see pages 45 and 168). Not all shrimp are created equal, however. Buy wild-caught American shrimp or quality farmed shrimp without water-retention agents for the best results. This ingredient category is of particular concern in terms of sustainability and human rights. As shrimp has become a cheap commodity market, the industry is rife with abuses. That said, there are best-in-class fishers and farmers whose work we should be supporting.

**Brown shrimp** are predominantly from Texas and are known for their robust flavor with a distinctive iodine tang.

**Northern shrimp**, sometimes called pink shrimp, but a different species from that listed below, swim in cold Northern waters. They are sweet and small, offering versatility for everything from pasta to seafood salads. These have a softer texture than many other shrimp, lacking the elastic snap, but showing a delightfully yielding, smooth texture.

**Pink shrimp** from Florida are snappy and elastic with a noticeably sweet flavor.

**Rock shrimp** are often battered and fried to create that irresistible popcorn shrimp. Don't overlook these deepwater gems.

**Spot prawns (side stripe shrimp)** are a grouping of multiple species that share an incredibly sweet flavor and tender texture. They are a cherished delicacy of the West Coast, from California to Alaska, are delicious raw, and are sometimes sold live.

**Tiger shrimp**, most often available farmed, have a large range of taste and texture depending on how they are raised. They are generally very mild in flavor and have a medium-body texture.

**White shrimp**, primarily from Louisiana and Florida, are celebrated for their clean taste and delightful snap. In the Gulf, these shrimp aren't just seafood; they're essential to the region's rich traditions of hospitality.

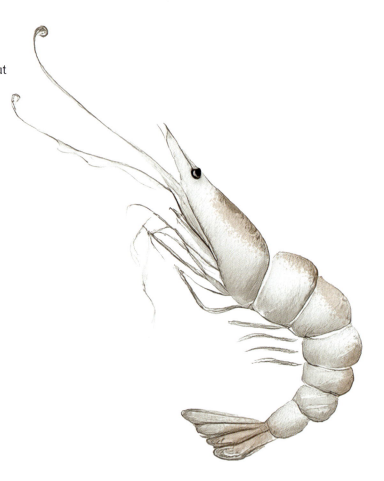

# Bivalves, Shellfish, and Cephalopods

## Crab

Crab is among America's favorite seafood, a cultural and culinary icon of different regions throughout the country. From the succulent sweet blue crab of Atlantic shores to the prized king crab of TV fame and cold Northern waters, each type brings unique flavors and textures to our tables. Whether fresh, frozen, or canned, all crabmeat should be carefully inspected for shell remnants before indulging in its sweet, briny goodness.

**Blue crab**, the darling of the Chesapeake and Southern Gulf shores, is typically boiled with lager and Old Bay for its quintessential regional flavor profile. Blue crab yields several meat types: The coveted jumbo lump is sweet, while claw meat adds a gamey richness. Don't overlook the delicious yellow fat and creamy liver inside the shell—it enhances any dish with a peppery-acidic bite. Crab paste, made by further processing shells for all remaining meat, is highly flavored and great for bisques or adding incredible flavor to a batch of gumbo.

**Dungeness crab**, harvested from the cold West Coast waters, delights with its intricate flavor and generous yield. Its super-sweet meat shines simply with lemon or butter or simmered into a rich broth.

**King crab**, often found precooked and frozen, is a delicacy that is great served on its own or the meat is picked and made part of a salad. Its impressively large chunks of meat are easy to eat, impossible not to enjoy.

**Jonah/peekytoe/rock crabs**, while less renowned, offer tender, flaky meat that is perfect for crab cakes and seafood stuffing.

**Soft-shell crabs** aren't their own species but are rather a seasonal phase of the blue crab. These crabs shed their hard shells from May to September and are a treat when prepared whole; they just need a little trimming.

**Stone crab** is a delicacy of Southern shores, mostly found on raw bar platters or famously served with a mustard-spiked mayo sauce. These are typically found as individual claws, precooked still in the cracked shell, and need only a gentle rewarming to enjoy.

## Squid

While many know this species only in the fried form of calamari (which is certainly delicious!), its culinary potential extends far beyond that. Fresh squid, often called "dirty," features a beautiful, mottled purple skin that signals freshness. This skin not only enhances the flavor but also pairs perfectly with char and smoke. Versatile in cooking methods—poached, sautéed, grilled—squid shines in every preparation. The meat consists of tubes and tentacles; use both for texture and presentation. The key to cooking squid? Keep it brief or long—anything in between leads to toughness.

# Urchin

Urchin is unique in the seafood world. In their whole state they don't seem much like a foodstuff, but rather something more likely to be found in a *Game of Thrones* battle scene. Intimidatingly spiked balls on the outside yield an intensely briny-of-the-sea flavor in "tongues" of sweet orange roe. Anyone familiar with them has likely come across them in fine sushi restaurants served as they are with nothing more than a drizzle of great quality oil. They can also be tossed into a ceviche (page 213) or thrown in with pasta at the last minute to enhance a creamy sauce. Bright yellow and firm are top-tier; darker, softer ones indicate lower quality.

# Crawfish

The Atchafalaya Basin, America's largest wetland, is a treasure trove of wild crawfish, and at its heart lies Breaux Bridge, the self-proclaimed crawfish capital of the world. Here, a crawfish boil is an event—a vibrant celebration of flavor. Create your own using our recipe (page 374). While crawfish—also known as crayfish or crawdads—can be found from Oregon to Maine, Louisiana's Creole charm extracts the most character from these "mudbugs." Crawfish season kicks off in early winter, as they emerge from hibernation. By Mardi Gras, they peak in size and flavor, with females bursting with colorful roe. Although most crawfish today are farmed and available year-round, the wild catch is a seasonal delight. You can also find crawfish as precooked meat, both frozen and fresh.

# Lobster

**American lobster**, also commonly known as Maine lobster, is the epitome of luxury, though this wasn't always the case. Once considered a food of last resort by early European settlers, it is now among the most cherished and valuable of all seafood. The majority of the catch comes from the coastal waters of Maine, where the fishery is a vital and heritage part of the culture and economy. As good presented "in the rough" (page 350) as it is shelled to be included in pasta, ceviche, salad, etc., it is among the most versatile of all seafoods. Use the shells for a rich stock and the roe for a delicious butter, but discard the liver as it's toxic.

**Spiny lobster/Warm water lobster** comes to us from Caribbean waters, and we only get to use the tail (as opposed to claw, knuckle, and tail from American lobster). It has a much more nuanced flavor than American lobster but shares the same snappy/elastic bite. Keep accompanying flavors lighter/brighter to fully experience its delightful flavor. It is typically sold as frozen tails—be sure to thaw them just before cooking for the best flavor.

# Octopus

The key to a great octopus dish is tenderness. There are multiple techniques for cooking octopus and plenty of legend/lore (page 332) associated with it. You'll almost always find octopus in frozen form, either cleaned, whole animals ready to cook, and increasingly the very delicious and precooked, thaw-and-prepare/eat-frozen tentacles. Octopus is quite versatile, as delightful served cold as it is hot. Roasting releases its delightful juices, which make for an exceptional sauce. Octopus is also a great match for smoke, whether from a hot grill or a sprinkle of smoked paprika.

# What's in a Name?

What's in a name? A lot. Given that seafood is caught the world over, with the same species in many regions and locales, naturally there are myriad names, not only in different languages but also in colloquial vernacular. For purposes of consumer confidence and truth, the FDA regulates what fish can be called what, so consumers get what they pay for. The inexpert consumer might not recognize that the snapper they're buying is actually tilapia, which is far lower priced. This is called seafood fraud. Farm-raised salmon cannot be sold as wild caught, and vice versa. Haddock cannot be sold as cod. Blue crab cannot be sold as Dungeness crab. But fish fraud is not always a malicious act. Sometimes the person you're talking to just doesn't have the right information. Sometimes people simply make mistakes.

The consumer bears some of the blame for the existence of fish fraud. Why? We're only willing to eat a few species of fish, rather than participate diversely in what the waters have to offer. No one needs to lie to us and call the pollock "cod" if we would only be willing to celebrate going home with the pollock. By demanding such a small number of species, we create irrational value for those few species while diminishing the rational value of all the others.

In recent years, there have been great advancements, especially in restaurants, in celebrating this diversity. Unfortunately, it's largely been done under the moniker "trash fish." Trash fish is a term used by fishermen for species incidentally caught while targeting popular species, which were largely shoveled overboard dead or dying, never bringing profit to the economy or dinner to the table. But there's nothing trashy about them. We're thrilled that species such as sheepshead, bearded brotula, and tautog, among hundreds of others, are swimming their way onto menus everywhere, so we can celebrate these unique species as a delicious dinner.

# The Physiology of Flavor

Fish, just like land animals, are made up of two types of muscle: fast twitch and slow twitch. Some species are more sedentary and use quick bursts of movement to capture prey, while others migrate thousands of miles and are constantly in motion. These two types of activity require different types of physiology to fuel those muscles. Species with high movement (think tuna, mackerel, bluefish) need constant access to fat in order to sustain their activity. Much of this fat is stored in the muscle structure and also running beneath the skin in a band of dark-colored tissue, known as the bloodline. These fatty fish, fat equaling flavor as a universal rule of cooking, tend to be more pronounced and robust in personality. In contrast, white fish (think cod, halibut) are far less active, and their muscles don't require the same processes. The fat in these fish is typically stored in the liver, giving the flesh its characteristic leanness and taut texture. Sedentary fish also have a much smaller bloodline, and their overall flavor is less pronounced. A good analogy is chicken breast, a seldom-used muscle in the animal, and chicken legs, an always-used muscle in the animal. One is less colored and demure in flavor, while the other is dark and flavorful.

The bloodline on high-activity fish can be highly flavored and not to everyone's liking. Think of the dark red band coursing through swordfish or the deep mahogany color of the bloodline of red-fleshed tunas. The bloodline on very large species such as these is often removed before cooking. With species such as mackerel or bluefish where the bloodline is more a lamination directly under the skin, it's less feasible to remove the bloodline prior to cooking. It is entirely edible, though, and we find it provides a delicious variety in flavor that punctuates the eating experience.

# Merroir

The idea that seafood tastes of its place isn't a hard concept to grasp. Everything we eat is reflective in one way or another of the environment it comes from. Think wine and the concept of terroir. It's the same with seafood, especially shellfish, such as filter feeders like oysters, clams, and mussels that sieve their food from the water. The salinity, type of microscopic food, water temperature, and dissolved nutrients all combine to render uniquely flavored products, even from areas located only yards away from each other.

With finfish, there's a striking difference between those from fresh water and salt water. Much of this has to do with the physiology of the fish and how they regulate the salt content of their bodies, called *osmoregulation*, if you care to know. Saltwater fish hydrate by intaking water through their digestive system, whereas freshwater fish absorb water through their skin, thus giving the water a greater impact on the taste of the fillets of freshwater fish. Any murkiness or off flavors in the water, such as pollutants, can be absorbed into the flesh and become part of the culinary experience. Fish living in a saltwater environment must keep salt inside and outside their bodies in equilibrium. There are amino acids in their cells that help with this regulation, and these add sweet and savory flavors to the flesh. There's simply more going on in the physiology of saltwater fish compared to fresh, resulting in greater complexity and diversity of flavor. All of this to say that while there can be great differences between fish from salt, brackish, or fresh water, and you will likely develop your personal preferences, it is our belief that great seafood is just that: great.

There's also a range in flavor between fish caught in warm and cold waters. This is in part due to differences in the nutrient availability across cold and warm water ecosystems and the life-forms they support. Because of their density, colder waters allow for easier ocean mixing. This allows for upwelling, a process that brings cold, nutrient-rich waters from the deep ocean to the surface. Once at the surface and exposed to sunlight, a profusion of microscopic planktonic life explodes and forms the base of the food chain. Think about the murky, moody personality of New England waters versus the crystal-clear seas of the Caribbean. Warmer waters tend to trap cold ocean waters in the deep and are typically less nutrient rich. The basis of the food chain in warm waters stems from a more limited amount of plankton and algae, which, counterintuitively, leads to an explosion of biodiversity as fish become specialized and adapted to a low-food/high-competition ecosystem (think coral reefs!). This difference in food sources and biodiversity of specialized diets and life histories leads to different flavors throughout the food chain, not for better or for worse. While this may be of more academic than culinary importance, it's fun to understand how the ecosystem comes to define the products we so adore.

# Part 2
# The Seafood Cook's Provisions

WE ARE LUCKY in that food is our life: careers, hobbies, interests, and lens through which we view the world. As such, peeking into our pantries at home you'll immediately see that we are collectors, and we are overly fortunate with the diversity and volume of discoveries we keep at hand. It would be another book entirely for all of our thoughts on all of the ingredients we successfully pair with seafood, as everything goes well in some form or another. But we do of course have favorites that we reflexively reach for time and time again. These lists are not meant as a shopping list or as an exhaustive inventory. While few or none of the ingredients that we recommend may be new to you, their particular affinity for seafood might be. In addition to ingredients to pair with seafood, seafood itself has a place in our pantry. We use these staples for a broad range of cooking and recommend you do the same.

# Seafood Pantry Items

## Dried Seaweeds, Rubs, and Sprinkles

Seaweed is big on flavor, especially when dried, concentrating its funky minerality and flavor-enhancing properties. Because of the potency of various types of dried seaweed, such as dulse, kelp, and sea lettuce, they are often used sparingly and in combination with other ingredients, such as nuts, spices, and seeds. In this way, it's kind of like celery seed: it is best as a team player, overwhelming when alone. There are many variations out there, such as the commonly used furikake of Japanese cuisine to sprinkle over a simple bowl of steamed rice. It's amazing how it can turn a blank canvas of rice into a deeply flavorful and satisfying dish. You can of course make your own blends that suit your preferences. Given that dried seaweeds can burn easily when exposed to heat, they are usually added at the end of sautéing, grilling, or roasting. For dishes that use moist cooking methods, such as stews or soups, they are added at the beginning to allow their flavor to bloom and meld into the larger dish. Simple seasonings and spice rubs are good for introducing this somewhat novel, new-to-the-American-palate flavor profile into your cooking. See more about seaweed on page 189.

## Fish Sauce

This potent ferment has a long history in cuisine all over the world. Before refrigeration, salt was a principle means of preserving any catch by pulling moisture out of whatever it would touch. That liquid, the salty, funky essence of the once fresh ingredient, has long been celebrated as among the greatest condiments. The use of such sauces dates back centuries in the Roman area in the Mediterranean and throughout Asia. Today it is commonly used to add a punch of umami, that meaty, rich, back-of-the-mouth flavor that gives every ingredient it's paired with a platform to shine. A couple drops in a marinade, sprinkled on fresh herbs with lime juice, or a dash in braising liquid for meats and fish adds a subtle yet powerful and transforming presence. In Southeast Asia, fish sauces are made from a variety of ingredients, all with their own nuances. In Italy, the modern colatura, known as *garum* in the Roman era, is made from Mediterranean anchovies. And Pacific Islanders make one from the salted innards of sea cucumbers providing the base of this unctuous ingredient. In America, we have our own Anglo version called Worcestershire sauce, bolstered by fermented anchovies to provide the same oomph. While Worcestershire sauce is perfect in a marinade for meats, you might give fish sauce a try with your next steak or lamb chops, or finish that steak, still sizzling off the grill, with a few dashes of fish sauce, some lime, and herbs. You'll be amazed at how much more *steaky* that steak tastes.

# Fish Stocks and Clam Broth

In our freezers are often multiple bags of stock, whether paella, fish, or shellfish, and we greatly enjoy the slow, intricate, intentional process of capturing the essence of bones and shells to make something beautiful in its own right. We include a number of recipes for stocks, as they are the base of dishes such as bouillabaisse and paella. Stocks keep in the freezer for many months to have on hand as a convenience product. But you know what? Sometimes you don't have any on hand. Luckily, there are some really good bottled and boxed shelf-stable seafood broths and stocks to choose from.

Another staple is clam juice/nectar. These bottled products of varying degrees of intensity are all super useful to give a dish some backbone and sea-salty tang. Clam juice and broth are generally interchangeable as ingredients: They are both the strained liquid remaining after steaming clams. Clam nectar is a concentrated reduction of this liquid. These ingredients can have varying levels of salinity, so be sure to taste them before using them in any recipe. You don't need much of them to achieve the goal of deepening the flavor of whatever they are included in. You can also sip them on their own. On a cold winter day, pop open a bottle, warm it up, top with a pat of butter, and enjoy as a post-snow-shoveling snack.

# Anchovies

Anchovies are a secret weapon of most great cooks and hold a place of high esteem in nearly every cuisine. Like fish sauce (which can be a by-product of curing anchovies), they add a depth and richness of flavor that is simply beautiful.

When used well, anchovies don't make food taste like anchovies, they just make food taste more interesting, somehow more alive. Many people think they don't like anchovies. We reckon this is due to a bad experience with poor-quality anchovies or a misunderstanding of the ingredient rather than any inherent undesirable qualities about these little fish.

*Anchovy* is the name of a specific fish but as a market term refers to dozens of different species that are legally sold as what we know of as anchovies. The resulting cured products all share the

# Umami

Umami is the elusive fifth taste that makes everything taste fuller, meatier, just a little more interesting. I love the science of it all. We love tomatoes, cheese, and fermented foods like beer, wine, mustard, and soy sauce. Ketchup that has tomatoes and fermented ingredients in it is a double winner. I adore preserved salted foods and mushrooms. When you marry them the way I do by hard-searing mushrooms with soy sauce, fish sauce, butter, and a smidge of brown sugar, the results are mind-boggling. Why is that? Glutamates. All of the above foods are high in naturally occurring glutamates. Skip the single salt and stick to the glutamates part. Foods with a high glutamate content make your mouth and brain happier. Cook with ingredients that have naturally occurring glutamates and your food will taste better and inspire more craving for deliciousness.

And use my MSG/salt mix (see page 54). Boom.

*Andrew*

same basic flavor and use, but given this diversity of raw ingredient, different brands will rely on different species depending on where they source the fish. So, experiment with different brands until you find one that you really like, and stick with it.

Fresh anchovies are bright and light in flavor. They are, well, just little fish. When pickled in acid, as are Spanish boquerones, the flesh is white. But it's a cure and fermenting process, called a red cure, by which these little gems mature, deepen, and expand in flavor to become the unctuous, funky, culinary gold they are. Anchovies are put under heavy salt, causing liquid to be pulled out of the fish and creating a brine in which they slowly ferment and darken in color. This liquid fish sauce is delicious in its own right (page 42). The salted fish are then filleted and typically packed in 2-ounce cans with oil. The curing process happens in fifty-five-gallon drums, so those little fish on the bottom have a lot of weight on top of them and lose their form as fillets. This lower strata is processed as anchovy paste. An advantage of the paste is that it can be doled out in small bits from a tube that can be resealed and stored in the refrigerator for many weeks. The 2-ounce cans of fillets, on the other hand, should be used up within a day or two max. In our kitchens, it's rare that any left over from a recipe doesn't find its way onto a piece of bread with butter or is popped into our mouths as is.

For salt-packed anchovies, the salt-curing process happens within a can, typically of a kilo or less in size. Now that's a lot of anchovies. But so long as the top layer remains covered in salt, they will last for months in the refrigerator, allowing you to pull out one or two fillets as needed. To use a salt-packed anchovy, simply brush off any caked-on salt, then soak it in cool water for about 20 minutes. Once slightly rehydrated, you can easily peel the fillets off the bone structure. Don't worry about any tiny pinbones remaining, as they will virtually disappear into whatever you are using them in. Sardines are similarly packed and used in the same ways.

In the recipes that follow, you will see anchovies appear in various ways, from straightforward dishes, where they sit atop roasted red peppers as little flavor bombs, to vinaigrettes. And if you don't think you'd like an anchovy vinaigrette, ask yourself if you like Caesar dressing, because it is little more than an emulsified anchovy vinaigrette.

One of the greatest revelations about anchovies is how well they partner with meat. Lamb and anchovies is a pairing of astounding harmony. Try a lamb leg marinated in lemon juice and zest, tons of garlic, and several cans of anchovies minced up. Let that rest overnight before giving it a turn over a smoky grill. It may be the best iteration of surf and turf you'll ever taste.

*I use so many anchovies* that I have them on standing order of at least one, sometimes two, cases a month. Yeah, I use cans of anchovies by the dozen and think you should too. (See page 16 for more on eating lower on the food chain.)

## Artisan Tinned Seafood

There's an ancient tradition of preserving seafood, from air-drying to salt curing and fermenting to more recent technologies such as canning. All of these were vital to the seafood economy before the advent of refrigeration and freezing. It wasn't until 1923 that Clarence Birdseye invented the quick-freeze machine and food systems everywhere were revolutionized as seasonal bounty could be prolonged in a raw state. There remain some fisheries—and here we're talking about Alaska—where the volume is so high and the location is so isolated that a good percent of the catch is destined for the can.

Though tinned seafood, such as sardines, were once a very popular foodstuff, it has mostly fallen out of favor. For example, in the early twentieth century, during the height of the canning industry, there were eighty-nine canneries operating in Maine alone. Today that number is one. Canned tuna, of course, is among our favorite and most consumed seafoods. But aside from that mass-market commodity product familiar to all, there has been a renaissance of small-scale canneries that set their product apart through artisan methods and the quality of raw ingredients used, from the fish to the olive oil and flavorings. These artisan producers crafting products wholly worth our attention are popping up all over the US.

Sardines, anchovies, squid, octopus, cod, you name it—someone has tried or is canning it (or should we say tinning it?) to a delicious result. In Europe, these traditions never faded and producers there have led the way in the recent resurgence in tinned products. These days there are restaurants menus entirely built upon a tinned product, because it can be that good. Increased appreciation for quality tinned products would not only improve our access to convenient and healthful seafood, it could also have a great impact on small-scale and regional fisheries, creating jobs and capturing more of the value of the product and keeping it in the home port.

*I think the lack of love* for canned seafood in America is that most folks have only eaten mass-produced, twice-cooked commodity tuna. The fish is cooked and then stuffed in a tin or bag with water and heated again, under pressure, to make it food safe. The results are lackluster. European seafood is generally either cooked once with olive oil or with fatty small fish, like sardines, and packed with olive oil before a secondary heating. The results are infinitely better.

*Andrew*

## Quick Canned Shrimp Pasta

A perfect and quick weeknight meal my wife taught me is as simple as boiling some pasta and sautéing some garlic in olive oil and adding a can of shrimp. My wife, a Mainer, grew up with the little pink shrimp as one of her staple and cherished foods, both fresh and from the can. This pasta couldn't be easier, though it can be enhanced by any number of flavoring combinations, such as fennel seeds, herbs, white wine, or whatever else you've got on hand. While your pasta is boiling, sauté some garlic in a good glug or two of olive oil, then add some canned shrimp along with its liquid. Add a bit of the pasta water and the al dente pasta. Toss and bring to a simmer while stirring until the sauce is reduced and thickened. (Add any desired seasonings when cooking the garlic, and add any herbs to finish.) And that's it. The hardest part of this recipe is waiting for your water to boil.

# Oil vs. Water-Packed

Canned/tinned seafood usually includes a medium to fill out the can, most often water or oil, but sometimes other ingredients, such as tomato sauce, mustard, or hot sauce. There are different reasons for choosing water- or oil-packed canned seafood.

In water-packed seafood, a lot of the flavor of the seafood leaches into the liquid, and we don't typically use that liquid in whatever dish we're creating. For example, water-packed tuna doesn't make for a great tuna sandwich, as the water is drained off and discarded. For ensalada rusa, a Spanish potato and tuna salad, for example, the water can be added to the vegetables as they simmer. But otherwise, unless you have a cat or dog trained to the sound of a can popping, that liquid goes down the drain along with its nutrients and flavor. Of course, if you are trying to reduce the amount of fat in your diet, then water-packed tuna offers more pros than cons.

Packing seafood in oil adds flavor, and of course fat adds richness. The quality of that oil is of the utmost importance, as it is as much an ingredient as is the seafood. The oil in a tin of lightly smoked sardines is delicious when whisked with some hot sauce and maybe a little whole grain mustard and chopped fresh herbs and poured back over the top of the sardines as a dressing. The oil in anchovies is a wonderful start to sautéed zucchini or drizzled over broccoli before roasting, carrying with it all the umami punch of the anchovies themselves.

Oil-packed tuna destined for a sandwich, well, you're likely mixing it with aioli or mayonnaise already, so replace some of that with the oil and achieve the same textural outcome, with a more flavorful result (plus the added nutrients the oil itself carries).

All this to say, there's no right or wrong, just factors worth considering when choosing which version to buy.


In my kitchen there is a right answer: oil-packed.

Andrew

# Bonito Flakes

Shaved from cured and dried bonito (a member of the tuna family), these feathery thin flakes are an essential flavor in Japanese cuisine. Many of us are familiar with their funky, salty presence as part of a dashi or miso soup. Though recipes for these can vary greatly, it's often a combination of dried seaweeds simmered with aromatics, then steeped with the bonito flakes to infuse their flavor in a gentle way that retains the delicate nuance. (See page 83 for Andrew's Favorite Dashi.) Making a minestrone or silken butternut squash soup? Start with a dashi or throw in a sprinkling of bonito flakes. Making a chicken stock and want to add a greater complexity of flavor? Toss in a handful of bonito flakes, turn off the heat, let steep for 10 minutes, then strain. The flakes are delicious little punctuations of flavor when scattered over the top of a salad of spicy greens, such as arugula and radicchio, adding a wonderful visual component and unexpected flavor akin to anchovies. Another fun way to use them is to scatter them over a hot dish to make a recipe known as dancing eggplant. A variation on this theme is to roast a sweet potato whole, in its skin, and when tender, pop it open as a you would a baked potato, drizzle with a little soy sauce and olive oil, add a scattering of scallions, and shower with bonito flakes. The heat of the sweet potato causes them to flutter and dance as the dish is served. Bonito flakes come in shelf-stable bags. Once opened, store them in an airtight container and they'll last for months. Though we think once you learn to use them, they won't sit around your pantry for long.

# Plankton

In addition to macroalgaes/seaweeds (think kelp), the oceans are full of microscopic life, both flora and fauna that serve as the very basis of the marine food chain. Known as plankton, this profusion of life is what gives the ocean its moody color. In the Bible, there's a passage that reads "all flesh is grass." Well, so too can it be said that all fillet is plankton. We rely on filter-feeding species, such as oysters or anchovies, that feed on microscopic life to aggregate Earth's greatest bounty into forms that we can easily eat. But we can also directly eat it ourselves. Available in dried, powder form with a muted pastel green color, plankton can be used as a powerful seasoning. Add a few pinches to a risotto for an instant deep marine flavor profile. Add it to your steak seasoning or an herby salsa to serve over roasted fish and the result is a satisfying and nutritious umami burst.

# Ingredients for Seafood Cookery

## Condiments

*Calabrian chile paste, prepared horseradish, giardiniera (Italian pickled vegetables), mayonnaise (we prefer making our own aioli), mustard (ground and whole grain), preserved lemon, soy sauce, vinegars (red wine, white wine, sherry, rice wine), Worcestershire sauce*

Cooking is often less about following a recipe and more just surviving a Tuesday night and getting dinner on the table. Great seafood cookery doesn't require much complexity. Sometimes just a few drops of a great-quality soy sauce is all that's needed to make a piece of roasted fish shine. That can of clam chowder? Throw a dash of Worcestershire sauce in it and you've got a wholly more compelling meal at hand. Whole grain mustard with a dash of good-quality vinegar and some olive oil makes a sauce that will complement just about anything you can think to cook. Rarely are the condiments treated as the focus of a dish, but these flavors can elevate your confidence in simple and delicious cooking.

# Vinegar

It's hard for us to imagine great food absent a bit of acidity to balance and brighten. Using vinegar is a particularly good way to add acidity, as it also brings complexity derived from whatever ingredient it was made from, whether it's beer, wine, cider, sake, you name it. Each iteration carries with it an evolved essence of its original state. Like most foodstuffs, there is commodity product and artisan product. With vinegar, it couldn't be more important to use the highest quality you can find.

*I'm a huge fan of adding* spice to nearly everything often during the cooking of the dish. But if the dish needs some spice after the fact, among my favorite ways to do so is with Calabrian chile paste. It has a fresher flavor than dried chile flakes and is salty, fermented, funky, and fiery. Calabrian chile paste mixed with some grated parmesan and extra-virgin olive oil is a quick and perfect sauce for just about anything. Try it tossed with chicken wings instead of buffalo sauce!

## Butter and Olive Oil

Most of the recipes in this book are built around inspiration from a given cuisine or region, and therefore will often call for a fat that is appropriate to its origin. Great seafood cooking can be as simple as a piece of fish topped with a pat of butter or drizzled with a bit of olive oil. These fats bring all that's needed to flatter the seafood at hand. As such, it's worth thinking about the flavor profile each fat brings. Just as you would consider which wine to pair with your seafood, you can think about whether butter, with its round, nutty flavor and hint of acidity, will best flatter a piece of fish, or whether olive oil, with its grassy, fruity, floral aromas and sometimes pungent back-palate bite is a better partner. To be clear, you can't go wrong. But it's amazing to taste the difference between the two fats. Try it for yourself sometime. Cook two pieces of the same fish in two different pans, one with butter and one with olive oil, and do a taste comparison. Do this with a couple different types of seafood and you'll develop a sense of what to reach for with each fish.

Extra-virgin olive oil is a staple in the recipes that follow. Given its ubiquitous presence in our cooking, the quality of the oil affects the overall quality of the dish. This doesn't mean you need to spend a whole lot of money—great-quality extra-virgin olive oil is available at reasonable prices. The brighter and less spicy varieties of olive oil tend to pair better with seafood, as the heavy green/spicy varieties can sometimes compete with its nuanced flavors.

The only time we do not recommend olive oil is for deep-frying. Blended, vegetable, and peanut oils all work better for this technique because of their higher smoke points.

The same principle of quality applies to butter. If you're going to use it, make it count. Again, you don't need to go over the top and buy $20 a pound imported, hand-churned coastal French butter (which is delicious). In the same vein, the commodity produced, lowest price butter off the shelf just doesn't cut it. In most places, you'll find regionally and lovingly produced butters that not only support an important local dairy farming economy but also are just more interesting, with a deeper and more complex flavor than the relatively bland product America has come to accept. Unsalted butter will give you better control over the seasoning of your dish (see page 371) and unless otherwise indicated is what our recipes call for.

# Canned and Jarred Ingredients

*capers, fire-roasted diced tomatoes, San Marzano tomatoes or high-quality canned tomatoes from California, olives, tomato passata (a vibrant Italian tomato puree)*

A couple other quick-fix go-tos in our pantry make it easy to throw together a meal in mere minutes. Combine a can of fire-roasted tomatoes with a couple olives and capers straight from the brine and you've got a great simmer sauce for salmon, shrimp, chicken, cauliflower, whatever. Because such a sauce is so simple, having the highest quality of these staple ingredients is important. If half of the dish you're throwing together is tomato, it's worth it to spend a dollar or two extra for a product that's compelling on its own.

# Citrus

*lemons, limes, oranges, especially Cara Cara and blood*

Aside from salt, adding citrus might be the easiest way to make your food delicious. Acid, like salt, helps to punctuate flavors and enliven the palate. Think about eating something fatty—it gets boring pretty quickly because the flavor is one-dimensional. Food that has been punched up with acid, whether citrus, vinegar, or wine, on the other hand, has a lot more lasting appeal.

Lemons in particular are just the thing for any seafood dish. Acid can be used throughout the cooking process, but even a few drops squeezed over the top as the dish goes to the table really amplifies the flavor. One particular gem is the Meyer lemon, a cross between a mandarin orange and a traditional lemon. It has a thin skin and a sweet, juicy flesh that is aromatic and can fill a room with its gin-like floral scent. It's like a grand cru version of a regular lemon. Meyer lemons are usually available in stores from fall through early spring. Use them just like regular lemons, but notice that their flavor is a bit more balanced.

Oranges, while typically rather sweet, are still a great companion to seafood, as their acidity brightens. The sweetness can be balanced with pungent herbs and chiles to build a beguiling blend of flavors.

When most of us think of limes and seafood, we think of ceviche, in which the seafood is "cooked" in a tangy marinade. But lime can be used just like lemon, a few drops drizzled over the top of any seafood just prior to serving. Replacing lemon with lime on a platter of raw seafood like oysters and clams is a revelation and a delight—it brings out slightly different flavor nuances from the shellfish.

And, of course, don't miss the ebullient but deep flavor profile of the zest of all citrus varieties. The zest doesn't carry the same acidity as the juice, but it has all those essential flavoring oils. Think of juice as an ingredient, and think of zest as a perfume to apply. Mixing zest with some olive oil and chopped parsley and garlic to make a quick gremolata-type sauce brings levity to anything it touches. In the recipes that follow, we call for fresh-squeezed juice, as that is always best, but you always have the option of using pre-squeezed juice.

# Spices

*allspice, black pepper, chile flakes, cinnamon, coriander, cumin, fennel seeds, mace, nutmeg, oregano (dried), saffron, smoked sweet paprika*

Spices offer an instant passport to global cuisines. Sumac, coriander, and cumin dusted over a piece of salmon and you're in the Med. Chinese five-spice added while you sauté shrimp and you're Far East. A pinch of oregano evokes the classic flavors of Italian American cuisine.

There are a number of spice merchants who've done the hard sourcing work to get the boldest, brightest, and best versions to us. Like any product, there is run-of-the-mill and there is truly outstanding. Given the impact spices can have on your cooking, it pays to seek out high-quality products. It's also important to preserve that high quality. The best way to do this is to actually use up your spices by using them regularly. We all have that relative who has those antique tins in their cabinets holding the original spices from the 1950s. Please don't use such spices. While the tins are an interesting artifact, your ingredients should be more of the moment. Buy spices in relatively small containers. Use them often. And cull your inventory, perhaps once a year. Purchase new-to-you spices just before you use them.

Beyond the usual partners, there are some friends of seafood living in your spice cabinet that may surprise you. What are often considered warm or baking spices are mostly relegated to just that: baking. Mace, nutmeg, cinnamon, and cloves are partners to pumpkin pie, but, used judiciously, bring a gorgeous and still-savory note to seafood. In particular, mace, the lacy outer hull of nutmeg, has a spicy twang that's particularly well-suited to shellfish. A little cinnamon added to tomato gives a hauntingly delicious dimension to soups and stews. Give a pinch a try.

We think of bay leaf, fresh or dried, as a hard herb, see page 55.

We prefer fresh herbs to dried. Dried herbs are more a vestige of eras past when fresh herbs were not widely available. But now that every grocery store carries a broad selection, their usefulness, with the exception of dried oregano and thyme, has passed. These two are outliers because their dried form offers a maturation of their flavor rather than a diminution, and we see them as wholly different from their fresh counterparts.

# A Couple Missives from Barton on Pepper and Fennel

## Pepper

I adore peppers of all kinds—chile peppers to pickled green peppercorns, and black pepper of all varieties. But I think that most cooks use pepper incorrectly in that they apply it in the very beginning and often haphazardly so, without much thought for whether it belongs in that preparation. Surprisingly, I'm a bit stingy with using pepper, not in volume, but in that I don't believe it belongs in every dish. Most recipes automatically call for salt and pepper. But think about it. Salt makes things taste more like themselves and enhances flavors. Pepper makes things taste more like pepper. And that's not always necessary or desirable. In my kitchen, pepper almost never stands alone. It is made better when paired with fennel and allspice, what I consider like ingredients. To me, this pepper blend is best used in its freshest, brightest form, meaning just at the point of service, freshly cracked over the plate after being toasted within the last couple of days to bloom the aromas (see Fennel, below). Of course, for a pepper-crusted steak or the fennel-pepper-crusted bluefish (page 304), I apply it on liberally at the beginning of the cooking process. Part of the charm is the deep nuttiness developed through the hard sear on the spices.

## Fennel

Oh, how we love fennel. Andrew and I got into a little competition while writing this book, each boasting our bona fides as the true fennel king. Andrew even texted a few of his old colleagues asking them to serve as witness, bolstering his claim to the throne. We put fennel in everything, and you'll see it appear throughout this book. It's because in our opinion there are few more delicious ingredients than fennel: its seeds, bulb, feathery fronds, and liqueurs, such as Pernod and Herbsaint, made from it. The charismatic flavor and savory floral character of this ebullient, beautiful, and beguiling vegetable/herb/salad green/ spice/flavoring is particular, and you're likely familiar with it as the defining ingredient in Italian sausage. Fennel is much more demure in flavor than its close relative anise, which has pseudo-licorice flavor and may not be for everyone. But fennel adds a gorgeous accompanying and uplifting presence to seafood of every sort that truly helps all things salty, scaled, and shelled to shine their brightest.

> In my pepper grinder is always a blend of fennel seeds and peppercorns, usually in a 50:50 ratio, sometimes with allspice berries joining the party.

I buy fennel seeds (and use them) by the pound. In my pepper grinder is always a blend of fennel seeds and peppercorns, usually in a 50:50 ratio, sometimes with allspice berries joining the party. Try adding fennel seeds to sautéed zucchini or crushing them into a paste with whole cumin seeds, chile flakes, salt, and olive oil to toss with broccoli or cauliflower before roasting. Every stock I make has a literal handful of fennel seeds in it. (Again, I buy by the pound, so this is not prohibitively expensive, as the price difference between an ounce and a pound is much lower than you might think. This is true of all spices, which makes them very economical if you actually use them all.)

Fennel bulbs are always present in my refrigerator and on my farm in the growing season. I use the bulb as a stand-in for onions when building recipes. Or I will use it raw, shaved as a crisp, cool-flavored base for or addition to a salad. I use the delicate and feathery fronds as an herb or salad green or to spin into a pesto. I take little nips of the liqueurs while I cook and use them to deglaze pans or flambé finished dishes.

So, if you've never cooked with fennel, please give it a try or several tries, as it is included in a number of the recipes that follow. With its beguiling flavor and versatility, I think it will become an absolute must in your kitchen, as it is in ours.

# On Salts and Salting

Salt is a foundation of good eating, as it helps determine how we perceive flavor and how foods cook. Plus, it's an ingredient in and of itself.

The minerals in salt and the environment in which it was formed cause it to crystallize into many different forms. This affects the ratio of seasoning power to volume of salt. The texture of the salt also greatly impacts how it integrates into the food. Chunky, clunky, coarse sea salt is of course delicious, but it takes some time to fully dissolve onto and into whatever it's used with. Flaky, voluminous kosher salt, with its vast surface area, integrates very quickly, giving the cook much more immediate control over the seasoning. Sexy salts, such as the large geometric flakes of Maldon or Jacobsen salt, are somewhat unique, adding a pleasant crunch and textural/visual appeal to a dish along with their seasoning spark.

In our cooking, we are very consistent in how we use salt. And we recommend the same for you. Sure, there are great-quality salts out there that come from all over the world, some of them glowing with seemingly magical colors. Is this sexy? Yes. Do they season dishes well? Yes. Are they worth the price? Maybe. Is it fun to collect them? Absolutely. But as the workhorse salt and your go-to in the kitchen, we recommend picking one salt and using that for most of your seasoning.

In Barton's kitchen, where the red box of kosher salt reigns supreme, if you were to replace that red box with iodized salt, you probably wouldn't want to eat the resulting food. Even if you replaced that red box with the blue box, he'd be totally off his game. Seasoning a dish is a process that over time becomes a physical memory. When you cook dish after dish, day after day, you learn what impact a pinch of salt from *your* fingers does to a dish. Over time, it becomes an instinct, an intuitive ability to season a dish to your preference without thought or measure of the salt used. This is a good thing. It's your own expertise, developed in your own cooking environment. But if you change the kind of salt you're using, you throw the whole learning curve out of whack.

As you become truly expert in seasoning, begin to experiment with how other salts can bring additional nuance to your food. Andrew counts nine other salts in his cupboard that he uses alternatingly. Pickling salt is work-specific and my sharp Italian sea salt is vastly different in flavor than the rose salt he collected from Senegal. While a huge pot of kosher salt from Jacobsen's out of Netarts Bay sits on his countertop, so do six other salts, including a bowl of MSG mixed with salt in a 1:2 ratio. He uses the MSG-salt all the time to finish dishes—it cuts down on salt intake by a third and makes everything taste better.

# Fresh Herbs

We think of herbs in two different categories: those you add at the end, intending to maintain their vibrancy, and those you add during the cooking process to steep and infuse flavors into the broader dish. It is helpful to put herbs into two categories: soft herbs and hard herbs.

*Soft herbs: basil, chervil, chives, cilantro, dill, mint, oregano, parsley, tarragon*

Using fresh herbs is among the easiest ways to enliven your cooking, especially seafood dishes. From a simple salad of mixed herbs dressed with a little lemon and olive oil as an accompaniment/sauce to chopped herbs tossed with melted butter before being poured over a piece of fish, herbs are versatile and add vividness, color, and nutrition to your meal. Having fresh herbs on hand is easy and economical, as long as you use the whole bunch or package that you buy. To this point, we think many cooks underutilize herbs, as their ebullient and fresh flavors can be hard to overdo. If a recipe only calls for a half tablespoon of herbs, well, that herb is probably still sold by the bunch, so just go ahead and use a lot of it. Any not used in a sauce can become a component of your salad. This is a far better use of extra herbs than pureeing and freezing or some other way to try to preserve their freshness. Just buy them often and use them always.

*Hard herbs: bay leaf, lavender, oregano, rosemary, thyme*

Hard herbs are tougher in texture than soft herbs (think stalky, woody rosemary versus feathery, soft chervil). The grace of hard herbs is found in how they meld into a dish, coaxed out through cooking, and they are most often removed before serving, as opposed to soft herbs, which are typically placed atop a finished dish prior to serving. Hard herbs share a somewhat resinous flavor, imparting a distinctly earthy/woodsy personality. And while soft herbs deserve a copious presence on your plate, even the smallest amount of hard herbs can have a big impact.

## Mint

When I showed up at the studio for this book's photoshoot, it took two minutes before the first comment about mint was made. The team had been hard at work for days and had been noticing some throughlines in my recipes. Namely, fennel and mint. I've written of our love of fennel (see page 52), and I feel the significant presence of mint deserves explanation as well.

I found my love of mint while living in Morocco, where it is ubiquitous in beverages and food. It was a dish of roasted red peppers, mace, and mint (page 167) that turned me on to how flattering the combo of mint and seafood can be. Of course, mint is also very common in Southeast Asian cuisines, often used in combination with basil and cilantro. I ask that you give mint a try so you can taste for yourself how versatile and deserving of our use it is.

Mint acts similarly to lemon and salt, accentuating flavors while lending its own. My above-average inclusion of mint is a bit of a window into my home life. On our farm on the coast of Maine, there are several long-established patches of mint, and dammit, the only ways to control them are to either mow it down or chow it down! So come mid-spring clear through the winter holidays, every water pitcher, most plates, and even flower bouquets are all beautiful representations of my struggle to contain mint's vigorous bounty.

# Wine and Alcohol

*Red, white, and rosé wines, sherry (drier styles such as amontillado and palo cortado), Madeira (drier styles), anise-flavored liquors (Pernod, Herbsaint, anisette, Ricard), dark rum, brandy*

It's important to always use good-quality wine with your cooking (though this doesn't mean the wine has to be expensive). The cooking process reduces the wine, amplifying inherent flavors and impact on a dish.

Hey, if you're going to open a bottle of chardonnay to eat with your meal, go ahead and cook with that too. This pretty much guarantees that your food and wine are going to be at least friendly if not great companions. But you don't have to approach it this way. You can use any variety that you have on hand—just make sure it's something you'd be willing to drink!

When it comes to the character a wine will impart to a dish, it's important to think about the structural components of the wine. A tangy, bright, fresh wine will add levity to a dish, while luscious, weighty wines will add richness. Both can be used to great effect depending on the other flavors in the dish and desired outcome.

The quality and style of wine matters most when the wine is incorporated into techniques such as poaching or braising, where you are typically using larger quantities than, say, just a splash to deglaze for a pan sauce.

And don't be afraid to venture past the old tropes. Red wine and seafood? Yup. Fully recommended. Think about it in terms of adding a layer of contrast, not comparison. Seafood simmered in a tart-tangy tomato sauce can be flattered by the addition of a robust jammy zinfandel. This fruity-floral wine meets the bright acidity and salty-savory seafood in a really fun way. Light red wines, commonly exhibiting light-bright-berry-fruity-woodsy flavors, can be a perfect foil for the richness of, say, salmon.

Aged and/or very tannic, heavy red wines are tricky, as they can contribute a bitter, conflicting note. But the truth is, there is no universal rule nor expert tip other than to enjoy the wine and food. If it tastes good to you, then it's a perfect pairing.

Our recommendations for the most common and most broadly flattering wines for seafood cookery are light-bright varieties such as sauvignon blanc and unoaked crisp chardonnay. In the red category, try gamay, pinot noir, and enthusiastically fruity grenache.

Fortified wines are a classic component of European cooking. Wines in this category include sherries and Madeiras that range in style, acidity, and sweetness. A dash of sherry in a shellfish pan roast, thick with cream, is a gorgeous pairing. A splash of Madeira to finish a pan of sautéed shrimp redolent of rosemary and butternut squash gives it an autumnal and hearty character.

The personality of fortified wines is always nutty and oxidized, often with a hint of caramel and dried fruit. They are heady and best used judiciously. Stick to lighter, less-sweet styles, as the more unctuous and weightier ones can easily overpower a dish. Particularly good are Manzanilla and fino sherries (the lightest in that category) and the brightly acidic and well-balanced Verdelho style of Madeira.

*Don't cook with anything you wouldn't serve a guest And avoid anything called cooking wine.*

*Andrew*

Spirits can be very useful in seafood cookery, and even heavily flavored liquors like bourbon and scotch can be surprisingly amazing partners to raw oysters. Just be careful not to overwhelm the subtle flavors of the seafood. Others, such as brandy, rum, and anise/fennel-flavored liqueurs such as Pernod and Herbsaint, can add a wonderful presence to a dish. It's best to avoid sweet, heavy liqueurs such as sambuca and Grand Marnier, as the sugary richness easily throws a dish out of balance. The key to using any spirit in cooking is to manage the punch of the alcohol. Most often the alcohol is simmered or flamed off, leaving subtle flavor nuances rather than the back-of-the-throat harshness of raw alcohol.

Flambéing highly flavored seafood such as bluefish is a particularly dramatic show to put on for guests. Just be careful of your eyebrows and don't overdo it.

# Equipment for the Seafood Kitchen

Is your kitchen set up to cook breakfast? Great. You've got a kitchen that's set up for cooking seafood too. You can buy all kinds of fancy gadgets, but you don't really need them. Start with these:

- A good nonstick pan
- A large baking dish
- A heavy-bottom pot
  - Lids for all of the above
- A Microplane (a tool we find entirely useful for all kinds of cooking)
- Zip-top bags for marinating and storing
- A thin, metal fish spatula
- A heatproof spatula
- 3 knives (chef's, flexible fillet, paring)
- Tongs
- An oyster knife

- An instant-read meat thermometer/candy thermometer for poaching and frying

**For next-level seafood cooking:**

- A pair of tweezers for pulling pin bones
- A fish poaching dish with a removable platform
- A bamboo steamer
- An offset spatula set, including large spatulas
- Kitchen string
- Parchment paper
- Sheet pans and cooling racks for drying, curing, and aging
- A clam knife

# Part 3
# Cooking Techniques

COOKING SEAFOOD happens in so many different ways—or doesn't, as it's often eaten raw. Below you'll find a narrative of ideas for each of the techniques commonly used. For a more step-by-step illustration of each technique, see the technique's associated recipe.

A fundamental precursor to all successful cooking is having a good idea of your desired outcome before you set out. Throwing a piece of fish in a hot pan without any real strategy diminishes your control and likelihood of success. So, before you start any recipe, put a picture in your mind (or, hey, check out any of the incredible photos in this book). Don't just think about the finished product, but read through the recipe steps before starting, and visualize yourself undertaking each step. Do you have the right equipment at hand? Are all your vegetables and seasonings cut and gathered before you start the high drama of sautéing? Do you have a plate nearby onto which you'll remove the fish from the pan so it doesn't keep cooking while you go frantically scurrying around the kitchen? This is a concept foundational to restaurant cooking and successful home cooking, known in French as *mise en place*, meaning "things in place." It's just like parents getting kids all set and ready to go to school the night before so the morning isn't harried (or at least those are our intentions, when we're not busy just surviving the moment). Having things in their place—both physically and mentally—makes for a much nicer experience.

So, let's dive into the mental mise en place of cooking seafood.

# Slow-Roast

The goal: succulent, moist, consistently textured seafood throughout. Cooking very low and slow, at temperatures such as 275°F, the process couldn't be any simpler. Heat an oven (or toaster oven) to the desired temperature. Place your preseasoned fish on a suitable platter, then put it in the oven. Yep, that's it. The benefits of this method are the same as the cons: patience and time. Yeah, it takes a little longer. But it also gives you time. Time in which your attention does not need to be on the fish but rather on your spouse and how their day was. It gives you time to cook the brown rice and steam the broccoli. Chop up a nice salsa (page 146) to spoon over your plate. Relax, have a glass of wine. The time it takes for fish to go from raw or even frozen (see page ooo) to cooked can be 20 minutes or more depending on thickness.

It also takes a lot of time for fish to go from cooked to overcooked when you're slow-roasting, so

you've got some leeway. This is a perfect method for entertaining, as you are bound to be distracted, and your attention is better gifted to your guests anyway. Note that given the very low heat of the cooking method, the fish itself never gets very hot. Unless you're serving it directly from the oven to the table, don't expect a piping hot dish. Room temperature sauces and salsas are great with decadently flavored, very moist roasted fish. Or serve it with something that does retain heat well—you could perch slow-roasted fish atop a steamy, creamy risotto.

If the skin is present when we buy it, we like to slow-roast fish with the skin on. Placed down in direct contact with the pan, the skin both helps to preserve moisture and gives flavor to the flesh while protecting it from the metal roasting pan or other direct conduit of heat. This helps to ensure a luxurious and even texture throughout. Before serving, you can certainly remove the skin if you like. The texture can be a little gelatinous, an esteemed quality in many cuisines but not often celebrated in American fare.

Checking for doneness is as easy as applying gentle pressure with your thumb. If flaky fish, such as cod or salmon, yields to pressure and breaks apart, then it is cooked, even if the color hasn't changed much. For meatier fish such as swordfish, use an instant-read thermometer, looking for 130°F in the center. The end result of slow-roasting will be gorgeous flakes, lacquered with an amazing amount of moisture, dripping even. You don't get any flavor development (for example, caramelizing the surface to create textural and flavor contrast), but this method serves to intensify the inherent flavors of whatever you are serving. For this reason, slow-roasting demands the highest quality raw product, possibly more so than any other method.

See: Slow-Roasted Salmon with Dulse Butter (page 252).

# What Fish to Slow-Roast

Varieties of seafood best for slow-roasting are ones that don't have much connective tissue, thick bands that course through fillets that are typically found in more active and larger fish. That tissue requires higher heat or longer cooking time in order to break down and become palatable. Species that work best for this low slow method are those that flake easily (think cod, halibut, sablefish, and salmon).

The overall ratio of skin to flesh for a piece of salmon is low enough that the resulting gelatinous texture in the skin can be a pleasant part of the eating experience. On the other hand, a fillet of flounder's skin is much greater in relation to the fillet, and it would only serve to distract. Most fish that lend themselves to this technique are sold skin-off, so this is not usually an issue.

Species such as tuna or swordfish are perfectly fine slow-roasted, but they might be better when cooked with higher heat, which allows their inherent fats to create textural contrast and enhance their flavor.

## Pan-Roast

This is a hybrid technique where the food goes from stovetop to oven. The goal is to create flavor and texture contrast from the direct heat contact with a hot pan and the gentler and moisture-preserving ambient heat of the oven. This technique is good for thicker skin-on fish, such as salmon, as the time and heat it takes to cook a piece of salmon in the pan alone makes it difficult to retain moisture and balance of browned outside to succulent meat inside.

Pan-roasting is often employed in restaurant kitchens, as it gives a little more control over the cooking time and frees up precious burner space. These same benefits hold true for you at home—your front burner space is freed up after only a few minutes of heating up the pan so your attention can be directed elsewhere as the oven finishes the work for you.

**NOTE:** Pan roast is also the name of a traditional dish of cream-stewed shellfish.

The process: Preheat your oven to the relatively low temperature of 300°F. After pre-seasoning your fish and letting it rest, scrape the skin (if present) with a knife, in effect shaving it to remove excess surface moisture. This will help prevent sticking while increasing the resulting crispness. Put your oven-safe pan over medium-high heat and get it hot. Pan selection matters a lot here. A heavy-bottom, thick pan, such as cast-iron that can both get raging hot on the stovetop and transition directly into the oven, is perfect. Put a small amount of fat in the pan, either butter or oil depending on your accompanying flavors. Once the fat comes to temperature—when the foaming of butter subsides or the oil begins to shimmer—place the fish skin-side down (if the skin is present) or presentation-side down. Cook for 20 to 30 seconds, giving the pan a very gentle shake to help prevent sticking. Transfer the whole pan to the oven and cook until it reaches the desired doneness. The ideal results are a lightly crisped skin or flesh, a desirable textural contrast to the still-moist and succulent interior of the fillet.

See Pan-Roasted Salmon with Horseradish Gremolata (page 251).

### I pan-roast in a different way.

I preheat my oven to 475°F or 500°F. Then I preheat my pan over medium heat for 4 minutes or so, place my fat of choice in the pan, and when it gets hot enough to cook, a relatively short amount of time, I add my fish and aromatics (garlic, herbs, ginger, chiles, shallots, etc.). I place my fish show-side down—sometimes that's the skin side, sometimes not—and sear. When it looks the way I want to serve it, I flip it and place it in the oven for several minutes—it will vary depending on the species and size of the fish. I like the effect I get from higher temperature roasting, locking in moisture and creating a crust on both sides.

Andrew

# Sauté

The purpose of sauté is to create contrast and to add or develop flavor through caramelization. Sauté is meant to be quick. It's medium to high heat applied consistently, directly through contact with the pan. The word *sauté* in French means "to jump," indicating that when you place whatever ingredient in the pan, it should jump and spit and sizzle just a little bit. It's important to note that it is the contact with the pan that does the cooking.

Do not replicate the showy behavior of some TV chefs who are constantly flipping and tossing and digging the pan into the flame, creating bursts of smoke and flame and drama. F that—meaning forget that—for a couple reasons:

**1.** It's the pan that conducts the heat, cooking by contact. So, the more time your shrimp spend flying, the less time they're actually cooking, and the less consistent your heat is because you are taking the pan away from the heat. Sure, seafood needs to be flipped or tossed every now and then, but for the most part, leave it be.

**2.** When you flip the pan, you expose the aerated particulates, created by the high heat, directly to the flame. This can create those big balls of fire that look really cool and make you feel like you're doing something. "Man, look at me. I'm cooking!" But that flamed oil doesn't taste very good. It's burned and acrid and adds a bitter flavor to the dish. (And it doesn't need to be a show! You're just trying to put dinner on the table.) In some cases, this developed bitterness is actually part of the final flavor profile, but this is done strategically and is balanced by other flavor components of the dish.

Moisture is the enemy of sauté. Why? Because moisture steams. The peak temperature steaming attains (not under pressure) is 212°F, but the sought-after results of sauté are achieved above 212°F. So, if moisture is present, you sacrifice potential crisping time to evaporate the moisture first. And on a thin fillet, that is time not well spent.

The results of sauté are the development of a pleasant, desirable texture on the surface and a still-moist interior. Whether we are using the skin or not, we tend to sauté on one side only for the majority of cooking time. This maximizes the contrast achieved while protecting against moisture loss. This mostly-one-side approach also helps to ensure that it doesn't stick. Speaking of pans, a heavy-bottom pan, such as a seasoned cast-iron, is great, as cast iron helps to mitigate any sudden decrease in temperature in the pan when the cold fish hits the surface. Consistent heat is easier to manage than constant flux.

We could wax poetic about using your grandmother's seasoned-never-been-washed heirloom pan, and that would certainly be great if you're so lucky to have one, but so is a good-quality nonstick pan. We both have our trusted sauté go-to that is always within reach, if not found living on the stovetop. Use one pan, get to know it really well, and it'll become a great sauté partner.

Sautéing smaller seafood ingredients, like shrimp, is a little different than thicker, broader ones, like fish fillets, in that it's more about very quick cooking and often with the intention of combining it with other flavors, such as garlic, shallots, and herbs. Here the heat of the pan is of particular importance in that you are layering ingredients, often starting with oil or butter, then adding your aromatics and cooking until desired doneness, say golden brown, crisped garlic slices. Then you add your shrimp and toss to combine, and the deeply flavored fat becomes the medium for cooking the shrimp. You cook, flipping as needed, either individually with tongs or chopsticks for greater control, or by flipping the whole pan away from the heat so it doesn't erupt in flames and quickly return it to the flame so the whole pan doesn't cool down.

Given the very high ratio of surface area to interior on an ingredient such as shrimp, cooking should be very quick. Applying heat to the outside means there's going to be a lot of residual heat that pushes to the interior, so shrimp don't necessarily need to be fully cooked before removing them from the heat. In fact, we'd argue that they shouldn't be, because the carryover cooking will ensure they are fully cooked, the proper texture, and safe to eat. This is why it is important to get your accompanying ingredients cooked to your desired doneness first. Don't overcook your shrimp because you added the garlic too late and it's still a bit raw.

The steps: Pre-season your seafood and let it rest. If the skin is present, scrape it with the back of your knife, shaving it in effect, to remove any surface moisture. Blot dry with a paper towel. Preheat your pan over medium-high heat. Put a small amount of fat in the pan—butter or oil, depending on your accompanying flavors. Once that comes to temperature, either the foaming of butter subsides or the oil begins to shimmer, add your ingredient presentation-side down. (Meaning the side that you will serve and on which it will do the vast majority of cooking.) Carefully swirl it a bit in the fat. This motion, while the seafood is in contact with the hot fat, can prevent sticking. Even a subtle and slight motion for just a few seconds helps. Cook until the fillet is 80 to 90 percent cooked through, as visible by a color change that gradually creeps

up the fillet vertically. Turn the heat off and flip the fish. Cook for an additional 30 seconds just to heat the surface area, as the remaining interior will cook from the carryover heat after it is removed from the pan.

Don't crowd your pan! If the portions are very broad, say a 4- to 5-ounce snapper fillet, which takes up a lot of surface area, consider using two pans or cooking in batches, as adding too much product to a pan all at once can dramatically decrease the temperature of that pan and work against you in achieving your goals. This is such a quick cooking method that you're not going to lose much by having the first two of four fillets wait a few minutes on the side as the remaining fillets take their turn over the heat.

*Butter basting is a sexy way* to add flavor and fun to this technique. See page 138 for more.

*J.T.*

See: Seared Snapper and Spicy Mango Basil Salad (page 297).

# Broil

Broiling is the application of direct heat from above. (As opposed to grilling, which is the application of heat from below.) This has all the drama, sizzle, and flair of grilling, except it happens in our house and largely out of sight in our ovens. What you're looking for with broiling is flavor that comes from caramelization, and when fat and liquids erupting from the cooking seafood hit the heat source, they explode into little bursts of flame and flavor that are then deposited back on to the surface. Flavor comes not just from those explosions, but also from the caramelization and charring that comes from the application of very high heat. Like grilling, you need to think about how to cook both sides evenly when the heat source is coming from only one direction. So, flipping at a strategic point in the cooking process is recommended unless the fillets are very thin or crusted.

The pan you use must be able to withstand high heat. In our home kitchens, we have the restaurant-staple oval sizzle pans and quarter sheet trays—both supremely useful all-around kitchen equipment. A pair of tongs is probably a good idea for helping to reach into the hellaciously hot oven environment for any necessary movement of the ingredients.

The controls you have in broiling are level of heat, distance from heat, and to open or close the oven, allowing for the capture or dissipation of ambient heat. Not to be too obvious, but the closer something is to the heat, the faster it will cook and the more char you will get. Also, the more potential for smoke in your kitchen. Positioning the rack higher or lower gives you control over how much of that spit-sizzle-smoke you get. And to be clear, it takes a bit of practice to understand your broiler, your kitchen, your airflow, etc. Closing the oven door focuses the cooking effort and adds an oven-like/roasting effect to the cooking process. This is particularly helpful with thicker fillets, meaty dense fish (like swordfish), or thick-crusted fillets (like the Broiled Tilapia with Lemon-Parmesan Mayonnaise on page 236).

The size of your broiler also matters—at least in terms of convenience. We find that a countertop toaster oven with its small compartment, thus easily managed for heat, is a perfect tool for broiling, and it allows us to see what's going on more easily.

To begin, pre-season your fish and let it rest. Decide what your desired level of char/browning is and gauge via the thickness of the fillet how long it will take to cook. A general rule is 8 to 10 minutes of cooking per inch of fillet, but given the vast array of densities, this is very much a broad scope of guidance. If the fillet is particularly thick and you'd like to cook without flipping, consider preheating your broiling dish for several minutes before putting the fish on it. This will provide some contact heat, allowing the fish to cook a little more evenly from both sides. Place under the broiler at the desired distance and heat setting. Cook until it reaches your desired doneness, measured either by using an instant-read thermometer reaching 130°F, or when a fillet such as salmon or cod breaks under gentle pressure from your thumb but is still moist throughout. If broiling a crusted or coated dish, medium temperatures and greater distance are recommended. You can always blast it for the last minute to get any unachieved color or char, but it's hard to undo that if you start too high and go too far.

See: Miso Broiled Carp (page 267).

# Grill

Grilling is the original and undisputed best cooking method in our eyes. Cooking over direct fire, outside, engaged with your surroundings, attuned to the environmental factors that impact the process from wind to temperature, airflow, and fuel. This is as sensuous and intentional as cooking gets. In contrast to broiling, which is the application of heat from above, grilling is the application of heat from below. The purpose of grilling is to develop the flavors inherent in the ingredient but also to add the flavor of smoke and singe and sear.

As fats and moisture are exuded from the ingredient or the marinade, they drip into the fire, combusting into a cloud of flavorful smoke. This then adheres to the item but also alerts your neighbors to the fact that you are awesome and that you are living well, and hopefully entreats them to come join you (provided you enjoy their company).

Grilling inherently happens outside, unless you are among the lucky few to have a Rumford stove in your kitchen. Grilling calls for us to be meticulously organized because we are taking the meal prep away from the kitchen, that epicenter of cooking where all of our tools and familiars are at hand.

Before you even light your fire, make sure you've got everything that you need to accomplish every task ahead of you. This includes everything from salt to all the other ingredients to serving utensils, marinating plates, resting plates, and perhaps a beverage to keep you hydrated (fire is hot and grilling can be sweaty!). It's not a good thing to have to go running back into the house to get something while the high-heat drama is underway.

Whether using a live fire of charcoal or wood or the far-more-common-in-America gas grill, grilling is all about managing heat, distance, and time. Once you've gotten all the tools and ingredients you need to successfully grill and have all your accompanying dishes ready and prepared, it's time to think about heat. Indirect heat is a lower, slower, more soulful process, one that perhaps employs the cover to capture rising heat from the grill and is great for creating a flavorful ambient environment. This method works well for big cuts or anything you want to add smoky richness to, such as a fatty piece of wild Alaskan king salmon. High, direct heat is good for getting the most char and developing textural and flavor contrast.

You can also use a hybrid technique, such as starting with a thick piece of salmon, skin-side down, over the highest heat, and then after a few minutes of char and crusting rotate the fish to a lower heat area, cover the grill, and cook. This takes advantage of the best of both heat levels, much like pan-roast makes the best of the stovetop and the oven.

Direct and indirect grilling require us to have a strategy for where we locate our heat. If you're using wood or charcoal, simply put all the coals and embers on one side of the grill, thus creating gradient temperature zones depending on the proximity. If you're using a gas grill, it will likely have multiple burners—simply turn one to high, one to medium, and one to low. Even if all you're going to do is direct heat grill, it still makes sense to have a lower heat zone to hold the other foods warm while you make final preparations at the table, sultry smoke rising and billowing around the food imbuing one last little kiss of fire's perfume.

As with any other cooking method, the less you touch the food the better. When it comes time to move that salmon from high heat to low heat, why move just the salmon when you can pick up the whole grill grate and rotate it 180 degrees? This lets the protective layer of skin do its work, helping to retain moisture in the fillet above while continuing to gain crispness. It also greatly reduces the chances that you'll feed the fire rather than your family, or those now-invited neighbors.

The biggest and more-often-that-not overlooked part of grilling is that before you put anything on the grill, you should have a strategy of how to get that thing off the grill. Notice that your grill grates are straight lines. You can put your piece of seafood either parallel or perpendicular along those lines. Consider long, thin fillets of mackerel that are best removed by skimming your spatula directly along those grill grates, using them as a guide. For best results, you'd better make dang sure those fillets are lying parallel with those grates. Otherwise, you've gotta lift it by the tail and tease the fish from each grate individually as you go, the whole time uncomfortably grilling your hands and greatly increasing the likelihood that the fish will break or stick. A simple act of mental mise en place employed ahead of any action is the key to enjoying the process.

One set of grill marks is sexy enough. Sure, those perfect chevrons of crosshatch beauty are awesome and a signifier of grilling prowess. But they require a high-touch approach, and every time you touch that fish, there's a greater likelihood of something going wrong. Also note that good grill marks take time to develop, and on a thin fillet, the time needed to make cross-hatch marks might very well be more time than you have for a successful outcome. Don't overcook for vanity's sake.

Good grill marks are mostly the result of proper preheating of the grill grates. Just as putting a piece of fish into a cold pan almost guarantees sticking, putting a fish on anything less than screaming hot grill grates diminishes the prospects of both success and vanity.

*When my grill grates are hot enough,* I find that getting grill marks on my fish is easy. The more of that crust, the better for me.

*Andrew*

See: Grilled Spanish Mackerel Panzanella with Chorizo–Red Pepper Salsa (page 144).

# Live Fire

Cooking over live fire, the sultry, primal process of coaxing heat from wood or charcoal, managing flame and fuel, airflow and proximity, makes cooking an all-senses event. Now we're not against cooking over gas, or even griddle pans on the stovetop, but the sensuous flavor of flame-and-smoke-embellished food simply can't be matched. The fuel itself becomes an ingredient, adding a flavor of its own. Think of it this way: Grilling over gas or griddle is like driving a motorboat. Hey, you're out on the water, you're getting places, it's an awesome experience. But grilling over live fire is like sailing, the process an attunement to every aspect of your environment, a constant, considered calculation of the best course of action and adjustment. Sure, it's easier to just flip the gas grill on, no doubt about it. And the flavor achieved from fats dripping onto the flame and sizzling back up onto the food certainly flatters and improves a meal. But, whenever possible, we choose the romance and enduring elemental process of live fire.

# Poach

Along with slow-roasting, poaching is all about gentle, low and slow, and uses a highly seasoned broth as the medium to not only maintain the moisture in the fish but also to infuse it with flavor. There are two methods for poaching: shallow and deep. Both are based on the same principles. In shallow poaching, the seafood is not fully submerged, and oftentimes the resulting broth is used as a component of a sauce to be served alongside. With deep poaching, typically used with larger, thicker pieces of fish, the entire seafood item is submerged in a flavorful liquid, and sauces for deep poach dishes are usually made separately. In French the poaching liquid is known as the *cuisson* and is a choose-your-own adventure of additional flavors. This cuisson is infused ahead of time, even if just for a few minutes, to achieve maximum flavor.

As you can imagine, poaching does not add texture to the cooked seafood, as the heat is extremely gentle (160°F to 170°F is our preference). The goal is really to flatter and augment the naturally silken smooth, delicate flake of the seafoods to be served.

Shallow poaching tends to be used for very thin fillets. Flaky white flesh fish, fish such as flounder and sole are usually cooked skin-off, while mackerel or black seabass-type fish are mostly cooked skin-on. This is mostly due to the structural integrity of such fillets—if you remove the skin, they become extremely delicate and hard to work with and lose a good bit of yield. If you keep the skin on, it takes on a pleasantly gelatinous texture and adds a huge amount of flavor.

Important components of a poaching broth are:

· Acidity, usually introduced in the form of wine or the brightness of citrus.

· Heady, flavorful aromatics, such as ginger, shallot, rosemary, thyme, allspice, and cardamom, work well here; their flavors are so gently steeped that they contribute their most elegant nuance without adding any competing characteristics.

· And, of course, the presence of elegant fresh herbs, especially tarragon, can be so beguiling.

You can make a poaching broth (especially a deep poach broth), use, strain, and freeze to use again later. It will be more flavorful from the seafood that has been poached in it. This is not an endless opportunity—you can use it perhaps three or four times maximum before starting anew.

A particularly great way to employ this technique is to plan ahead and serve poached dishes chilled later or even the next day. As the fish nears fully cooked, simply turn off the heat and allow the dish to cool to room temperature; the fish will finish cooking from the residual heat. Then chill the fish in the broth, and the broth will continue to enhance the flavor of the fish as it regains moisture from its aqueous environment. The well-integrated and developed flavors become a decadent treat. Flake the fish over a salad or marinate it in a vinaigrette and serve over crostini for a perfect picnic dish or something to take to the office, as it's unlikely to offend any seafood-phobic colleagues. The same is true in your home, as this technique doesn't send any aromatic clouds of cooking vapor into your kitchen. It keeps its aroma to itself. See page 8 for more of our thoughts on the subject.

See: Deep-Poached Halibut with Green Goddess Dressing (page 224)

## Chilled Seafood Dishes

Chilled seafood dishes were once a staple of fine American cuisine. A quick flip through the great James Beard's *New Fish Cookery* reveals that the father of American cuisine was quite fond of seafood cooked then chilled before serving. There are myriad iterations of the idea: an escabeche, where seafood is cooked and then marinated in a punchy vinegar, spice, and vegetable mix, often served the next day; in saor, an Italian variation on that theme, nestles cooked seafood into what is basically acid-spiked braised vegetables and is served at room temperature. Another great method is to poach seafood in a flavorful broth and then chill it in the broth overnight. The next day the seafood can be flaked while the broth is used as part of a vinaigrette to dress a salad that the seafood is scattered over. Or the broth can be reduced until highly concentrated and whisked into an aioli to be served with the fish.

Not only does this type of recipe strategy offer a great deal of convenience for entertaining (all the work has been done ahead of time), it makes seafood a viable breakfast item or a lunch-on-the-go option to take to the office, to school, or on a picnic.

# Fry

Frying is all about texture. And, of course, it adds richness, as whatever fat you're frying in becomes an integral part of the dish. Like poaching, there are two strategies to go about this. One is to shallow-fry, meaning to have a relatively thin layer of fat in which you cook an ingredient one side at a time. Think piccata or a delicate crusted flounder fillet. And then there's deep-frying, where foods are fully coated and fully submerged in the fat. The type of crust or batter used is determined by the nature of the recipe and its flavor profiles. And there are different techniques, coatings, and batters from cuisines all over the world. It is of the utmost importance that the fat you are cooking in is fresh and clean. Fats can go rancid and add an acrid, unpleasant aroma to anything they touch. Even fresh oils used for frying quickly take on the character of anything that previously touched it, including those golden crusty bits that fall to the bottom and the flavors inherent in whatever food was cooked. The high heats used in frying

accelerate the breakdown of those fats. And while frying fat can certainly be reused after straining, we don't recommend reusing it too many times, as you'll lose the distinct flavor of contemporary ingredients. They'll be haunted with the ghosts of seafood past.

Frying is a quick cook method, and achieving and maintaining consistent high temperatures is fundamental to a successful outcome. Different batters or coatings may call for different temperatures, ranging from 350°F to well over 400°F. And when your fat has reached temperature, it's important that the temperature doesn't drop too precipitously after adding your items. The lower the temperature, the more fat that item absorbs, the greasier it becomes, and the heavier it eats. Properly fried foods feel light on the palate—the crisp is ethereal, not weighty. To do this, maintain or even increase the heat just before adding your ingredients and don't add too much at a time, as those ingredients need room to sizzle and sputter about. It actually takes less time total to fry in smaller batches than to drop everything in at once.

Frying is also inherently entertaining: it's fun, it's sexy, it smells great. (Though be sure to have good ventilation humming. And think about removing any hot oil to outside as it cools.) A succession of seafoods and vegetables, fried crisp in the minute and served piping hot, is a wonderful way to welcome guests into your house.

Last, be mindful and careful. Frying can be dangerous. Wherever possible, use tongs, clear out some space, and make your guests (especially children) aware that this is the cook's work area for the time being.

*I always fry on a back burner* to maximize the efficiency of the exhaust, but more so to prevent the catastrophe of hot oil accidentally falling off the stove.

*John*

Sauces for fried foods are made separate from the frying and should always include a bright burst of acidity to help balance the richness. Many classical sauces served with fried foods are fatty in themselves—think remoulade and tartar sauce, for example. This is certainly a delicious serving style, but a pile of lemons to squeeze on a moment before popping the food into your mouth is truly all that is needed. And don't think that frying is just for proteins—in fact, a good fritto misto is as much vegetable as anything else. Super crispy see-through Japanese tempura is perfect to enrobe sprigs of herbs such as parsley or cilantro, super-thin shaved lemon slices, or bite-sized broccoli or cauliflower florets.

Shallow-frying, where you use a sauté pan and just about 1/3 to 1/2 inch of fat, is meant for dishes where you are crusting one side of the fish or possibly two. The fat should come about halfway up the sides of whatever you are cooking. It requires the cook to flip the ingredient about halfway through cooking.

Either method of frying is generally hands-off. Give the items a very delicate swirl before dropping them fully into the fat. This ensures that the very outer layer cooks just a little, helping to prevent the crust from falling off or items getting stuck to the bottom or glomming together. Once the items are in the fat, you can perhaps give it a gentle stir, but otherwise let the fat do its thing.

What you're aiming for is color and texture. Given the high, high heat, try not to fry foods that are particularly thick. Generally, bite-sized or a couple of bites are as big as you want to go, so the ratio of cook time for the outside and inside is equal. An exception would be a giant hunk of cod for fish and chips, where you would employ a slightly lower heat for a longer time. Before starting, have a receiving setup ready, meaning a platter lined with paper towels and a bowl of salt or whatever seasoning you're using to sprinkle on at the end.

Speaking of salt, it's important to pre-season any delicate seafoods and let them rest for a few minutes (see page 80), as this helps augment structural integrity. It's also important to think about how the crust or batter is seasoned, given its proportionally high surface area. It's usually best to season lightly at the outset and sprinkle with salt again after cooking as needed rather than guessing wrong at the beginning.

Seasonings other than salt in a batter or coating are directly exposed to the fat, and their delicate flavor and oils can burn very easily. So, it's best to sprinkle these on after cooking (think a dusting of Old Bay Seasoning).

Just as you need a strategy for getting the fried items out of the fat and resting them, you should have a strategy for getting them into the fat. The prep for this technique is inherently hands-on, so have a system whereby you keep one hand clean and the other dedicated to dipping into whatever coating you're using. Have a linear flow setup, so you're never reaching across yourself or the stove to get a dripping battered food to the fat.

See: Fritto Misto (page 147)

# Steam

While other methods create contrast in texture and flavor, steaming lends just the subtlest waft of perfume, a beguiling scent meant to alight interest as the most elegant use of perfume or cologne is meant to. Steaming is different from poaching in that you're placing seafood above an infused liquid rather than submerging it within. By capturing the rising steam that carries the delicate aromas with it, the inherent flavor of the seafood itself is greatly intensified while visited by just a whisper of additional flavor. Cooking fish whole via this method is best, as it takes advantage of the additional flavor, structure, and beauty of presentation that serving on the bone provides.

For additional flavor, wrap your fish in banana, fig, or grape leaves before steaming. There are specialized steaming vessels, such as bamboo steaming baskets, available online and at Asian markets for just a few dollars. In the absence of such equipment, a deep pot with a rack in the bottom to create separation between the liquid and the food

works perfectly well. If you don't have a rack that fits, this is a perfect use for those fennel fronds or some chunked-up onions, carrots, or celery—anything that will provide a raft upon which the seafood can sit above the liquid. The flavors don't have to be Asian-inspired, of course. Fennel, thyme, allspice, and black pepper give a distinctly Mediterranean feel. Bay leaves, onion, fennel seed, cardamom, cloves, and cinnamon stick provide invitation to Western Africa.

Recognizing doneness comes with practice. Using an instant-read thermometer to measure 125°F to 130°F at the thickest part of the seafood tells you it's time to serve it. For thin fillets the rule is when it flakes it's done. But for whole fish, using a thermometer is important, as the density of the bone in the center will hold its cool far longer than the delicate fillet surrounding it.

Whole fish are extremely delicate, so make sure the pot you're using is either going to be

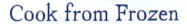

the serving vessel or that you have enough room to work in order to wedge a large spatula, perhaps even two, underneath the fish to support it in its entirety as you lift it out. The pot should be large enough so that using a top, you are capturing the heat and creating an environment of consistent, even steam. As you are not going to turn or flip the fish as it cooks, building up and capturing the heat is essential.

Sauces for steamed dishes are made separate, though some of the infused liquid beneath, now enriched with flavorful drippings from the fish itself, can be incorporated. This technique is most often found in Asian cuisines, and commonly the sauces served have an acidic, salty, and possibly spice component.

See: Steamed Black Bass with Ginger, Garlic, and Scallions (page 301)

## Cook from Frozen

Quality frozen fish is now the norm and available in nearly every grocery store. While this is a result of improvements in freezing technology, of equal importance is how that fish is thawed. But who says you need to thaw it when you can cook it right from frozen? If the seafood has been glazed with a protective sheath of ice, thaw that glaze quickly under cold running water. Now, this doesn't work with all species or methods of cooking. But as long as the heat is gentle and evenly applied—especially with slow-roasting, poaching, or braising into a stew—you can achieve incredible results while keeping the timeframe from freezer to plate short and convenient.

We love cooking from frozen, because it makes seafood truly a convenience food. On a busy Tuesday night with no plans for dinner, you can forgo the chicken nuggets from the freezer and grab the seafood instead.

I find it better to defrost seafood under cold water and cook from there on, but indeed seafood is a convenience food.

Andrew

Part 4

# The Recipes: From Simple to Stunning

# Our Culinary Approach to Seafood

## Andrew

Less is more. In everything. And that's how I cook. That's also how I cook seafood because of the delicate nature of many finfish species. Less is more when it comes to a broiled piece of flounder (butter and salt?) or a fried hake fillet (salt and lemon?), but just look at all the intense flavors in my recipe for whole black bass (page 301). That's because when a saltwater fish with a decent amount of fat like bass is cooked on the bone, it will develop a throughline of flavor that can stand up to the hot peppers and garlic.

I approach seafood cookery in general as a minimalist, but there are exceptions. Consider the bold nature of a shucked cherrystone clam, which can take on a horseradish-spiked cocktail sauce and still be the dominant flavor. As a globalist I have been taught all about the range of possibilities for when and where to play with bigger flavors. I have had the chance to cook around the world more times than I can count. I've sat in kitchens with grandmothers in Okinawa and fishermen in Sicily, with tribal leaders in the Amazon cooking river fish wrapped in leaves over open fire and three-star Michelin chefs with a battery of cooks lending support to one diner's pleasure. I've seen a lot. And what I have learned has informed my way of cooking fish and shellfish.

Sure "less is more" is easy to say, it's almost cliché. When I eventually write my memoir, I'll share my life's journey as a chef across a few hundred pages. But in the meantime, how I've learned to cook seafood over the past forty-five years is simple knowledge that I can share to illustrate the point. It was 1980, and I was working in Venice at Al Colomba, a superb restaurant at the time, for a day rate as a glorified grunt peeling vegetables and cleaning fish and doing whatever I was asked to do. I had lots of ideas. Very few were any good. I remember once getting some local razor clams that were so thin and delicate. I thought I would process them for days, cure them, dry them, grind them, rehydrate them, then turn that into a mousseline and season it with everything I could get my hands on. It was the dumbest idea ever but a necessary part of being a young cook. In the midst of my experiment, a line cook who must have been sixty, an old hard-drinking fellow who always had a cigarette in his mouth and knew how to cook everything superbly, discovered me in the back with my Frankenstein creation and tasted it. He spat it out.

I was horrified and my pride was hurt, but I'll always remember what he told me (prefaced by a lot of swearing): "Incontra la vongola dove si trova!" *Meet the clam where it's at.* Forty-five years of tasting, experimenting, asking questions everywhere I've gone, constantly learning, and eating and I'm finally at the place where I can meet an ingredient where it's at.

That's how I cook seafood.

# Barton

As a child of the Chesapeake and son of an intrepid seafood cook, I have always appreciated the savor of salt water and all that comes from it. I have photos of myself in utero, my mom perusing the seafood wharf at 12th and Maine in D.C. So, it made sense that when I started my career as a cook, I was drawn toward chefs with a passion for seafood and precision to their cooking, and I adopted their skills as I charted my course. I've had the good fortune to live and cook all over the world. Not to the extent that Andrew has, of course. Who has? But enough to see and appreciate distinct cuisines and cultures dedicated to seafood as well as the similarities among them. Seafood begs for a straightforward approach and is often best flattered by one. This is the approach reflected in the recipes that follow. On a Tuesday night, when dinner is needed now, a piece of fish straight from the freezer into the toaster oven for slow-roasting with nothing more than a delicious-in-its-own-right olive oil and salt is my go-to. And while my ladyfish and kidsquids certainly appreciate this, we also very much enjoy exploring many global forms and flavors of seafood.

One of the things I appreciate most about seafood is that it does not lend itself to highly manipulative cooking processes. Even on the loftiest of Michelin tasting menus, where the chef's hand and personality are very present, the seafood dishes generally feel more ingredient-forward, less done up. I have a feeling that this is why many chefs don't take to seafood as a throughline in their creative process. It distinctly edits our actions and is really a reflection of our intentions, so it might not feel as rewarding to the cook. Our intentions for seafood cooking must always be to serve forth the very best quality we can find and flatter it only so much as is needed with ingredients and ingenuity. I cannot stress this enough—90 percent of getting a dish right is starting with great-quality ingredients. Let the inspiration of what looks best in the market be the first humble step in any recipe.

While the recipes in this book are designed with particular species in mind, we have ordered the book around culinary categories, grouping together seafoods with like culinary qualities. So if the spicy mango and basil salad piques your interest but the snapper called for just doesn't sing, then the barramundi or tautog or branzino that does will certainly play the role well. Like all ingredients, seasonality provides a significant parameter to available quality.

The ultimate ingredient in every recipe I cook is gratitude. We are aware of how fortunate we are to be well-fed, to have choice, and to give those gifts to others. To cook for anyone is an act of love, an act of kindness, and when we set forth with such intention, our meals are better for it. This isn't some new-age hokey mantra, it's just that, damn, I'm really glad to have dinner. And I'm really honored to be able to give dinner to my kids. Such a mindset is the foundation of sustainability: Why do the work to sustain something if we're not happy to have it?

# Seafood for Breakfast

Breakfast in America nearly always excludes seafood from the menu. The chicken contributes (eggs), the pig participates (bacon), but seafood just isn't invited to the table. We think this should change. (Of course, the classic brunch food smoked salmon is the exception. And while we certainly adore silken, suave, smoky salmon, we encourage you to think outside the cereal box.) Not only can seafood provide a powerhouse of healthful and nutritious fuel for the day, it's also unexplored culinary country in which we can find all sorts of creative opportunities, whether it's canned salmon integrated into your scramble or last night's fish turned into a cake and used as the base for a Benedict brunch. Swordfish bacon, anyone?

## From England to Japan, Chile to

South Africa, fish plays a role at breakfast. We have served Japanese breakfast at my house since my son Noah was a baby. A small portion of rice, broiled fish, pickles, and miso soup has been my preferred big breakfast (that and a big mess of Russ & Daughters cured and smoked fish) ever since I was young!

Andrew

# Pre-seasoning Seafood

Salt is a magical ingredient. Not only does it accentuate flavor, making foods taste more like they do, but it also has a significant impact on texture and moisture retention. It's a long-held practice to season seafood and meat just prior to cooking, especially with methods like sautéing or grilling where you are aiming for char and crispness. This goal can be more difficult to achieve in the presence of salt, as salt draws water to the surface, and water is the enemy of crisp. Given enough time, though, salt draws that moisture to the surface, but then the salt is reabsorbed into the flesh as it is drawn deeper throughout the fillet. Salt helps to enhance the structural integrity of cells, thus helping to maintain the moisture within while cooking. But it also leaves the surface covered in water-soluble proteins that were drawn out by the salt and then left there on the surface as the salt and water migrated. These slightly desiccated proteins can aid in crisping, charring, and flavor development. You'll notice the recipes in this book call for seasoning fish at different times but generally fifteen minutes before cooking—enough time for this process to happen. Another benefit of pre-seasoning is that the same flavor enhancement is achieved with less salt than from a surface coating of salt.

# Cooking to Doneness

Given the extreme diversity of size, shape, texture, and even basic life form of seafood (i.e., clam vs. cod), cooking to doneness is not as simple as it is for meat or chicken. Sure, you can use a thermometer for thick fillets such as salmon or whole roasted fish (125°F to 130°F is our suggested range). But when cooking very thin flounder fillets or dozens of shrimp, a thermometer just isn't the best or most accurate tool. Here's a general outline of how to tell when various seafoods are cooked. The rule of thumb for flaky fillet fish (pollock, flounder, salmon) is more physical and visual—it uses your thumb. When a fillet is cooked, it will separate under gentle pressure. Even if the color of the fish has not changed significantly (as with very slow-roasted salmon), as soon as the fish flakes, it is cooked.

# 4.01

# Stocks and Broths

These are great culinary foundations to have on hand in the freezer. They are useful in so many ways, from sauces to soups, and they can help minimize waste by making good use of bones and trim.

# Andrew's Favorite Dashi

**MAKES 4 QUARTS**

Dashi is the all-purpose cooking broth of Japan, used in soups, braises, and sauces. Cooks the world over have taken to dashi because it is loaded with glutamates, making it a natural healthy umami bomb of flavor to add to any dish you can think of. Its two ingredients—seaweed and dried smoked bonito—should be a staple in every cook's pantry.

*Andrew*

**5 six-inch squares kombu (dried kelp)**
**2 cups tightly packed bonito flakes (katsuobushi)**

Pour 4 quarts water into a large stockpot and add the kombu. Bring to a strong simmer over medium heat, uncovered.

When the water is about to boil, turn off the heat and let it rest, uncovered. Return to a strong simmer, and when it's about to boil, turn off the heat. Remove and reserve the kombu. Add the bonito flakes and bring it back to a boil and cook for 10 to 20 seconds.

Turn off heat, skim the foam, and let stand for 8 minutes, uncovered. Strain and use or refrigerate up to a week or freeze for up to many months.

To make a second stock for simmered dishes or recipes that require a less refined stock, simmer the used kombu and bonito flakes in the same volume of water for 10 minutes. Strain and serve immediately or store in airtight containers in the refrigerator for up to a week or freeze for up to many months.

# Barton's Dashi

## MAKES 3 QUARTS

Dashi is one of the foundations of Japanese cuisine, but don't think it needs to be confined as such. This delightfully nuanced broth has a big impact through its umami-rich, briny flavors and is a perfect base for everything from bouillabaisse to chowder. It's also a perfect stand-in for fish or shellfish stock if those ingredients are not on hand. I take a bit of liberty with my version by adding white wine, a hit of acid and aroma that helps to bridge any mash-up of East-West cuisine. As a little treat, serve it on its own with a dash of mace, dried chile, and fennel seeds. To keep the flavors of this broth light and bright, take care to keep it at a low simmer and don't let it boil.

1 cup white wine

2 strips lemon zest

2 slices fresh ginger

2 star anise pods

2 ounces kombu (dried kelp)

½ cup bonito flakes (katsuobushi)

Combine the wine, lemon zest, ginger, and star anise in a large pot or small stockpot. Place over medium heat, bring to a simmer, and simmer until the alcohol dissipates, about 5 minutes. Add 3 quarts water and return to a simmer. Add the kombu, reduce the heat to maintain a gentle simmer, and cook for 15 minutes, uncovered throughout. Using a slotted spoon, remove the kombu and reserve it for another use.* Add the bonito flakes, remove from the heat, and let steep for 10 minutes. Strain, discarding all solids.

Use immediately or store in airtight containers in the refrigerator for up to 4 days or the freezer for up to 1 month.

*The kombu used to flavor both of our dashis rehydrates as it cooks and is typically removed from the finished broth. This "refreshed" kelp can be diced up and used in vinaigrettes, salads, or sauces like tzatziki in place of some of the herbs. Or just eat it—it's delicious.

# Basic Fish Stock

A tip for making fish stock is to not disturb it. The less you move the stock while you're cooking it and straining it, the clearer both the liquid and the flavor will be. Stock captures the essence of its ingredients, so using the highest quality is of the utmost importance. If you don't have fish bones on hand, you'll be able to find them at a specialty fishmonger. Seek out the cartilaginous fins, heads, and collars, as they are particularly good for giving body, richness, and depth of flavor to stock. In this recipe, we call for bones from the flaky white flesh fish category—fish with lean, clean flavor—but that doesn't mean you can't make a great stock from more robust-flavored species. For example, salmon head stock is delicious, but the process of making it is more like making tea, as you steep it rather than simmer it.

*Jet*

I buy bay leaves by the pound and use them copiously, especially in stocks and soups. If you are more modest with your bay leaf consumption than I am, you don't need to include all ten as we do here. Even one will add a noticeable depth of character to the broth.

¼ cup extra-virgin olive oil or butter

10 allspice berries

1 knob fresh ginger (about the size of your thumb)

10 bay leaves

1 or 2 cardamom pods

10 black peppercorns

2 tablespoons fennel seeds

1 pound vegetable trim (fennel and fronds, onion, celery, carrots, leeks)

3 pounds fish bones and/or trimmings (preferably from mild-flavored fish such as flounder, cod, and halibut)

Heavy pinch of salt

2 cups white wine

Heat the oil or melt the butter in a large, wide pot (8 quarts or bigger) over medium-low heat. Add the allspice, ginger, bay leaves, cardamom, black peppercorns, and fennel seeds and toast until aromatic, about 1 minute. Add the vegetable trim and cook, stirring, for about 5 minutes. Add the fish bones, salt, and wine. Increase the heat to medium, bring to a simmer, and simmer until the alcohol aroma has dissipated, about 5 minutes. Add 3 quarts cold water and bring to a low simmer. Simmer uncovered for 20 minutes, then turn off the heat. Let the stock rest for 10 minutes, allowing the solids to settle. Ladle the liquid off and pour the rest through a strainer into a bowl. Once you reach the bottom of the pot, pour the remaining liquid through a strainer into a separate bowl. Let it rest for a few minutes to allow the particles to settle. Ladle off the clear liquid from the top, discarding any liquid that is murky. Discard all the solids and combine the two stocks. Use immediately or store in airtight containers in the refrigerator for 2 to 3 days or the freezer for up to 6 months.

# Andrew's Rich Fish Stock

**MAKES ABOUT 1 GALLON**

Rich fish stock is a step away from broth, makes sauce making a breeze, and is economical in its use of vegetable trim, water, and fish bones/heads to turn good food into great food. Stock is a vital ingredient in the kitchen. It has good flavor but is light; watery if you wanted to think of it that way. Rich stocks are fortified in some way, a greater bone-to-water ratio, more veg, some cooked and raw bones or all three. I use those types of stocks a lot. Broths are fortified even more and frequently are reduced as well to concentrate flavors and they are servable on their own.

**3½ pounds fish bones from a saltwater white-fleshed fish, heads included (I love to use halibut or snapper)**

**3 cups mixed diced leeks, celery, and onion**

**2 bay leaves**

**1 tablespoon black peppercorns**

**8 parsley sprigs**

**3 garlic cloves, smashed**

**1 cup white wine**

Rinse the fish bones and heads under cold running water for 10 minutes. Place them in a 3-gallon pot and cover with 1 gallon cold water. Add the diced leeks, celery, and onion, the bay leaves, peppercorns, parsley, garlic, and wine and bring to a simmer over low heat. Lower the heat to maintain the barest of simmers and cook for 2 hours, uncovered. Let the stock cool in the pot for 1 hour.

Strain slowly, tipping the pot into another pot in the sink and letting the solids stay. Discard the solids. Strain again through a strainer lined with cheesecloth.

Use immediately or store in airtight containers in the refrigerator for up to 1 week or the freezer for up to 6 months.

# Barton's Rich Fish Stock
# (for Paella, Bouillabaisse, or Any Braise)

**MAKES ABOUT 3 QUARTS**

In many broth-based and braised dishes, the outcome is largely determined by the quality of stock that is used. This stock provides a rich texture and incredible, well-developed flavor and is versatile for use in soups, stews, risottos, and more. Where clarity is key to flavor and quality for our Basic Fish Stock (page 85), that's not the case here. The key is fresh, fresh, fresh ingredients. That said, it's fine to accumulate the shrimp or lobster shells over time. Just keep them in an airtight container in the freezer until you're ready to use them.

*J.L.*

2 garlic heads

8 tablespoons extra-virgin olive oil

2 pounds lobster bodies or shrimp heads

1 onion, sliced (about 1 cup)

1 fennel bulb with fronds, sliced (about 1¹/₂ cups)

2 celery stalks, sliced (about 1 cup)

¹/₄ cup tomato paste

2 tablespoons smoked sweet paprika

2 star anise pods or ¹/₂ teaspoon ground star anise

2 tablespoons fennel seeds

5+ bay leaves

1 pinch ground cinnamon

2 cups rosé or white wine

3 to 4 pounds white fish bones, such as halibut or cod head

Salt

There's a surprise spice in here: cinnamon. This gives the stock an unassuming nuance, depth, and fullness. Don't overdo it; a healthy pinch will do.

Preheat the oven or toaster oven to 325°F. Coat the garlic in 1 tablespoon of the oil and wrap it in aluminum foil. Roast for 45 minutes.

Heat 4 tablespoons of the remaining oil in a large heavy-bottom pot such as a dutch oven over high heat. Add the lobster bodies and sear them until deeply colored all over, 4 to 5 minutes. Remove from the pot to a bowl. Lower the heat to medium-high and add 1 tablespoon of the remaining oil to the pot. Add the onion, fennel, and celery and cook, stirring, until colored, 7 to 8 minutes. Scrape away a small space in the bottom of the pan and add the remaining 2 tablespoons oil. Add the tomato paste to the oil and cook, stirring, for about 2 minutes, until it no longer smells raw. Add the paprika, star anise, fennel seeds, bay leaves, and cinnamon. Cook, stirring constantly, for 2 minutes to toast the spices. Add the whole heads of roasted garlic, smashing them with the back of a spoon to release the cloves. Add the wine and cook, stirring, until the alcohol smell has dissipated, about 2 minutes. Add the bones and seared lobster bodies and 3¹/₂ quarts water and bring to a simmer over medium heat. Reduce to medium-low and simmer, uncovered, for 45 minutes. Strain and let cool.

Serve immediately or store in the refrigerator for 2 to 3 days or the freezer for up to 6 months.

# Andrew's Shellfish Stock

The is the stock that arguably makes the biggest difference in my seafood cookery. It's transformative for carrying flavor in seafood pastas, risottos, soups, and braises like bouillabaisse and cioppino, and in sauces it simply is a must.

*Andrew*

If I am feeling frisky, I will supplement the plain shells with a pound of chopped shrimp with the heads on.

2 tablespoons extra-virgin olive oil

2 tablespoons tomato paste

Shells from 5 to 7 pounds shrimp

2 carrots, diced (about 1 cup)

2 celery stalks, diced (about 1 cup)

1 medium onion, diced (about 1 cup)

1 leek, greens trimmed and discarded, split and washed, minced (about 1 cup)

2 bay leaves

1 teaspoon black peppercorns

8 parsley sprigs

6 garlic cloves, smashed

1 cup chopped tomatoes

2 cups dry white wine

Heat the oil in a 2-gallon pot over medium heat. Add the tomato paste and shrimp shells. Cook, tossing frequently, for about 4 minutes, until the paste is caramelizing but nothing is burning, then add the carrots, celery, onion, leek, bay leaves, peppercorns, parsley, and garlic. Cook for 10 minutes, stirring occasionally. Add the tomatoes and the wine, cook for a few minutes, then and add 6 quarts water. Bring to a simmer, then lower the heat to maintain a simmer and continue cooking, uncovered, for 1 hour.

Let cool for 1 hour on the counter, then strain through a fine chinois lined with cheesecloth, pressing down on the solids. Discard the solids.

Use immediately or store in airtight containers in the refrigerator for up to 3 days or the freezer for up to 1 year.

# Barton's Shellfish Stock

## MAKES ABOUT 3 QUARTS

Like fish stock or dashi, shellfish stock is useful for any seafood dish that calls for a bit of added liquid, bringing its own iodine-rich, shellfishy flavor. This differs from Andrew's Rich Fish Stock (page 86) in the flavors and spices it incorporates. It's also a bit lighter in both body and flavor and is better for dishes where you don't want color added, such as a white chowder. Don't be afraid to mix your seafoods up a bit. Clam chowder with a bit of lobster stock in it? Yes, please. A West Coast cioppino with a heady shellfish stock as its base? Now you're talking. Though this recipe calls for quite a few ingredients, they are all things you likely have on hand. And it is a great way to take full advantage of something you've already paid for: the shells of shrimp or lobster left over from another meal. This version gives you a nice, brightly colored, intensely aromatic stock that is versatile in its uses. You can darken the stock and give it more body by adding 2 to 3 tablespoons tomato paste.

*[signature]*

1/4 cup vegetable oil
6 lobster bodies or 3 cups shrimp heads/shells
1 onion, chopped (about 1 cup)
1 carrot, chopped (about 1/2 cup)
2 celery stalks, chopped (about 1 cup)
1 1/2 cups chopped fennel bulb and/or fronds
5 to 10 bay leaves
1 star anise pod
1 tablespoon fennel seeds
1 1/2 cups white wine
1/4 cup dark rum or brandy
Salt

Heat the oil in a large, wide stockpot over high heat. Add the lobster bodies or shrimp heads and shells and cook, stirring occasionally, for about 4 minutes. Remove the bodies and reserve them. Lower the heat to medium-high and add the onion, carrot, celery, fennel, bay leaves, star anise, and fennel seeds and cook, stirring occasionally, until the vegetables just begin to wilt, about 5 minutes. Return the shells to the pot. Add the wine and rum. Bring to a boil and cook until the alcohol smell dissipates, about 5 minutes. Season generously with salt. Add 3 quarts water and bring to a simmer. Reduce the heat to medium-low, cover and cook for 30 to 40 minutes. Remove from the heat and let the stock rest for 10 minutes, allowing the solids to settle.

Ladle the liquid off and pour it through a strainer into a bowl. Once you reach the bottom of the pot, pour the remaining liquid through a strainer into a separate bowl. Let it rest for a few minutes for the particles to settle. Ladle off the clear liquid from the top, discarding any liquid that is murky. Discard all the solids and combine the two stocks. Use immediately or store in containers in the refrigerator for 2 to 3 days or the freezer for up to 6 months.

# Chicken Stock

This chicken stock is rich and takes on a lovely color thanks to the roasting of some of the bones. Two things we'll call out. We are using dashi as a base for this stock. Please give it a try. The results are decadent, and this stock is filled with craveable flavor. And you might be wondering why chicken stock is in a seafood cookbook. Well, the answer is simple: Some recipes for soups, stews, and sauces, even ones that are rooted in the world of blue foods, taste better with a base of poultry broth. You won't be disappointed.

5 pounds chicken backs, necks, and wing bones

2 gallons dashi (pages 83 or 84) or water

4 carrots, diced (about 2 cups)

4 celery stalks, diced (about 2 cups)

2 onions, diced (about 2 cups)

1 leek, greens trimmed and discarded, split and washed, chopped (about 1 cup)

1 bay leaf

1 teaspoon black peppercorns

4 parsley sprigs

2 cloves

2 garlic cloves, smashed

Preheat the oven to 350°F. Place half of the bones on a baking sheet and roast until browned, about 50 minutes.

Meanwhile, bring 2 quarts of water to a boil. Place the remaining raw bones in a large colander in your sink. Rinse with cold water first, then with the boiling water.

Pour the 2 gallons water or weak dashi into a 3- or 4-gallon stockpot and place over low heat. Place both the cooked and the rinsed raw bones into the pot. Add the carrots, celery, onion, leek, bay leaf, peppercorns, parsley, cloves, and garlic. Bring to a bare simmer.

Lower the heat to maintain a 200°F temperature, with no bubbling or movement of the stock. (This can be done in the oven as well. If you use the oven method, set your oven to 225°F.) Steep for 24 hours, adding the occasional cup or two of cold water if needed. And, yes, it's very safe to cook something for this long "unattended," as long as you are in the house! If you're steeping on the stovetop and need to leave, throw the pot into a 225°F oven.

Skim the fat. Slowly strain the stock through a cheesecloth-lined colander placed over a large bowl, discarding the solids and scum at the bottom of the pot. Let the stock cool for at least 1 hour, uncovered, on your counter. Skim the fat from the top again if needed.

Use immediately or store in the refrigerator in airtight containers for up to 4 days or the freezer for up to 1 month.

# 4.02
# Bivalves

# Cleaning and Cooking Bivalves

Bivalves are among the few seafoods that we buy live (along with lobster, crabs, and live fish from Asian and other markets). Once taken from the water, they can last up to several weeks if properly stored. As such, there's an incredible diversity in that each batch has multiple creatures, some of which have different levels of remaining vigor.

Bivalves, in particular clams and oysters, are often grown in, on, or just above the bottom of the water column. Grit can get lodged in their shells and crevices. This is especially true of oysters, particularly at the hinge—precisely the point you start at to open them. So, it's important to wash them before working with them, so you don't introduce any of that grit into the edible portion or broth made from cooking. It's best to wash them with a brush under cold running water. Never soak them in fresh water.

Mussels affix themselves to rocks and pilings in the wild and to ropes on which they are farmed. They do so with what's known as the beard, or *byssus*, fibrous tendrils that grow from the creature out through the split of the shell. This is not edible. In fact, engineers have discovered that these threads are stronger than Kevlar! The beard is best removed just prior to cooking. To do so, simply hold the mussel in one hand and, using the thumb and forefinger on the other hand, grasp the threads and pull them away from the shell. This is not good for the well-being of the mussel, so they should be cooked immediately after cleaning.

If any mussels have open or gaping shells prior to cooking, this could be a sign that they are dead, and you *do not* want to eat those. But sometimes the mussels just relax a little and their shells gape open. So lightly tap one side of the shell on a table, and if the mussel shows any movement in closing its shell, it is fine to eat. Discard any that are cracked.

Mussels can cook at slightly different rates: After 5 minutes many will have opened, after 8 minutes most will have opened, and after that a couple more might open, but there may be some that never open at all. Simply discard the ones that haven't opened and enjoy the ones that have.

How to
Shuck an
Oyster

# Poached Clams with Pecans, Orange, and Basil

**SERVES 4**

Clams are often served raw on the half shell, but they are even more versatile when cooked then returned to the shell to be eaten chilled with various accompaniments. I love the unexpected bright and cheerful combination of orange and clams, along with the textural punctuation of crunchy pecans and cooling, aromatic basil. You can also try this with mussels or a combination of mussels and clams.

*J.T.*

1-inch knob fresh ginger, cut into large pieces*
Zest and juice of 1 orange (about ¼ cup juice)
24 littleneck clams
3 tablespoons extra-virgin olive oil
½ small red onion, diced (about ¼ cup)
1 garlic clove, grated on a Microplane or minced
½ cup pecan pieces
1 teaspoon sherry vinegar
Salt
Freshly cracked Black Pepper–Fennel Blend
(page 53) or black pepper
Fresh basil leaves

*Instead of ginger, you could use a few cardamom pods and bay leaves to flavor the water.

Pour ½ inch of water into a wide-bottomed pot and add the ginger, orange juice, and clams. Cover and cook over high heat until the clams have opened, 6 to 10 minutes, shaking the pan halfway through. Discard any that do not open. Remove the clams and reserve them. Strain the liquid, reserving ¾ cup.

Meanwhile, heat the oil in a medium sauté pan over medium heat. Add the red onion, garlic, and pecan pieces and cook until toasted and aromatic, about 4 minutes. Add the orange zest, vinegar, and the reserved clam cooking liquid. Stir to combine and bring to a simmer.

Remove from the heat and season with salt if needed. Remove the clam meats from the shells, discarding one shell from each clam. Spoon the pecan mixture evenly into the remaining shells, placing a clam on top of each. Garnish with pepper-fennel blend and torn basil.

Left to right: Chilled Mussels with Aioli (page 95) and Poached Clam with Pecans, Orange, and Basil (page 93)

# Chilled Mussels with Aioli

**SERVES 8 AS AN APPETIZER**

This is such a crowd-pleasing recipe, full of color, flavor, and texture from herbs, pepper, and fennel. There's something lovely about the flavor of mussels that are cooked and served chilled; it brings out the sweetness in them. This is equally good with clams or a blend of mussels and clams.

The remaining broth is the cook's treat. Strain into a mug, season with a dash of lemon juice and a touch of salt, and float a pat of butter on top for a delightful sip.

*[signature]*

¾ cup white, red, or rosé wine or water

2 pounds mussels

¼ cup plus 1 tablespoon extra-virgin olive oil

1 fennel bulb, finely diced (about 1½ cups)

1 bell red or yellow pepper, finely diced

Salt

Zest and juice of 1 lemon (2 to 3 tablespoons juice)

2 tablespoons chopped chervil

2 tablespoons chopped chives

2 tablespoons chopped tarragon

¼ cup Aioli (page 96)

¼ cup breadcrumbs, such as panko

Pour the wine into a wide pan large enough to hold all the mussels in no more than a double stack/layer.

Add the mussels, turn the heat to high, and cover. You'll start to see steam after a few minutes, and when it audibly comes to a boil, give the mussels a quick stir. Return the lid and cook for another 1 to 3 minutes, until the shells begin to open wide. Using tongs or a slotted spoon, transfer those that have opened to a large bowl. Continue to cook until all (or at least most) have been transferred. Discard any shells that do not open after 7 to 9 minutes. Chill the mussels in the refrigerator uncovered. Strain the cooking broth through a fine-mesh strainer.

While the mussels are cooling, heat ¼ cup of the oil over medium heat. Add the fennel, bell pepper, and a pinch of salt and sauté until tender, about 4 minutes. Remove from the heat and set aside. When the mussels are cool enough to handle, remove the meat and reserve it along with one side of the shell per mussel for serving. Combine the mussel meats with the fennel-bell pepper mixture, the lemon juice, chervil, chives, tarragon, and 2 to 3 tablespoons of the reserved cooking broth. Cover tightly until ready to serve.

In a small saute pan, heat the remaining 1 tablespoon oil over medium heat. Add the breadcrumbs and stir/toss constantly until golden brown. Remove from the heat and add the lemon zest and a pinch of salt.

Add a small dollop of aioli to each shell, place 1 mussel and a spoonful of the fennel-bell pepper mixture on top, and top with a few crunchy breadcrumbs.

# Aioli

**MAKES ABOUT 2 CUPS**

Aioli, or more simply put, a mayonnaise flavored with garlic, is a recipe absolutely worth having in your canon. It is a perfect partner to seafood of all kinds, whether slathered on a delicate piece of cod before broiling, used as the base of a remoulade sauce, or dolloped atop a simple grilled fish. Aioli is infinitely variable in the flavors it can provide a platform for. Try whisking in a few pinches of smoked sweet paprika for a smoky, sunset-hued twist, adding chopped fresh tarragon and a few dashes of Tabasco for elegance and punch, or subbing out the vinegar for lime juice if you're thinking more tropical for your flavoring.

The amount made here is more than is needed for most recipes, but it's always good to have on hand. It will keep for a few days in an airtight container in the refrigerator.

This is my favorite sauce, and it graces our table several times a week. I like a very garlicky aioli, so I add several more cloves than this recipe calls for. But if you want a more neutral mayonnaise, 1 or even ¼ clove will do to gently perfume it. I also like mine very punchy with vinegar. If you prefer a little less tang, you can replace some or all of the vinegar with water or lemon juice.

4 garlic cloves, grated on a Microplane or minced
2 egg yolks
2 tablespoons sherry vinegar
Salt
2 cups vegetable oil (or 1½ cups vegetable oil and ½ cup extra-virgin olive oil for a stronger flavor)

Combine the garlic, egg yolks, vinegar, and a healthy pinch of salt either in a medium bowl or a food processor. Whisk or process into a fine paste. While you are whisking or the machine is running, slowly drizzle in the oil until the mixture is thickened. If it becomes too thick, add a couple of drops of water to thin it. Season with more salt as needed.

# Merguez Sausage with Oysters and Clams, Two Ways

Merguez, a highly spiced North African lamb sausage, is a seemingly unusual but perfect pairing with the briny tang of ice-cold raw oysters or clams. We present two versions of this pairing. The first is hot merguez straight off the heat served alongside the oyster, providing a fire and ice approach, each bringing the best out of their partner. The second is merguez crumbled and cooked down with the bright acidity of tomato and the cooling flavor of parsley and then spooned atop the shellfish.

*Jat*

A light red Bordeaux wine, served lightly chilled, is a surprisingly wonderful pairing for this meaty/salty combo.

## Version 1: Spicy Icy

12 oysters or clams
8 ounces merguez sausage

Shuck the oysters and keep them very cold until ready to serve. Grill or broil the merguez until heated through and slightly charred. Remove from the heat and slice into bite-size rounds. To serve, eat a cold briny oyster immediately followed by a bite of hot sausage.

## Version 2: Crumble Jumble

12 oysters or clams
2 tablespoons extra-virgin olive oil
1 shallot, diced (about 3 tablespoons)
8 ounces merguez sausage, bulk or removed from skin
Salt
1 plum tomato, cut into 1/4-inch dice
2 tablespoons chopped parsley
Zest of 1 lemon
Red chile flakes, such as Aleppo or gochugaru

Shuck the oysters and keep them very cold until ready to serve.

Heat the oil in a medium sauté pan over medium heat. Add the shallot and merguez and cook until the shallots are softened and the merguez is lightly browned, breaking up any chunks of sausage as you go. Season lightly with salt. Mix in the tomato. Cook for about 1 minute, until the tomato is softened. Remove from the heat. Add the parsley and lemon zest and stir to combine. Spoon over the oysters and sprinkle with chile flakes.

Merguez Sausage with Oysters
and Clams, Two Ways (page 97)

# Scallop Aguachile

**SERVES 4**

I love raw seafood; I love spicy, sour, and tart things; and I love herbs and cucumbers. So it's no surprise that long ago when I first ventured to coastal Mexico, I fell in love with aguachile, the dressing of seafood with "chile water." I found a lot of success with recipes of varying kinds. Then I ate several aguachile dishes cooked by the brilliant Claudette Zapeda and I realized I knew nothing about the dish. Claudette is the queen of aguachile. I paid keen attention to her demos and, luckily, since she is a close friend, she parted with some of her secrets. The result is a perfect aguachile verde.

*Andrew*

**8 ounces tomatillos, chopped**
**1/2 bunch cilantro, chopped**
**1/3 cup chopped scallions**
**1 1/2 teaspoons honey**
**1 serrano chile, stemmed**
**1 cup coconut water**
**1/4 cup lemon juice (about 2 lemons)**
**1/4 cup lime juice (about 4 limes)**
**1/2 large English cucumber, chopped (about 1/2 cup)**
**Salt**

**1 pound fresh jumbo dry-pack sea scallops, sliced across in half or thirds**
**1 teaspoon toasted fennel seeds**
**1 carrot, steamed and cooled, thinly sliced into rings (about 1/2 cup)**
**1 small Persian cucumber, thinly sliced into rings (about 1 cup)**
**1 shallot, thinly sliced into rings (about 1/4 cup)**
**1/2 cup mint leaves (from about 4 sprigs) and mint flowers if you have them**
**1/2 cup cilantro leaves (from about 4 sprigs)**
**1/2 cup of your favorite edible flowers**

Combine the tomatillos, cilantro, scallions, honey, chile, coconut water, lemon and lime juices, English cucumber, and salt to taste in a blender and blend until homogenous. Strain though a fine-mesh strainer or a strainer lined with cheesecloth and discard the solids. Season the liquid again as needed, then cover and refrigerate for at least 2 hours.

Place 4 to 5 ounces of aguachile into 4 ice-cold low-sided wide bowls. Divide the scallops among the bowls. Sprinkle each with the fennel seeds and salt. Arrange the carrot discs, Persian cucumber rings, and shallot rings around each bowl. Arrange the mint and cilantro leaves and flowers around the bowls. Serve immediately.

# Oysters with Vadouvan Creamed Leeks

**SERVES 4**

Vadouvan is a French take on an Indian curry spice blend. In this recipe, the sensuous tones of the spice meet the silky texture of creamed leeks, all of which to bubbly-top the oysters, heated through until their frilly edges curl and their liquor joins the sauce in this epic flavor bomb.

*J-L*

**6 tablespoons butter**

**2 tablespoons vadouvan**

**3 cups ½-inch diced leeks, white and light green parts (about 2 large leeks)**

**¾ cup heavy cream**

**½ cup white wine**

**24 oysters, shucked, liquor and bottom shells reserved**

**Zest and juice of 1 lemon (2 to 3 tablespoons juice)**

**Salt**

**1 cup breadcrumbs, such as panko**

**½ teaspoon ground allspice**

**Freshly cracked Black Pepper–Fennel Blend (page 53) or black pepper**

**Rock salt (or folded aluminum foil)**

Make sure to clean your leeks before dicing. Peel back the layers of the leeks and rinse well under cold running water to ensure no dirt remains hidden.

Melt 3 tablespoons of the butter in a medium saucepan over medium heat. Add the vadouvan and toast for 30 seconds. Add the leeks and cook, stirring, without coloring for 4 to 5 minutes. Add the cream, wine, oyster liquor, and lemon juice and season with salt. Bring to a simmer and cook until the sauce is thickened and the leeks are softened, 8 to 10 minutes. Remove the pot from the heat and reserve.

Melt the remaining 3 tablespoons of butter in a small sauté pan over medium heat. Add the lemon zest, breadcrumbs, allspice, and pepper-fennel blend. Cook, stirring frequently, until very light golden brown and aromatic, 3 to 4 minutes. Reserve.

Preheat the broiler.

Line a baking tray with rock salt or folded aluminum foil and arrange the empty oyster shells on top. Drop 1 oyster into each shell. Evenly divide the leek mixture among the shells. Top with the breadcrumb mixture. Broil until sizzling, 3 to 5 minutes. Serve hot.

# New Orleans–Style Sizzling Oysters

**SERVES 4**

I fell head over heels for this dish while visiting legendary chef Tenney Flynn's restaurant in the French Quarter, GW Fins. I loved it so much I ordered a couple more plates of them for dessert. His is a labor-intensive dish that I have somewhat simplified here. Tenney dries the shells in an oven overnight, and when they are ordered, the shells are super-heated in an 800°F broiler. Then butter and oysters are added to those shells, creating a fajita effect, bubbling and spitting as it's then walked through the dining room for all to see and smell.

My home version has all the same flavor but without the drama and danger (oyster shells tend to explode at such high temps!). And, of course, I also added fennel seeds.

For this recipe it's best to use a large deep-cup oyster with a hearty shell. Oysters from the South are particularly well-suited for this.

*J.L*

24 oysters, shucked, liquor and bottom shells reserved

1 teaspoon ground fennel seeds

Zest and juice of 1 lemon (2 to 3 tablespoons juice)

2 garlic cloves, grated on a Microplane or minced

Freshly cracked Black Pepper-Fennel Blend (page 53) or black pepper

1 cup (2 sticks) butter, melted

Rock salt or aluminum foil

Crystal Hot Sauce

Crusty bread

A way to take this recipe truly over the top, as Tenney does, is to cold-smoke the oysters for a few minutes before making the recipe. I call for this step in the recipe below, but note that it is optional. I use a PolyScience smoking gun, which is perfectly suited for this task.

In a baking dish, combine the oysters with their liquor, the fennel seeds, lemon zest, garlic, and pepper-fennel blend. Using a smoker or smoking gun, cold-smoke the oysters for 5 to 10 minutes, just long enough to gently flavor them.

Set an oven rack to the highest level and preheat the broiler to high.

Line a baking tray with rock salt or folded aluminum foil and arrange the empty oyster shells on top to stabilize. Place 1 oyster in each shell and pour the melted butter over the top. Place under the broiler and broil until the oysters have plumped and their edges are frilled, 4 to 5 minutes. Remove from the broiler, drizzle with the lemon juice, and serve with hot sauce and crusty bread.

# Mignonettes to Serve with Raw Oysters

Traditional mignonette, a French sauce to serve with oysters, brings a beguiling acidity and slight spice to the briny oyster. We add two variations here. The first uses a sweet white balsamic vinegar, because sweet and salty is a great flavor combo that reveals a distinct personality in the oysters. The second is a West Coast-style mignonette inspired by Hog Island Oyster Company and their famous Hogwash. This herby and spice-rich sauce is a particularly good pairing for West Coast oysters.

## TRADITIONAL MIGNONETTE

**MAKES ABOUT 1/2 CUP**

2 tablespoons finely chopped shallot (about 1 small shallot)

2 teaspoons freshly cracked Black Pepper–Fennel Blend (page 53) or black pepper

3 tablespoons best-quality red wine vinegar

Juice of 1/2 lime (about 1 tablespoon juice)

Combine all the ingredients in a small bowl. Add up to 1 tablespoon water to tame the acidity. Make the day of use.

## WEST COAST MIGNONETTE

**MAKES ABOUT 3/4 CUP**

1 garlic clove

1/4 cup seasoned rice wine vinegar

1/4 cup best-quality red wine vinegar

2 tablespoons finely chopped shallot (about 1 small shallot)

1 tablespoon finely minced pickled ginger

1 small chile, such as Fresno or jalapeño, grated on a Microplane or minced (seeds are okay)

1/4 cup finely chopped cilantro

Juice of 1 lime (about 2 tablespoons)

Smash the garlic with the back of a knife, but do not obliterate it, as you are going to retrieve it. Combine the vinegars in a small bowl, add the garlic, and steep the garlic for 5 minutes. Remove and discard the garlic and add the shallot, pickled ginger, chile, cilantro, and lime juice. Make the day of use.

## WHITE BALSAMIC MIGNONETTE

**MAKES ABOUT 1/2 CUP**

3 tablespoons white balsamic vinegar

Juice of 1/2 lemon (about 1 tablespoon)

2 tablespoons finely chopped shallot (about 1 small shallot)

2 teaspoons toasted fennel seeds, roughly chopped

1/2 teaspoon red chile flakes, such as Aleppo or gochugaru, or more to taste

Combine all the ingredients in a small bowl. Add up to 1 tablespoon water to tame the acidity. Make the day of use.

# Corn–Oyster Fritters

**SERVES 6 TO 8**

Fried, fresh seafood, especially
oysters, are spectacular, and I love
corn fritters. I perfected this recipe
about twenty-five years ago, and I've
never needed another one. I love
corn and shellfish together-sweet and
briny, hot and crunchy with a soft
interior-with a cool spicy sauce for
dipping. Contrast equals perfection.
I serve cold poached seafood of all
types with the remoulade. I have some
on hand all the time, especially in
the warm weather months.

**Vegetable oil**

**2 cups shucked and chopped fresh oysters (about
40 oysters), oyster liquor included***

**3/4 cup milk, plus more if needed**

**1 egg**

**5 tablespoons minced scallion**

**2 serrano chiles, minced**

**2 cups freshly cut corn kernels, gently mashed**

**1 cup finely ground cornmeal**

**2 cups all-purpose flour, plus more if needed**

**1 tablespoon baking powder**

**1/2 teaspoon sugar**

**Salt and freshly ground black pepper**

**1 cup remoulade, homemade (recipe follows) or
store-bought**

**Lemon wedges**

**Crystal Hot Sauce**

* I like to use large West Coast oysters for this recipe.

Pour vegetable oil into a deep-frying pan 3 inches
deep. Heat over medium heat to 375°F.

Combine the oysters and their liquor, milk, egg,
scallion, chiles, and corn in a large bowl. Combine
the cornmeal, flour, baking powder, and sugar in
a separate bowl and season with salt and pepper.
Fold the wet ingredients into the dry ingredients
with a rubber spatula, adding more milk or flour if
needed. The batter should be fairly stiff.

Drop golf ball-size spoonfuls of the batter into
the oil using a slotted spoon or spider and fry
until golden brown, about 4 minutes. I do them in
batches, 8 or so at a time. Remove from the oil and
drain to paper towels. Season with salt. Serve with
the remoulade, lemon wedges, and hot sauce.

# Remoulade

**MAKES ABOUT 1 QUART**

3 celery stalks, chopped (about 1½ cups)

4 garlic cloves

3 medium eggs

1 teaspoon Chesapeake Bay seasoning

3 tablespoons smoked sweet paprika

2 tablespoons Worcestershire sauce

¼ cup whole grain mustard

¼ cup Zatarain's Creole mustard

¼ cup prepared horseradish

¼ cup Heinz Chili Sauce

½ cup cider vinegar

6 scallions, chopped

1½ cups vegetable oil

1 tablespoon hot sauce

Salt

Place the celery, garlic, eggs, Chesapeake Bay seasoning, paprika, Worcestershire sauce, mustards, horseradish, chili sauce, vinegar, and scallions in the bowl of a food processor. With the machine running, slowly pour the oil in to emulsify. It should be thinner than a typical mayonnaise. Season with the hot sauce and salt. Place in the refrigerator while you finish the dish you're serving it with. The longer it rests, the better—I let mine go for at least 12 hours and in the fridge for up to 3 days without issue. Bonus tip, it actually freezes well.

# Andrew's The BEST Clam Chowder

SERVES 6 TO 8

Well, clams are one of my desert island foods for sure. I've dug them out of the bays of Long Island Sound since I could walk. This soup reminds me of cold fall and early winter meals at our home out on Long Island. The fennel, chile, and chives are my additions from forty years ago. The rest is my family chowder recipe that my dad created. Grandma and Grandpa were observant Jews, so there wasn't a lot of clam chowder at their house. I don't keep kosher, nor did my parents. Maybe that's why my dad loved this recipe so much-the forbidden fruit rebound effect and all that. I will tell you this: Make this with Basic Fish Stock (page 85) or Andrew or Barton's Shellfish Stock (page 88 or 89) and call me if you don't find it to be your new favorite chowder recipe.

*Andrew*

4¼ cups Basic Fish Stock (page 85) or Andrew or Barton's Shellfish Stock (pages 88 to 89)

6 pounds cherrystone clams (about 48 clams)

⅓ pound salted butter (1½ sticks or six 1-inch cubes)

1 fennel bulb, minced (about 1½ cups)

1 serrano chile, finely minced

1 large yellow onion, diced (about 1½ cups)

3 celery stalks, diced (about 1½ cups)

2 carrots, thinly sliced (about 1 cup)

1 teaspoon celery seeds, toasted and crushed*

1 teaspoon fennel seeds, toasted and crushed*

3 small Yukon Gold potatoes, peeled and diced (about 3 cups)

3 cups heavy cream

Salt and freshly cracked black pepper

½ cup minced parsley

¼ cup minced chives

Buttered toast

* I find the best way to toast celery seeds and fennel seeds is in a small dry sauté pan set over medium heat. It should take just a couple of minutes. Be careful not to let them burn. Cool slightly, and then crush them using a mortar and pestle.

Pour the stock into a large pot and bring to a boil over medium heat. Add the clams and cover. Cook until JUST open, about 8 minutes. Remove the clams and strain the broth through a strainer lined with cheesecloth (or a coffee filter) and reserve.

Shuck the cooked clams and coarsely chop them. Reserve.

Heat the butter in a large heavy pot over medium heat. Add the fennel, chile, onion, celery, and carrots. When the vegetables appear glassy, 12 to 15 minutes, add the celery seeds and fennel seeds and cook for another minute. Add the potatoes and the reserved broth and bring to a simmer. Cook until the potatoes are tender, about 20 minutes.

Add the clams and heavy cream and season with salt. Reduce the heat to low and simmer very gently for about 20 minutes to thicken the cream a little. Spoon into bowls and garnish the clam chowder with minced parsley and chives. Serve with buttered toast.

# Barton's New England Clam Chowder

**SERVES 6 TO 8**

My clam chowder incorporates a bit
more spice than is traditional. I add
coriander, mace, fennel seeds, and
garlic for depth and sultriness. In
addition to the acidity of the white
wine in the clam broth, I finish my
chowder with a bit of lemon juice to
bring the whole into balance.

*J. L.*

Like most soups and stews, making the
recipe ahead of time, cooling overnight,
and rewarming before serving gives the
flavors a chance to integrate.

1 cup white wine

4 bay leaves

18 top neck clams or 24 littleneck clams (1½ to
2 pounds total)

8 ounces bacon, finely diced

4 tablespoons (½ stick) butter

1 yellow onion, diced (about 1 cup)

1 fennel bulb, diced (about 1½ cups)

1 celery stalk, diced (about ½ cup)

4 garlic cloves, grated on a Microplane or minced

1 tablespoon fennel seeds, crushed

1 teaspoon ground coriander

½ teaspoon ground mace or nutmeg

4 medium red potatoes (about 1 pound), skin on,
diced (about 4 cups)

3 cups half-and-half

2 cups water or Basic Fish Stock (page 85) or
Barton's Shellfish Stock (page 89)

Salt and freshly cracked black pepper

Zest and juice of 1 lemon (2 to 3 tablespoons juice)

¼ bunch parsley, chopped (about ¼ cup)

Combine the wine and bay leaves in a large stockpot
with a lid and bring to a boil over high heat. Add the
clams, cover, and cook until they open, 6 to 10 minutes,
depending on size. Discard any that do not open.
Remove the clams from the broth, then shuck and
chop the meat. Strain and reserve the clam-wine broth.

Render the bacon in a large heavy-bottom stockpot
over medium heat until crisp. Remove the bacon to
a plate and reserve, leaving the fat in the pot.

Return the pot to medium heat and melt the butter
in the bacon fat. Add the onion, fennel, celery, and
garlic and sauté until translucent, 5 to 7 minutes.
Add the fennel seeds, coriander, and mace and toast
for 30 seconds. Add the reserved clam broth, the
potatoes, half-and-half, chopped clam meat, and
water or stock. Season with salt and pepper. Bring
to a simmer and cook until the potatoes are just
soft, about 15 minutes.

Add the lemon juice and taste for seasoning. Spoon
into bowls and garnish with the reserved bacon, the
lemon zest, and parsley.

## Purging Clams

Clams must be cleaned well before
using. I scrub them using a brush
under running water and go a step
further by purging them in salt
water for 30 minutes, then I lift
them out of the water, leaving any
grit in the bottom of the bowl. Do
not pour through a strainer or the
grit will find its way back to the
clams. Purge the clams just before
cooking them; don't leave them in
the salted water for more
than 30 minutes.

*Andrew*

Left to right: Andrew's The BEST Clam Chowder (page 110) and Barton's New England Clam Chowder (page 111)

# Butternut Squash and Mussel Soup

**SERVES 4**

So often we see butternut squash soup as a pureed, velvety smooth dish. This version is a brothy one in which tender chunks of squash and charred and caramelized onions are simmered in a mussel broth. While on the surface this recipe is very simple, the addition of miso gives it an unbelievable depth of character and umami punch. And the tarragon oil adds a decadent and elegant richness to the dish. Any leftover tarragon oil can be incorporated into your next vinaigrette.

This is great when cooled and reheated, as it gives the flavor of the mussels the opportunity to meld with the butternut squash.

**2 pounds mussels**
**1 medium butternut squash (about 2 pounds)**
**1 yellow onion, halved and sliced vertically (about 2 cups)**
**10 tablespoons extra-virgin olive oil**
**Salt**
**3 tablespoons white miso paste**
**Juice of 1/2 lemon (about 1 tablespoon)**
**Dash of Angostura bitters**
**1 garlic clove, sliced**
**1 bunch tarragon leaves, blanched and shocked**
**Crusty bread**

Pour 6 cups of water into a large pot and bring to a simmer over high heat. Add the mussels, cover, and cook until open, 5 to 8 minutes, shaking halfway through, then remove them from the pot. Remove the mussels from their shells and reserve, discarding the shells.

Peel the butternut squash and cut it into roughly 3/4-inch cubes, about 6 cups. Reserve the cubed squash. Add the peels, seeds, and trim to the mussel cooking liquid and simmer for 10 minutes. Strain and reserve the liquid, discarding the solids.

Heat a large heavy-bottom pot (such as a dutch oven) over high heat. Add the onions to the dry pan and let them rest untouched to char slightly, about 3 minutes. Add 2 tablespoons of the oil, reduce the heat to low, season with salt, and cook until caramelized and soft, about 20 minutes.

Add the chunks of butternut squash and miso. Stir to break up the miso and coat the squash. Add the reserved mussel cooking broth, the lemon juice, and bitters. Adjust the seasoning with salt, if needed, and simmer, uncovered, until the squash is soft throughout but not falling apart, about 25 minutes.

To make the tarragon oil, heat 2 tablespoons of the remaining oil in a small pan over medium heat. Add the garlic and cook for about 30 seconds, just until no longer raw. Combine the garlic-oil mixture with the remaining 6 tablespoons oil and the blanched tarragon in a blender and season with salt. Blend until smooth, then pass through a fine-mesh strainer and reserve.

To serve, add the shelled mussels to the soup. Ladle into bowls and garnish with tarragon oil. Serve with crusty bread, grilled or toasted.

## Bitters

Bitters are used in cocktails to create balance between flavors. And they work the same with food. Naturally sweet roasted butternut squash soup with Dungeness crab garnish? Throw a few drops of bitters in and you'll find it comes into focus and is more mature in flavor than any soup you've ever had. Don't overdo it. Just a dash will do.

# Oyster and Parsnip Stew with Rosemary

SERVES 4

The oyster pan roast is a classic technique in which rich dairy is infused with flavors that shucked oysters and their liquor are added to. It is an à la minute preparation, to be made at the time of serving. A mark of success is barely cooked and plump oysters, their edges frilled from the heat. It's uncomplicated in the ingredients used but is dependent on the cook's attention to execute properly. In this version, tender sweet parsnips and heady rosemary are added for a savory autumnal character.

**8 ounces parsnips, peeled and cut into 1-inch pieces**

**4 garlic cloves**

**1 cup half-and-half**

**Salt**

**1 rosemary stalk**

**24 oysters, shucked, liquor reserved**

**Zest of 1 lemon**

**Freshly cracked Black Pepper–Fennel Blend (page 53) or black pepper**

**2 tablespoons chopped chives, parsley, or chervil**

**Crusty bread**

Combine the parsnips, garlic, half-and-half, and 3 cups water in a large pot and season with salt. Cover and bring to a simmer over medium heat and cook until the parsnips are tender throughout, about 20 minutes.

Transfer the parsnips and cooking liquid to a blender and blend until completely smooth.

Return the parsnip puree to the pot and add the rosemary. Let steep for 2 minutes. Remove and discard the rosemary. Bring to a simmer over medium-high heat.

Add the oysters and their liquor, stir to combine, and return to a simmer. Cook until the oysters begin to plump and their edges begin to curl, about 4 minutes. Adjust the seasoning salt if needed.

Remove the pot from the heat and divide the soup and oysters evenly among 4 bowls. Garnish each bowl with lemon zest, pepper-fennel blend, and the herbs. Serve immediately with crusty bread.

# Montauk Scallop and Oyster Pan Roast

**SERVES 6**

This is one of *those* dishes that's simply perfect. I liken it to the edible equivalent of "shut up and kiss me." There is a briny intensity here that is sublime.

When I was a young boy, I went to the Grand Central Oyster Bar in Manhattan with my father and was mesmerized by the pan roasts and stews that fronted the massive oyster bar. As I sat on worn wooden stools and stared at the custom miniature steam-jacketed kettles, I thought it was simply the finest example of show-off cookery I had ever seen. My father would always ask for scallops in his oyster pan roast. He knew they were a perfect briny, oceanic tandem, and this recipe marries them perfectly.

In larger portions, it's a meal-in-a-bowl dinner that only needs crusty hot bread and a salad with an acidic vinaigrette to make for a heavenly troika.

For parties, I make a large batch and serve it in smaller portions out of coffee mugs. I have no issues shucking forty, sixty, or eighty oysters at a time. When I need more than that, or for parties, I buy them shucked from my fishmonger.

*Andrew*

1 slice bacon, minced

2 celery stalks, thinly sliced (about 1 cup)

1 yellow onion, quartered and thinly sliced (about 1 cup)

1 thyme sprig

1 teaspoon smoked sweet paprika

1 tablespoon tomato paste

1 teaspoon chile paste*

3/4 teaspoon Old Bay Seasoning

1 quart freshly shucked oysters (about 80 oysters), drained, 1 1/2 cups liquor reserved**

1 cup Basic Fish Stock (page 85) or either Andrew or Barton's Shellfish Stock (pages 88 to 89), plus more as needed

1 tablespoon butter

8 ounces dry-pack sea scallops

Salt

2 cups heavy cream

2 tablespoons Worcestershire sauce

Freshly ground black pepper

Chives, for garnish

1 baguette, sliced 1/2 inch thick, toasted and buttered, or oyster crackers, for serving

* Available in the relish aisle of your supermarket, or you can use harissa paste.

** Oyster liquor is the liquid inside of the oyster shell. If you don't have 1 1/2 cups of oyster liquor, add more fish stock to reach the correct amount.

In a large pot, cook the bacon over medium heat until softened, about 1 minute. Add the celery, onion, thyme, paprika, tomato paste, chile paste, and Old Bay and cook, stirring frequently, until the onion is translucent, about 2 minutes. Add the oyster liquor and fish stock and bring to a boil. Lower the heat to medium-low and simmer for about 10 minutes, until reduced by one-quarter.

Meanwhile, in a medium skillet, melt the butter over low heat. Season the scallops with salt. Increase the heat to high and cook until the scallops are well browned on one side, about 2 minutes. Immediately transfer to a plate.

Stir the heavy cream into the pot, bring to a simmer, and cook until slightly thickened, about 3 minutes. Add the oysters and bring just to a simmer. Add the scallops and simmer for 30 seconds. Remove from the heat, stir in the Worcestershire sauce, and season with salt and pepper. Discard the thyme sprig. Spoon the stew into bowls, garnish with chives, and serve immediately with the toasted buttered baguette slices or crackers.

# Whole Bay Scallops in Coconut Green Curry

## SERVES 4 AS AN APPETIZER

Perry Raso is the amazing proprietor of Matunuck Oyster Bar in Rhode Island. He's also an organic farmer, oyster farmer, local (and beyond) legend, lover of great wine, and an admired friend. This recipe is adapted from one that he serves on his menu—it uses whole scallops (or mussels or clams) and is a great way to introduce eating the whole scallop (as we do with mussels). Typically, all we eat of the scallop is the adductor muscle, which is used to open and close the shell, and large scallops are rarely sold whole. Mostly this is for food safety reasons, particularly with wild-caught scallops. But the farming of scallops, a relatively new effort in the United States, allows for farmers to determine water quality, and thus food safety, enabling us to enjoy the entire delicacy.

If you can't find in-shell bay scallops, you can use scallops of any type, adjusting the cooking time depending on size.

2 tablespoons vegetable or peanut oil

1 red onion, very thinly sliced (about 1 cup)

1 large carrot, very thinly sliced (about 2 cups)

1 red bell pepper, core and seeds removed, very thinly sliced (about 1 cup)

1 yellow bell pepper, core and seeds removed, very thinly sliced (about 1 cup)

1 serrano or Fresno chile, core and seeds removed, thinly sliced (optional)

2 pounds (15–18 count) bay scallops in their shell (or 1 pound shelled)

1 recipe Green Curry Sauce (recipe follows)* or 32 ounces jarred green curry sauce

1 bunch cilantro, chopped

1 lime, cut into wedges

* While we certainly recommend the easily-made-from-scratch sauce here, there's no shame in reaching for what's on the shelf.

Heat the oil in a large sauté pan over high heat. Add the onion, carrot, bell peppers, and chile and cook undisturbed until they begin to brown, about 4 minutes. Add the scallops and toss to combine. Add the curry sauce, cover, and bring to a boil. Reduce the heat to medium and cook until the scallops have opened, about 5 minutes. Discard any that remain unopened. If using scallop meats, cook until they are barely firm, like the base of your thumb, when pinched.

Divide among the bowls and garnish with cilantro and lime wedges.

# Green Curry Sauce

**MAKES ABOUT 4 CUPS**

This curry sauce is delicious as a simmer sauce for white fish, salmon, and more!

2 tablespoons untoasted sesame oil (use peanut oil if you can't find untoasted)

1 shallot, diced (about 3 tablespoons)

2 garlic cloves, grated on a Microplane or minced

2-inch knob fresh ginger, grated on a Microplane or minced (2 tablespoons)

1 teaspoon curry powder

$\frac{1}{2}$ teaspoon ground cardamom

$\frac{1}{2}$ teaspoon ground nutmeg

1 tablespoon green curry paste

Two 14-ounce cans unsweetened coconut milk

2 teaspoons sugar

1 tablespoon fish sauce

Juice of 1 lime (about 2 tablespoons)

Salt

Heat the oil in a small saucepan over medium heat. Add the shallot, garlic, and ginger and cook until softened, about 5 minutes. Add the curry powder, cardamom, nutmeg, and curry paste, stir well to incorporate, and toast the spices for 1 minute. Add the coconut milk, sugar, fish sauce, lime juice, and salt to taste and whisk to combine. Bring to a simmer and cook for 5 minutes for the flavors to meld. Taste and adjust the salt as needed. Remove from the heat.

The sauce will keep in an airtight container in the refrigerator for up to 1 week.

# Andrew's Mussels Fra Diavolo

SERVES 4

I love mussels—maybe too much. For many years I was the restaurant critic for our local state glossy monthly magazine and my editor told me to stop eating mussels in every restaurant that offered them. I told him they were my barometer dish. I can tell you everything about a restaurant by their mussel dishes because of how fresh they have to be, how carefully they are stored on ice, and how they are cooked. For home cooks the job is easier: Just source them well!

I like to use big plump mussels from Maine, the Pacific Northwest, or the Mediterranean. Look for large shiny fresh mussels with beards intact that have a sweet oceanic smell and feel heavy in the hand. Beyond that, what more can I tell you? *Fra diavolo* is literally translated as "brother devil." It's a fitting description for a dish based around a spicy tomato-wine sauce. Food just doesn't get much tastier, especially when this sauce is paired with sweet, plump oceanic mussels.

*Andrew*

¹/₄ cup extra-virgin olive oil

¹/₄ cup minced shallot (about 2 shallots)

2 garlic cloves, thinly sliced

1 teaspoon red chile flakes

1 cup dry white wine

3 cups The Tomato Sauce (recipe follows)

3 pounds mussels

Salt

¹/₄ cup chopped parsley

Crusty bread

Heat the oil in a large saucepan over high heat until it shimmers. Add the shallots, garlic, and chile flakes and cook, stirring, until fragrant, about 1 minute. Add the wine, bring to a boil, and boil until reduced by half, about 3 minutes. Stir in the tomato sauce and bring to a simmer. Stir in the mussels, cover, and cook, shaking and tossing until the mussels open, 3 to 4 minutes. Discard any mussels that do not open. Season lightly with salt and transfer the mussels and sauce to a platter. Sprinkle with parsley and serve right away with plenty of crusty bread.

# The Tomato Sauce

**MAKES 3 CUPS**

2 tablespoons extra-virgin olive oil

¹/₂ onion, minced (about ¹/₂ cup)

1 basil sprig

2 garlic cloves, grated on a Microplane or minced

¹/₂ teaspoon dried oregano

Pinch or two of red chile flakes

Salt

¹/₂ cup dry white wine

1 tablespoon tomato paste

¹/₂ teaspoon sugar

One 28-ounce can San Marzano tomatoes

Freshly ground black pepper

Heat the oil in a large saucepan over medium heat until it shimmers. Add the onion, basil, garlic, oregano, chile flakes, and a generous pinch of salt. Cook, stirring occasionally, until softened, about 5 minutes. Add the wine, tomato paste, and sugar, bring to a simmer, and cook for 2 to 3 minutes. Add the tomatoes, crushing them by hand as you add them to the pot, and bring to a boil. Partially cover, reduce the heat to low, and simmer, stirring occasionally, until thickened and reduced to 3 cups, about 30 minutes. Season with salt and pepper. Serve immediately or store in an airtight container in the refrigerator for up to 5 days.

# Moules Marinière

SERVES 4

Is there a more classic seafood dish in the French culinary canon? I don't think so, and neither would any frites-loving bistro habitué. Wine and mussels, a little butter . . . the key to this dish is reducing the wine and veg before adding the mussels so the sauce is the kind you want to mop up with every scrap of bread in your house.

*Andrew*

½ cup (1 stick) butter

6 garlic cloves, sliced (about ¼ cup)

2 small shallots, minced (about ¼ cup)

8 parsley sprigs, minced (about ¼ cup)

½ very small leek (pale whites only), minced (about ¼ cup)

1 celery stalk, minced (about ½ cup)

1½ cups dry white wine

4 pounds mussels

¼ cup heavy cream

Juice of ½ lemon (about 1 tablespoons)

Freshly cracked black pepper

2 loaves crusty bread

Melt the butter in a large pot over low heat. When it begins to foam, add the garlic, shallots, parsley, leek, and celery. Sweat for 2 to 3 minutes, until aromatic and the garlic and shallots have sweetened and glazed. Add the wine and simmer for several minutes, until reduced by about half. Raise the heat to high and add the mussels. Place a lid on the pot and cook for 3 to 4 minutes. Every minute or so, lay a towel across the top of the pot, grip the sides of the pot, press your thumbs on top of the lid, and toss the mussels in the pot so they rotate from the bottom of the pan to the top. Keep doing this until the mussels have opened, 4 to 6 minutes total cooking time. Discard any shells that didn't open. Add the cream and cook, lid off, for 1½ minutes. Season with the lemon juice and black pepper. Divide the mussels into bowls and spoon the broth over the mussels. Serve with crusty bread.

# Mussels with Pistachios, White Wine, and Chile

**SERVES 4**

This is more of a bean dish than a mussels dish, and it makes for a hearty entree. Instead of dipping frites into the mussel sauce, beans are cooked into the mussel broth and served underneath the mussels, acting as both sauce and partner.

¼ cup plus 2 tablespoons extra-virgin olive oil

4 garlic cloves, sliced, or more if you like

½ cup shelled roasted pistachios

1 teaspoon red chile flakes, such as Aleppo or gochugaru

2 bay leaves

4 pounds mussels

1½ cups white or rosé wine

Two 15-ounce cans cannellini beans, drained, liquid reserved

½ cup basil leaves, roughly chopped or torn, or 2 tablespoons chopped tarragon

Crusty bread

Heat the oil in a wide pan large enough to hold all the mussels in no more than a double stack/layer over medium heat. Add the garlic and sauté until golden brown and just crisp, about 4 minutes. Add the pistachios, chile flakes, and bay leaves and toast for 15 seconds. Add the mussels and wine, turn the heat to high, and cover. You'll start to see steam after a few minutes, and when it audibly comes to a boil, give the mussels a quick stir. Continue to cook until all (or at least most) have opened, 7 to 9 minutes. Use a slotted spoon to remove the mussels to a large bowl, discard any shells that didn't open, and cover to keep warm.

Turn the heat down to medium-high and add the beans to the broth. Depending on how much liquid you have remaining, you may need to add the bean liquid to achieve a loose consistency, like a creamy sauce. Bring to a simmer. Use the back of a spoon to crush a few of the beans to encourage the sauce to thicken. Stir in the basil and divide the beans among bowls. Divide the mussels on top of the beans and serve with crusty bread.

# Clams in Black Bean Sauce

**SERVES 4**

This dish, inspired by the versions at Wo Hop and King Dragon (sadly gone) that I ate as a child with my family, is now my family's favorite. My dad and my son never got to share a bowl of this together, but if we all were magically together again, it would be the first thing I would make for them. No one likes to pick favorites, but this is one of my ten favorite recipes to make at home. Full stop.

This is one of those dishes that requires a small amount of prep and comes together in a hurry once everything hits the wok. I always get all my prep work sorted and ready to go next to my stovetop so I am ready to cook . . . and yes, that includes having a serving bowl handy as well.

3 tablespoons peanut oil

4 whole dried hot chiles

1 golf ball–sized knob fresh ginger, peeled and very thinly sliced

2 garlic cloves, thinly sliced

¼ cup salted Chinese black beans, slightly crushed to optimize flavor

3 tablespoons brown sugar, or more to taste

1 bunch scallions, chopped into 1-inch lengths

18 to 24 large littleneck clams, cleaned

2 carrots, very thinly sliced (about 1 cup) (I use a peeler to make long thin strips)

½ cup Shaoxing wine (sake is a fine substitute)

2 tablespoons cornstarch

½ cup chicken stock, homemade (page 90) or store-bought

½ bunch thinly sliced garlic chives

Preheat a large wok fitted with a domed lid over high heat. Add the oil and swirl.

Add the dried chiles, ginger, garlic, black beans, brown sugar, and scallions and toss. They should scorch right away. Add the clams and carrots and toss. Add the Shaoxing wine and bring to a boil, tossing. Cook for about 4 minutes, until the clams are almost open.

In a small bowl, whisk the cornstarch into the chicken stock. Add the chicken stock mixture, cover, and cook, tossing once or twice, for another 3 to 4 minutes, until the clams open. Discard any shells that do not open.

Spill out onto a platter or low wide rimmed bowl. Turn the clams so they are all facing up. Garnish with the garlic chives.

Andrew Peters, Scallop Farmer
Penobscot Bay, Maine

# Fregola with Sweet Corn, Mussels, and Clams

**SERVES 6 TO 8**

Fregola is a chewy, small-ball-shaped semolina pasta. When made with a bronze die and air-dried, it varies in texture and color from piece to piece. This is the orzo, if you will, of Sardinia. But WAAAAAY better. Rustichella D'Abruzzo makes a great one that you can find on Amazon or in Italian markets. The chewy softness of the cooked fregola sops up the liquid gold of the mussel and clam juices, and while this is a foreign ingredient to many readers, I insist you try this at home. When oregano and corn are married with white wine, they have an affinity for each other that has to be tasted to be believed. I can't think of a better dinner party showstopper than this Midwestern riff on a Sardinian classic.

*Andrew*

**½ cup extra-virgin olive oil**
**¼ cup sliced shallots (about 2 shallots)**
**A few pinches of red chile flakes**
**6 garlic cloves, thinly sliced**
**Small handful of basil leaves**
**2 teaspoons wild Italian oregano**
**1 cup white wine**
**2 pounds clams**
**2 pounds mussels**
**18 to 24 cherry tomatoes**
**Salt**
**8 ounces dried fregola sarda**
**2 cups corn kernels cut from the cob**
**2 tablespoons minced parsley**

Combine ¼ cup of the oil, the shallots, chile flakes, garlic, and basil in a large pot over medium heat and sweat the shallots for about 2 minutes. Stir in the oregano. Add the wine and cook for 3 to 4 minutes. Add the clams, cover, and cook, shaking the pot occasionally, until they open. Pull from the heat and transfer the clams to a bowl to cool. Add the mussels to the same pot, cover, and cook, shaking the pot occasionally, until they open, then remove the mussels and place in a bowl. Strain the cooking liquid into a large bowl. Discard any shells that don't open. Shuck the clams and mussels into the liquid. Discard the shells.

Preheat the broiler. Place the cherry tomatoes in a medium bowl and toss with 2 tablespoons of the remaining oil. Remove a few at a time with a spoon and place on a small metal baking tray. Broil until charred on top, 2 to 3 minutes. Remove the cherry tomatoes and reserve.

Bring a large pot of water to a rapid boil and salt it. Add the fregola and cook for 4 to 5 minutes to parcook it. Drain, reserving a mug of starchy pasta water.

Meanwhile, heat the remaining 2 tablespoons oil in a large sauté pan over high heat. Add the corn and cook until cooked through, 2 to 3 minutes. Season with salt.

Add the reserved seafood liquid and bring to a simmer. Add the parcooked fregola, toss, and cook until the liquid is almost evaporated. If it isn't cooked quite perfectly yet (you want it tender but not mushy), add some of the reserved pasta water a sploosh at a time until it is. Add the shucked clams and mussels and heat through with the fregola until the liquid has been absorbed.

Divide the fregola, clams, and mussels into low wide bowls and garnish with the blistered cherry tomatoes and parsley.

# Chilled Mussel Salad with Vadouvan Vinaigrette

**SERVES 4**

Plump, salty mussels pair with crisp, tangy apples and peppery greens all brought together by a provocative vinaigrette. Mussels alone marinated in the vinaigrette overnight are a great little bar snack/hors d'oeuvre served with toothpicks. These flavors pair perfectly with floral, tropical-scented IPAs or chilled fruity red wines. Picnic anyone?

For a summery variation, swap the apples and almonds for peaches and walnuts.

*Toasting spices in a dry pan is essential to bloom and maximize flavor, but be careful not to burn them—all you're trying to do is wake them up with a little heat.*

1 cup apple cider, wine, or Basic Fish Stock (page 85)

2 pounds mussels

4 to 6 cups greens mix, watercress, frisée, or arugula

1 cup cilantro leaves

1 cup parsley leaves

1 large crisp and sweet apple, such as Gala or Honeycrisp, thinly sliced

5 to 6 radishes, cut into matchstick-size pieces

¼ cup extra-virgin olive oil

⅓ cup almonds, chopped

2 tablespoons vadouvan spice blend or curry powder

3 tablespoons sherry vinegar or champagne vinegar

Salt

Freshly cracked Black Pepper–Fennel Blend (page 53) or black pepper

Pour the apple cider in a wide pan large enough to hold all the mussels in no more than a double layer. Add the mussels, turn the heat to high, and cover. When steam appears after a few minutes, give the pan a quick shake. Cook for another 1 to 3 minutes, until the shells are mostly open. Using tongs or a slotted spoon, transfer those that have opened to a bowl. Continue to cook until all (or at least most) have opened, 7 to 9 minutes. Discard any shells that don't open. Chill the mussels in the refrigerator, uncovered. Strain the cooking broth through a fine-mesh strainer. Return the pan to medium heat and reduce until about 2 tablespoons remain. Remove from the heat and reserve.

In a large bowl, combine the greens, cilantro, parsley, apple slices, and radishes, being mindful to separate any clumps of apple to evenly disperse.

Combine the oil and almonds in a small sauté pan over medium heat. Toss to coat and warm through. As soon as you begin to smell the warming almonds, turn off the heat and add the vadouvan. Stir to incorporate quickly, then add the vinegar and the reserved reduced cooking liquid. Season with salt if needed.

When the mussels are cool enough to handle, shuck them, reserving the meat and discarding the shells. Pour the vinaigrette over the mussels, then toss everything together to dress the salad and serve immediately. Garnish with fennel-pepper blend.

# Mixed Seafood Salad with Herbs, Butternut Squash, and Almonds (Frutti di Mare)

**SERVES 8**

This frutti di mare is a celebration of many types of seafood all brought together in an extremely crunchy, colorful, and gorgeous salad. A nontraditional addition is sexy ribbons of butternut squash. (This is a perfect use of the bulb of a butternut squash left over from another recipe.) The rawness of the squash is tamed by an ever-so-brief bath in boiling water but retains its integrity, crunch, and vibrant color. If you have leftover seafood from another meal, such as halibut or salmon, go ahead and throw that in.

**Salt**

**2 pounds small clams or cockles**

**2 pounds mussels**

**8 ounces calamari, tubes cut into very thin rings, tentacles (if present) cut into 2-tentacle sections**

**8 ounces shrimp, peeled and deveined, sliced lengthwise as thinly as possible**

**8 ounces (½ small) butternut squash, skin removed, then peeled into strips using a peeler**

**2 celery stalks, thinly sliced (about 1 cup)**

**1 red onion, thinly sliced (about 1 cup)**

**Zest and juice of 2 lemons (about ¼ cup juice)**

**½ cup extra-virgin olive oil**

**¼ cup slivered almonds, toasted**

**4 garlic cloves, very thinly sliced**

**1 teaspoon red chile flakes, such as Aleppo**

**¼ cup chopped parsley**

**1 baguette, sliced ½ inch thick, brushed with extra-virgin olive oil, and toasted**

**1 cup Aioli (page 96)**

In a large pot, bring 4 cups salted water to a boil. Add the clams and simmer until they open, 5 to 7 minutes, stirring occasionally. Remove from the water and reserve. Discard any shells that do not open. Return the water to a boil and cook the mussels in the same water until opened, 5 to 6 minutes, stirring occasionally. Remove the mussels from water and reserve. Discard any shells that do not open. Remove the clam and mussel meat from their shells and reserve. Reserve a few shells, if desired, to garnish the plates. Strain the cooking water through a fine-mesh strainer and reserve.

Combine the calamari, shrimp, and butternut squash ribbons in a large bowl. Sprinkle with a pinch of salt. Return the mussel cooking water to a boil and pour it into the bowl with the mixed seafood and squash. Stir and let rest for 30 seconds, or until the shrimp are cooked through. Strain and discard the cooking liquid (or save for another use, as it is a tasty, flavorful stock at this point).

Return the shrimp mixture to the bowl, add the celery, onion, and lemon zest, and toss to combine.

Heat the oil in a small sauté pan over medium heat. Add the almonds and garlic and cook until golden brown, about 4 minutes. Turn off the heat and stir in the chile flakes. Add the parsley and lemon juice. Stir to combine and pour over the mixed seafood. Season with salt and serve immediately, with the toasted baguette slices and aioli, or chill and serve cold.

Left to right: Andrew's Linguine with Clam Sauce (page 134) and Barton's Linguine with Spicy Clam Sauce (page 135)

# Andrew's Linguine with Clam Sauce

**SERVES 2 TO 4**

Well, as I've said, the Zimmern
family and clams are inseparable.
I've been making this recipe forever.
It's loaded with shallots and garlic
that get so sweet and aromatic in
the oil and broth that they perfectly
grace a plate that otherwise would be
overly salty from all the clams. I do
love a grassy green olive oil in this
recipe, and I like a sprinkle of wild
Italian oregano on this dish right at
the table. Carefully wash and handle
your clams to avoid chips and broken
shells. This will obviate the need
for straining and cleaning the broth.

**Salt**

**8 ounces dried linguine**

**¾ cup extra-virgin olive oil, a grassy green oil if you have one, plus more for finishing**

**5 medium shallots, thinly sliced (about 1 scant cup)***

**10 garlic cloves, thinly sliced**

**2 bay leaves**

**½ teaspoon red chile flakes**

**5 to 6 oregano sprigs, tied together**

**½ cup white wine**

**24 littleneck clams**

**¼ cup minced parsley**

**Zest and juice of 1 lemon (2 to 3 tablespoons juice)**

**Salt and freshly ground black pepper**

**Crusty bread**

* Shallots range in size, shape, and color: from the round yellowish French shallot to the rust-hued long bullet echalion or banana shallot and the purplish Jersey shallot most commonly found in American supermarkets. More nuanced and delicate in flavor than their related onions, I use these alliums with abandon. Throughout the book we list both count and amount, assuming medium Jersey shallots yield about 3 tablespoons of dice each. For this recipe, in particular, more is better!

Bring a large pot of salted water to a boil, add the linguine, and cook to al dente according to the package instructions. Drain and reserve.

Heat the oil in a large, wide pan with 3-inch sides and a lid over medium heat. Add the shallots, garlic, bay leaves, chile flakes, and oregano and cook for 4 minutes, or until the shallots are wilted and translucent. Add the wine, bring to a boil, and cook until reduced by half, about 2 minutes. Remove the oregano bouquet and bay leaves, and discard.

Add the clams, cover, and cook for 5 to 6 minutes, until they open, shaking the pan occasionally. When all the clams have opened, remove the clams and reserve them in a bowl. Discard any shells that didn't open. Add the parsley and lemon zest to the pan. Add the pasta to the pan, stirring and cooking the pasta in the sauce. Season with salt as needed (you won't need much if any) and pepper. Add the lemon juice and toss well.

Divide the pasta into bowls and top with the reserved clams, the sauce left in the pan, and a drizzle of fresh oil. Serve immediately with crusty bread.

# Barton's Linguine with Spicy Clam Sauce

**SERVES 4**

As is common in my cooking, I often reach for the spice rack and go heavy on fresh herbs as well. In this case, coriander, with its beguiling flavor, and tarragon bring an unexpected elegance and complexity to what is often a very simple, straightforward recipe. Not that I'm against simple. Since this is a dish that people expect to be garlicky, I take that as license to go overboard and indulge my preference for lots and lots of garlic. Feel free to dial it down if you'd like.

*Jet*

**Salt**

**8 ounces dried linguine**

**¹/₄ cup extra-virgin olive oil**

**4 to 6 garlic cloves, grated on a Microplane or minced***

**2 teaspoons red chile flakes, such as Aleppo, gochugaru, or Urfa**

**1 teaspoon ground coriander**

**2 teaspoons fennel seeds**

**Zest and juice of 1 lemon (2 to 3 tablespoons juice)**

**¹/₂ cup white wine**

**12 to 20 ounces canned, tinned, or jarred clams in brine****

**3 tablespoons butter**

**6 tarragon sprigs, chopped**

**1 bunch parsley or chives, chopped**

**Freshly cracked Black Pepper–Fennel Blend (page 53) or black pepper**

\* I like even more garlic, as in a whole head!

\*\* There are so many sizes of cans, but the more clams the better.

Bring a large pot of heavily salted water to a boil, add the linguine, and cook to about a minute less than the package instructions for al dente. Drain and reserve the pasta and 1 cup of cooking water.

Heat the oil and garlic in a large sauté pan over medium heat and cook until just starting to brown, about 3 minutes. Add the chile flakes, coriander, fennel seeds, and lemon zest and cook, stirring, for 30 seconds. Add the wine and lemon juice, bring to a simmer, and simmer until reduced by about half, about 2 minutes. Add the clams with their juice, the butter, pasta, and ¹/₄ cup pasta cooking water. Stir vigorously. Keep at a boil until the sauce is thick and coating the pasta, about 1 minute, adding more pasta water if needed. Remove from the heat and stir in the tarragon and parsley. Season with salt if needed. Garnish with pepper-fennel blend and more chile flakes, if desired.

# Seafood Egg Foo Young

**SERVES 4**

After being transplanted from NYC to Minnesota, I needed to come up with an egg foo young recipe in a hurry if I wanted to eat. The recipe for the eggs was easy, the sauce was not. I floundered for a month before asking a friend, Chinese chef Daniel Lam, if he had a good one, and he said, "They are all the same! Everyone knows this recipe," and he gave me this one. I changed it for cooking at home and have been using it ever since.

I serve this dish as part of a larger Cantonese meal or for breakfast. It is fantastic as a brunch dish. You can use any combination of seafood you like, but this one is pretty delicious. If you don't have oysters on hand, skip them or replace them with just about anything from the sea.

*Andrew*

1 tablespoon peanut oil

16 oysters, shucked, meat and liquor reserved

6 large shrimp, peeled, deveined, and chopped

1 teaspoon soy sauce

1 teaspoon oyster sauce

Salt and freshly cracked black pepper

8 extra-large eggs

3 to 4 Napa cabbage leaves, thinly shredded (a generous 2 cups)

1 carrot, shredded into fine strips (about ½ cup)

3 scallions, very thinly sliced

1 large handful of bean sprouts

½ cup frozen peas, rinsed in very hot water for 1½ minutes to defrost and drained

1 teaspoon grated ginger

8 ounces jumbo lump crab

1½ cups vegetable oil

1 recipe Egg Foo Young Sauce (recipe follows) or a generous cup of store-bought

Pour the peanut oil into a very hot preheated wok. Add the oysters and shrimp and cook for 1 minute. Add the reserved oyster liquor, soy sauce, and oyster sauce, and season with salt and pepper. Toss and remove the seafood from the wok to a plate to cool while you complete the recipe prep. Wipe out/clean the wok.

Crack the eggs into a large bowl and beat them. Add the cabbage, carrot, scallions, bean sprouts, peas, ginger, the cooled oyster/shrimp mixture, and the crab. Combine well. DO NOT SEASON. Salt will make these omelets watery.

Add the vegetable oil to the wok and return to high heat.

When the oil starts to smoke (around 400°F), scoop the mixture from the bottom of the bowl using a large stainless steel work spoon and move to one side of the wok. Cook for about 30 seconds. Add a second scoop on top of the first one. Baste with hot oil and repeat on the other side of the wok so you have two oval mounds going. Flip the first omelet over and cook for 2 minutes. A minute later, do the same with the second omelet. Take them out and put them on a hot platter. (If you don't have a wok, you can do this in a very hot cast-iron pan, but only make one omelet at a time.) Repeat until all your omelets are made.

Pour the sauce over the omelets and serve.

# Egg Foo Young Sauce

**MAKES ABOUT 1 CUP**

**½ cup Chicken Stock (page 90)**

**2 tablespoons high-quality naturally brewed soy sauce\***

**2 tablespoons oyster sauce**

**2 teaspoons toasted sesame oil**

**2 teaspoons sugar**

**2 teaspoons cornstarch**

**2 tablespoons Shaoxing wine (sake is a good substitute)**

\* I love Zhongba soy sauce and get mine at themalamarket.com.

Whisk all the ingredients together in a small saucepan and bring to a simmer over low heat. Simmer for about 1 minute, until it is the texture of a good Sunday supper gravy. Keep warm while you make the omelets, or cool and store in a container in the refrigerator for up to a week.

# Butter-Basted Scallops with Apple Cider Brown Butter

Butter-basting scallops is about as sexy as seafood cooking gets. Once the scallops are golden brown, add a couple tablespoons of butter, and once the butter is nutty, aromatic, and delightfully golden brown, use a spoon to lovingly pour the foaming butter over the scallops. This further enhances the flavor by depositing caramelized butter solids on top. And it's just a lovely way to spend time. The butter, now infused with scallopy goodness and a rich mahogany hue, is then combined with reduced apple cider and mustard to emulsify into a pungent, salty, sweet sauce that looks as beautiful on the plate as it is delicious. Try serving this over grits cooked with thyme and you will be autumnally happy.

2 cups apple cider

1 bay leaf

1¼ pounds large scallops

Salt

4 tablespoons (½ stick) butter

2 garlic cloves, grated on a Microplane or minced

4 thyme sprigs, leaves picked

1 tablespoon whole grain or dijon mustard

1 tablespoon chopped chives

1 teaspoon red chile flakes, such as Aleppo or gochugaru

Pour the cider into a small saucepan, add the bay leaf, and place over medium heat. Reduce the cider to ½ cup, about 10 minutes. Remove from the heat, discard the bay leaf, and reserve the liquid.

Place the scallops on a plate, season with salt, and let them rest for 10 to 15 minutes. Pat dry with paper towels. Melt 1 tablespoon of the butter in a large sauté pan over high heat. Place the scallops in the pan and cook, undisturbed, for 3 to 4 minutes, until deeply colored. Flip the scallops and add the remaining 3 tablespoons butter, garlic, and thyme to the pan. Tilt the pan toward you and use a large soup spoon to baste the scallops with butter. Cook this way for about 1 minute. Remove the scallops from the pan to a serving platter. Turn the heat down to medium and add the cider reduction and mustard. Bring to a simmer and whisk to emulsify with the butter. Remove from the heat and add the chives and chile flakes. Spoon the sauce over the scallops and serve.

# 4.03
# Small Silver Fish

# Parmesan-Crusted Sardines with Fiery Pine Nut Salsa

**SERVES 4**

Fish with cheese, you say? Yes! I first had the pairing at the famed Zuni Café in San Francisco, where they serve a delightful plate of salty cured anchovies with thick slices of parmesan, some olive oil, and celery. The flavors are a perfect match for each other. (Of course they are! It's basically Caesar salad.) The toasty, spicy pine nut salsa is perfect spooned over steamed veggies or atop rice.

*[signature]*

The parmesan crust is a great topper for nearly any fish, especially flatfish like flounder or sole.

8 fresh sardines
Salt
1/2 cup extra-virgin olive oil
1/2 cup panko breadcrumbs
1/4 cup grated parmesan cheese
1/2 teaspoon dried oregano
2 garlic cloves, grated on a Microplane or minced
Zest and juice of 1 lemon (2 to 3 tablespoons juice)
1/4 cup pine nuts or pecan pieces
2 tablespoons capers, rinsed, patted dry, and chopped
2 teaspoons (or more!) red chile flakes, such as gochugaru or Aleppo
2 shallots, finely minced (about 1/4 cup)
2 tablespoons chopped parsley

Set an oven rack to the top position and preheat the broiler.

Gently scale a sardine by running your finger from the tail toward the head. Do this under running water so the scales wash away. Using a paring knife, gently cut through the belly cavity and use the back side of the knife to scrape out the innards and discard. Wash the cavity under running water. Repeat with the remaining fish. Pat the fish dry and place in a large broiler-proof baking dish in a single layer. Season with salt, then brush with 1 tablespoon of the oil.

In a small bowl, combine the panko, cheese, oregano, garlic, lemon zest, and 2 tablespoons of the remaining oil and stir well. Evenly divide the mixture over the top of the sardines.

Broil until the coating is crispy golden brown and the fish are cooked through, 4 to 6 minutes.

While the fish is under the broiler, to make the salsa, combine the remaining 5 tablespoons oil, pine nuts, and capers in a small sauté pan. Place over medium heat and cook, stirring, until the pine nuts are golden brown, about 3 minutes. Add the chile flakes and shallot and toss to combine. Turn off the heat and add the parsley and lemon juice. Season with salt.

Serve the crispy fish topped with the salsa.

# Chilled Poached Mackerel with Fennel, Olive, Orange, and Chile Salad

SERVES 4

In eras past, chilled fish dishes were common in American cuisine, though they seem to have fallen out of favor. None other than the great James Beard included many such dishes in his classic cookbooks. Poaching is a particularly great way to prepare fish for a cold presentation: Cooking the fish in a highly flavored broth, then allowing it to cool in that broth to soak up a great deal of flavor and maintain the moisture in the fish. After use, the cooking broth can be strained and reduced to be included in a vinaigrette for another dish. The combination of ingredients in this salad is a classic, mixing sweet and salty to punctuate the crunchy, cool fennel.

1¼ pounds mackerel fillets
Salt
1 cup white or rosé wine
1-inch knob ginger, sliced
10 allspice berries
2 bay leaves
1 star anise pod
1 cinnamon stick
¼ cup pitted, slivered green olives, such as picholine or manzanilla, 2 tablespoons brine reserved
2 oranges, zest removed in strips, flesh segmented or cut into discs and quartered, seeds removed
1 shallot or small red onion, thinly sliced, trim reserved (about 3 tablespoons)
1 fennel bulb, shaved (about 1½ cups)

Juice of 1 lemon (2 to 3 tablespoons)
Red chile flakes, such as Aleppo or gochugaru
¼ cup slivered almonds, toasted
¼ cup parsley or mint leaves
Fennel-Chile Crisp (page 175) or chile oil (optional)
Crusty bread

Season the fish with salt and let it rest for 10 to 15 minutes.

Combine the wine, ginger, allspice, bay leaves, star anise, cinnamon, reserved olive brine, orange zest, and shallot trim in a shallow pot big enough to fit the mackerel in a single layer and bring to a simmer over medium heat. Add ½ cup water, cover, reduce the heat to low, and cook for 10 minutes to steep. Remove the shallot trim and orange peel if needed for the mackerel to fit.

Place the fish into the liquid skin-side down. Cook for 1 minute, then flip and cook for 1 more minute. Cover the pan, remove from the heat, and bring to room temperature, then chill in the refrigerator until cold.

Make the salad by gently tossing the fennel, olives, orange pieces, lemon juice, chile flakes, shallot, almonds, and parsley in a medium bowl. Remove the fish from the cooking liquid and flake the fish over the top of the salad, discarding the skin and any fine bones. Drizzle with Fennel-Chile Crisp, if using. Serve with crusty bread.

Ever wonder what to do with kumquats? This is a great dish to use them in. Sliced thinly, they add a perfect balance of bitter and sweet and a pleasantly chewy texture.

# Grilled Spanish Mackerel Panzanella with Chorizo–Red Pepper Salsa

**SERVES 4**

A grilled whole fish is striking to serve, especially one as beautiful as mackerel. This preparation calls for a butterflied fillet, meaning the bones have been removed but the fillets are left connected to retain the majesty of the creature. Head on or off, it's up to you, as some are less inclined for such a show. Key to all grilling: Before you put it on, have a strategy to get it off. Lay the fish lengthwise parallel to the grill grates so you can easily scoop it off.

The panzanella (an Italian salad based on yesterday's bread) that accompanies the fish has vibrancy and texture and, of course, a healthy portion of veggies. And the chorizo-pepper salsa is just dynamite in the huge flavor and color it brings.

*J.t.*

Panzanella is often served with croutons as the form of bread. But those croutons, despite becoming swollen with the dressing and juices of the other ingredients in the salad, are very hard to eat. They don't get onto your fork or easily integrate with the other ingredients, so instead of cubes, I make my panzanella with toasted baguette slices, or crostini.

I very gently crumble them into the salad so they act as leaves, thus becoming part of every bite rather than standing alone.

When grilling for sear and sizzle. I like to use a mixture of salt and sugar, roughly 4 to 1, as the sugar caramelizes, becomes sticky, and absorbs the smoke flavor better than a salt-alone-seasoned piece of fish would. This is not to add sweetness so much as to increase the depth and complexity of flavor.

1 or 2 whole Spanish mackerels, about 4 pounds, butterflied from top or bottom, bones removed (ask your fishmonger to do this)

3 tablespoons extra-virgin olive oil

Salt

Sugar (a hearty pinch should be plenty!)

1 fennel bulb, thinly sliced (about 1½ cups)

1 small red onion, thinly sliced (about 1 cup)

½ cup packed basil leaves, roughly chopped

½ cup parsley leaves, roughly chopped

Zest and juice of 1 lemon (2 to 3 tablespoons juice)

¼ baguette, sliced ½ inch thick, brushed with olive oil, and toasted

1 recipe Chorizo–Red Pepper Salsa (recipe follows)

Prepare a grill with a medium hot fire.

Brush the skin of the fish with ½ tablespoon of oil. Season the flesh side of the fish with salt and a hearty pinch of sugar (this should be about 4 parts salt to 1 part sugar) and let rest for 15 minutes.

Recipe continues >

Place on the grill over medium-high heat, splayed out skin-side down, and grill until the skin is crispy and the fish is nearly cooked through, 5 to 6 minutes. See page 69 for grilling instructions. Cover the grill to complete the cooking. Remove the fish and place on a platter skin-side up.

In a medium bowl, combine the fennel, onion, basil, parsley, lemon zest and juice, and the remaining oil and season with salt. Gently crumble the toasted baguette slices and add them to the mixture. Toss to combine. Serve the fish with the salad and spoon the salsa around the plate.

## Chorizo–Red Pepper Salsa

### MAKES ABOUT 1 CUP

This potent and gorgeous sauce keeps for up to a week in the refrigerator and only gets better over time. Spoon it over a fried egg, or a piece of simply roasted fish, or even into endive leaves and top with a little segment of orange for a delightful tapa.

**4 tablespoons extra-virgin olive oil**

**4 ounces dried Spanish chorizo, casing removed and finely diced**

**2 red bell peppers, roasted, skin and seeds removed (see page 165) and finely chopped**

**1 tablespoon sherry vinegar**

Heat the oil in a small pan over medium heat. Add the chorizo and cook, stirring, until crisp, about 5 minutes. Remove from the heat, add the peppers and vinegar, and stir to combine. Cool.

The salsa will keep in an airtight container in the refrigerator for up to 1 week.

# Fritto Misto

This dish of mixed fried seafood should be served with lemon and sea salt. Period. Let the flavors of the fish, squid, and shrimp shine through here. When I cook this at home, I serve it as an appetizer or hors d'oeuvre in my kitchen, with my guests bellied up to the counter, drinking aperitifs or a glass of champagne. I serve it by seafood type and insist on frying the seafood as guests gobble it up. Fried food this perfect, when eaten hot out of the oil, is heavenly. If it sits for a few minutes, it's good. If it sits for five minutes, the magic is gone. Try it once my way and you will be hooked forever.

*Andrew*

1 pound head-on shrimp, peeled and deveined, with head left on

1 pound anchovies, white bait, smelt, or other small whole fish*

1 pound cleaned squid, cut in 1/2-inch pieces

Salt

8 cups vegetable oil (I like grapeseed or peanut oil best)

4 cups all-purpose flour

2 teaspoons ground white pepper

6 tablespoons potato starch

2 cups very dry white wine

4 parsley sprigs

4 sage sprigs

2 basil sprigs

1/2 cup club soda, plus more if needed

1/2 cup ice

Lemon wedges

Sea salt mixed with red chile flakes and ground in a mortar and pestle

Special equipment: candy/fryer thermometer

* To prepare anchovies, make a shallow incision at the bottom end of the belly and cut upward toward the head. Under running water, gently rinse away the innards. Lay on paper towels to dry well. If you don't have small whole fish, use small fillets of fish a size up or fillets of thin fish like rouget or mackerel.

Prepare all the seafood. Make sure it is all very dry. Season with salt and set aside while you prepare your station.

Heat the oil in a large deep pot or, even better, in a wok (that's how I fry mine) to 300°F. Keep a thermometer in the oil at all times.

Mix 2 cups of the flour with 2 teaspoons salt and the white pepper in a pie tin and set it on the counter. I love pie tins for dredging, and you can use thin metal tins or disposable tins.

Mix the remaining 2 cups flour with the potato starch and 1 teaspoon salt in a very large bowl. Whisk in the wine.

Get organized on the side of the stove where your oil is. Place the batter next to the pot first, then place the flour dredge next to that, and put the seafood next to that. On the other side of the oil, place a tray lined with paper towels and a rack over that.

Have the lid of the pot ready beside the pot. When the oil reaches 300°F, add the parsley, sage, and basil, immediately cover (it will splatter), and fry until crisp; this will only take a few minutes, if that. Remove with a slotted spoon and reserve on the rack. Raise the temperature of the oil to 375°F.

Whisk the club soda and ice into the batter.

Working in batches, dredge the shrimp in the seasoned flour and knock off any excess. Dip it into the batter. It should coat but run off. Add more club soda if the batter is too thick. Fry the shrimp, in two batches, for about 3 minutes, until golden. Remove with a mesh or wire strainer, reserve on the rack, and season with salt.

Serve on a plate with some of the herbs, lemon wedges, and chile salt.

Clean the oil of any burnt batter pieces.

When the shrimp have been eaten and the oil in the wok is back to 375°F, repeat the battering and frying process with the anchovies and serve to your guests with some of the remaining herbs and more lemon and chile salt as needed. Repeat again with the squid (or whatever other seafood you are frying). The rings of the squid will cook very quickly, only 1 or 2 minutes.

# Mackerel Escabeche

**SERVES 4**

I love mackerel, but not everyone else loves this fatty, strong-tasting fish as much as those of us who grew up on it. Enter the technique that levels the playing field! Frying adds a pronounced layer of flavor, and the residual oil flattens out the oily nature of the fish itself, but it's the spicy confetti ribbons of pickle that make this dish a hit everywhere I serve it. Don't confuse this version of the dish with the Jamaican escoveitch, where the fish is cooked in vinegar pickle. This version is of Spanish/Portuguese origin, popular in the Philippines and South America, and is notable in that the fish is cooked and then marinated. Sweet, spicy, and sour go so well with fried fish, and the room-temperature marination means the fish never gets tight and cold—a flavor killer if ever there was one.

Andrew

1 recipe Escabeche Vegetables (recipe follows)*
2 pounds mackerel, cut into 3/4-inch-thick steaks, center bone included
Salt and ground white pepper
1 to 2 cups all-purpose flour
2 teaspoons dried oregano
2 cups vegetable oil

* For optimum results, make the pickled veg the day before you fry and serve the fish.

Bring the escabeche to room temperature by removing it from the refrigerator when you start to cook your fish.

Season the mackerel with salt and white pepper and let rest for 15 minutes as it comes to room temperature. Place the flour in a pie tin and season with salt and the oregano.

Heat the oil in a large skillet over medium heat. One side at a time, place the fish in the flour mixture; you don't need to coat the skin. When the oil is very hot, around 375°F, fry the fish steaks in batches until browned on both sides and just cooked through, about 1½ minutes per side.

Remove the fish to a platter. Pour the escabeche cooking liquid onto the platter of fish. Allow to marinate for 1 hour, flipping periodically. Top the fish with all of the vegetables and serve.

# Escabeche Vegetables

8 allspice berries

4 star anise pods

1 tablespoon black peppercorns

6 bay leaves

Bouquet garni* of several thyme sprigs

8 garlic cloves, sliced

1 cup distilled white vinegar

½ cup sugar

1 red onion, halved and sliced (about 1 cup)

4 small tomatoes

2 carrots, very thinly sliced (about 1 cup)

1 red bell pepper, seeds discarded, very thinly sliced

1 poblano chile, seeds discarded, very thinly sliced

1 habanero chile, seeds discarded, very thinly sliced

1 bunch scallions, cut at an angle into 1-inch lengths

4 garlic cloves, thinly sliced

* a small tied bundle of aromatic herbs

Place the allspice, star anise, peppercorns, bay leaves, thyme bouquet, and sliced garlic in a small bowl. Pour ¼ cup boiling water over the contents of the bowl and steep and cool for 10 minutes. Add the vinegar and sugar and whisk until the sugar is dissolved.

Bring a small pot of water to a boil. Score the tomatoes and dip them in the boiling water for about 20 seconds. Scoop them out with a slotted spoon and remove to the ice bath. Slip the skins off, then remove the cores and cut into quarters. Reserve. Leave the water on the stove.

Blanch the carrots in the boiling water for a few seconds. Remove with a slotted spoon and add to the vinegar mixture. Add the bell pepper, poblano and habanero chiles, scallions, and thinly sliced garlic and toss well. Discard the thyme bouquet. Place the contents of the bowl in a gallon-sized zip-top bag. Remove as much air as you, then seal and refrigerate for at least 8 hours or as long as 24 hours.

# Fried Smelts with Radish, Apple, and Lemon Zest

**SERVES 4**

Smelt is a delightfully gorgeous little fish, with a transcendent rainbow sheen that shimmers on its fully edible scales. These fish have a very small, delicate bone structure that has no noticeable presence once cooked, so there's no need to remove it. Plus, it's great added nutrition and time and money savings, so why not? This is an example of a shallow-fry technique where the smelt are cooked one side and then the other, though it could easily be done as a deep-fry technique, submerging them in oil. We do a shallow-fry here because we include butter along with the oil, which adds a flattering boost of flavor to these freshwater fish, though it is certainly not necessary. This is a perfect recipe to prepare in an air fryer.

Smelts are a springtime delicacy, as in northern waters they begin their activity mostly in the winter and early spring. They are available year-round as a high-quality frozen product but are particularly delightful when fresh. The fresh fish explode with aromas of watermelon, cucumber, and violet, surely welcome scents in northern climes at that time of year. The salad is bright, fresh, and packed with flavor and texture. It is great on its own or as an accompaniment to any other fish.

1¼ pounds smelts, dressed
Salt
¼ cup mayonnaise
1 lemon, ½ juiced (about 1 tablespoon), ½ seeds removed and sliced as thinly as possible on a mandoline
1 cup all-purpose flour
4 tablespoons (½ stick) butter
¼ cup vegetable oil
1 bunch radishes, very thinly shaved
1 apple, such as Honeycrisp, cored and thinly shaved on a mandoline
1 jalapeño or serrano chile, thinly shaved on a mandoline
½ cup packed basil leaves
½ cup packed parsley leaves
1 tablespoon extra-virgin olive oil
Freshly cracked Black Pepper–Fennel Blend (page 53) or black pepper

Season the smelts with salt and let them rest for 15 minutes. In a small bowl, mix the mayonnaise with ¼ cup water and the lemon juice. Spread the flour onto a plate.

Heat the butter and vegetable oil in a large sauté pan over medium-high heat. Once the butter is fully melted and beginning to brown, dip the smelts into the mayonnaise mixture and then into the flour to coat evenly. Carefully place the smelts in the pan and cook on one side until crisp, 2 to 3 minutes. Carefully flip the fish and cook until golden brown, about 2 more minutes. Remove to a tray lined with paper towels to drain.

In a medium bowl, make a salad of the lemon slices, radishes, apple, chile, basil, and parsley. Dress with the olive oil and season with salt and pepper-fennel blend. Serve the salad with the warm smelts.

# Sardines with North African–Style Tomato Relish

SERVES 4

If you suffer a dislike, or even phobia, of sardines, then this is the preparation to shatter your expectations. When grilled whole, these little fish present elegantly and the meat flakes easily off the bone. The summery, fresh tomato-based sauce doubles as a serving of vegetables and is made all the more enticing by the inclusion of herbs and heady spices.

8 fresh sardines

Salt

¼ cup plus 1 tablespoon extra-virgin olive oil

1½ cups diced plum tomatoes (about 4 tomatoes)

½ small red onion, diced (about ½ cup)

6 parsley sprigs, chopped (about 2 tablespoons)

6 cilantro sprigs, chopped (about 2 tablespoons)

Zest and juice of 1 lemon (2 to 3 tablespoons juice)

2 garlic cloves, grated on a Microplane or minced

1½ teaspoons smoked sweet paprika

¼ teaspoon ground cinnamon

1 teaspoon ground cumin

Crusty bread

Set an oven rack to the highest level and preheat the broiler.

Gently scale the sardines by running your finger from the tail toward the head. Do this under running water so the scales wash away. Using a paring knife, gently cut through the belly cavity of a sardine and use the back side of the knife to scrape out the innards and discard them. Wash the cavity under running water. Repeat with the remaining fish. Pat the fish dry and place in a large broiler-proof baking dish in a single layer. Season with salt, then brush with 1 tablespoon of the oil. Broil for about 5 minutes until the skin is crisped and the fish is firm to the touch. Remove from the broiler and keep warm.

In a medium bowl, combine the tomatoes, onion, parsley, cilantro, lemon juice, and salt. Toss to incorporate.

In a small sauté pan, heat the remaining ¼ cup oil over medium heat with the garlic until the garlic is lightly browned and fragrant, about 4 minutes. Remove from the heat and add the paprika, cinnamon, cumin, and lemon zest. Stir for 15 to 30 seconds to toast lightly. Pour over the tomato mixture and toss to combine.

Place the fish onto a serving plate. Spoon the sauce over the top and serve immediately with crusty bread.

# 4.04

# Preserved and Canned Seafood

# Boards for Entertaining

For a time, a board fetish swept social media. Butter boards, really? Smart cooks have
been setting out boards of all types forever. Charcuterie and cheese boards are the tip
of the spear, as it were. In the Levant and the Eastern Mediterranean, mezze has been
served up as a prelude to mealtime for thousands of years. When it comes to entertaining,
I always put out a table of snacks for grazing. I don't put them on a board because
liquids run everywhere and there can be cross contamination from foods touching other
foods. Instead, I use all my little bowls, plates, ramekins, leaves, and other vessels on a
big board, so I can easily move them from where I entertain over beverages to the dinner
table when the meal starts. Tinned fish like smoked mussels, clams escabeche, smoked
trout dip, soused shrimp, cured salmon, and broiled eel all sit on my board, especially in
wintertime. That board always includes roasted peppers and anchovies. Add some pickled
hot peppers and a basket of crusty bread or sturdy crackers and you are all set.

# Shaved Bottarga with Blood Orange, Fennel, and Dill

**SERVES 4 TO 6**

Bottarga is the cured and pressed roe usually of mullet or tuna. Once salted and pressed, it becomes almost like parmesan cheese in terms of its texture and the ability to shave it into beautifully thin strips. These shavings have a luscious mouthfeel as your tongue warms the fat in the pressed eggs and it blooms this wonderful sea-fresh, salt-fragrant, glorious taste.

2 fennel bulbs, very thinly sliced on a mandoline (about 3 cups)

3 oranges, preferably blood oranges, cut into very thin slices

1/2 small red onion or large shallot, very thinly sliced (about 1/4 cup)

1 cup picked dill and fennel fronds

1/4 cup extra-virgin olive oil

2 tablespoons red or white wine vinegar

Salt

1 to 2 ounces bottarga, outer membrane removed (if present), very thinly shaved on a mandoline or with a vegetable peeler

Freshly cracked Black Pepper–Fennel Blend (page 53) or black pepper

In a large bowl, combine the fennel, oranges, onion, dill, oil, and vinegar. Season with salt and toss to combine. Place on a platter and cover with the bottarga. Sprinkle with a few turns of pepper-fennel blend.

I love to leave at least one of the oranges whole as the bitterness of the pith and the aroma of the zest, when left intact, adds incredible dimension to the dish.

## Bottarga Forms

Bottarga is available as a block, the whole skein of roe, sometimes encased in wax that must be removed before using it. It's also available in a crumbled powder form. Either product is perfectly suitable for this dish.

# Bread with Tomato and Anchovies (Pan con Tomate)

MAKES 12 TO 15 PIECES

Of all the glorious tapas gifted to the world by Spain, one of the simplest is also one of the very best. Baguette is toasted and, while still warm from the oven, scraped with raw garlic to infuse just a hint of pungent spice. Grated tomatoes are punched up with sherry vinegar and then topped with herbs and vinegar-marinated anchovies, known as boquerones. It's elegant yet rustic and a perfect way to start the meal.

1 baguette, sliced ½ inch thick, brushed with extra-virgin olive oil, and toasted

2 garlic cloves, cut in half lengthwise

4 plum tomatoes, grated using the largest hole of a box grater

Flaky salt, such as Maldon

1 to 2 tablespoons sherry vinegar

7 ounces boquerones

¼ cup parsley leaves, torn

¼ cup mint leaves, torn

1 shallot, minced (about 3 tablespoons)

Extra-virgin olive oil

While the bread is still warm, rub each slice with garlic. In a medium bowl, whisk the tomatoes with a pinch of salt and the vinegar. Spoon the tomato mixture onto the garlic-rubbed toasts. Lay the boquerones over the tomatoes. In a small bowl, mix the parsley, mint, and shallot and arrange over the top and drizzle with oil.

# Sicilian Citrus Salad with Anchovies and Mint

**SERVES 4**

Winter is when citrus really begins to sing. This dish is always on my table for the Feast of the Seven Fishes dinner around Christmas. It's a mix of cheery-bright colors and fresh flavors and a real show-stopper. It's also a wonderful part of a multicourse meal in that its freshness offers a bit of reprieve to the palate in contrast to richer dishes. The salty-funky cured anchovy adds an elegant balance and brings out a nuance in the citrus, elevating its flavor. The key is to use only the highest-quality anchovies and really great olive oil. And, of course, I add chile and mint to this gorgeous, savory salad.

Trim off the top and bottom of each citrus fruit to expose the flesh. Using a knife, start from the top and cut toward the bottom to slice the peel off following the contour of the fruit. Try to cut strips 1 to 2 fingers wide, as this will help avoid cutting away too much of the flesh. Trim off any pith remaining on the fruit. Cut each orange into quarters vertically. This will help you see if there are any seeds to remove. Working across the segments of each quarter, cut ¼-inch slices.

Carefully transfer the citrus pieces to a medium bowl and chill until needed. Just prior to serving, add the mint, vinegar, and the oil from the anchovies. Mix gently to avoid breaking up the pieces. Divide the citrus among 4 dishes. Divide the anchovies on top, curling them like a ribbon so they rest proud atop the citrus. Sprinkle with the chile flakes and drizzle with the oil.

**4 whole oranges (a mix of varieties, such as blood orange, navel, and Cara Cara)**

**¼ cup mint leaves, torn**

**2 teaspoons sherry vinegar**

**One 2-ounce tin oil-packed anchovies (or more, and preferably smoked, if you can find them)**

**½ teaspoon red chile flakes, such as Aleppo or gochugaru**

**3 tablespoons extra-virgin olive oil**

# Roasted Peppers with Anchovies and Parsley Bagna Cauda

**SERVES 8 AS AN APPETIZER**

This recipe has a special place in my heart because of my love of anchovies and the cupboard crime I feel is perpetrated against all of us via the sale of the cheap tinned, dry, oversalty, commodity anchovies. I like imported anchovies from the Cantabrian sea. They are almost sweet/salty and infinitely more delicious than cheap brands. Portuguese, Italian, and Spanish anchovies hand-packed in olive oil are superb as the next best choice for me.

This dish, with sweet peppers, salty anchovies, oil and lemon zest, parsley, chile flakes, and garlic are on a platter at every event or dinner at my home. The leftovers go on pizza, in salads, in a sauce, in a sauté pan with chicken thighs or clams. I can't think of a dish in this book I want you to make more than this one. When I want to plus this up, I roll the pepper pieces instead of laying them flat. Fussy, yes, but stunning.

4 red bell peppers

4 yellow bell peppers

½ cup extra-virgin olive oil

1 garlic clove, grated on a Microplane or minced

½ teaspoon red chile flakes

Salt

½ bunch parsley, finely minced (¼ cup)

32 anchovy fillets, prepared as in Salt-Cured Fish Fillets (page 178) or purchased (three 2-ounce tins)

2 lemons

Crusty bread

Char your peppers as quickly as possible. I lay mine on coals in the grill, on coals in the fireplace, or over open burners on my stovetop as a last resort. But that works just fine. You want to completely char them and you want to do it quickly so the peppers don't cook. If you don't have a gas range, set your broiler to its highest setting. Place the peppers on a tray and place as close to the broiler as possible. Rotate as they char until all sides are blistered and black in color.

Pile the peppers in a bowl as they come off the heat and cover the bowl with a plate or another bowl that fits tightly over the top. Let rest for about 1 hour, then carefully pull all the charred skin off the peppers using a paper towel over the sink without using water. I don't like to wash away the charred flavor I spent so much time creating.

When all done, push your finger through the bloom end and open the peppers into a clover shape. Cut off the flesh at the base of the stem and discard the stems and seeds. You should have about 32 petals of roasted peppers.

Lay the pepper petals on a platter, alternating yellow and red colors, and set aside; don't refrigerate.

In a small pot, heat the oil, garlic, and chile flakes over the lowest heat until the temperature of the oil reaches 225°F or until the garlic has become fragrant. Turn off the heat. Let cool for 20 minutes. Pour over the peppers and season delicately with salt.

Sprinkle the platter with the parsley—yes, it's a lot. Lay the anchovies over each pepper petal. Zest the lemons over the platter and serve right away with plenty of crusty bread.

# Roasted Peppers with Smoked Mackerel, Mace, and Mint

**SERVES 4 AS AN APPETIZER**

When I lived in Morocco, I ate a lot of roasted peppers from the stalls at night markets. Often there were small grilled or cured fish to accompany the peppers. And, of course, gallons of mint tea. These flavors bring me right back to that delicious and cacophonous setting. In this dish, I bring all those elements together, perfect for entertaining. More often than not, I serve this with anchovies, using a whole 2-ounce can, the oil drizzled over top, the fillets cut into long thin strips. Salt-cured sardines (see page 178) work equally well.

Andrew entertains more than I do, so his recipe for peppers and tinned fish (page 165) serves 8 to my 4. This recipe is easily doubled if you too have a larger crowd.

3 red bell peppers

Flaky salt, such as Maldon

6 ounces hot smoked mackerel, flaked into small pieces

1 shallot, thinly sliced lengthwise (about 3 tablespoons)

½ chile, such as jalapeño or serrano, sliced as thin as possible

Juice of 1 lemon (2 to 3 tablespoons)

3 tablespoons thinly sliced mint leaves

½ teaspoon ground mace or freshly grated nutmeg

3 tablespoons extra-virgin olive oil

1 baguette, sliced ½ inch thick, brushed with olive oil, and toasted

If you are broiling the peppers: Arrange an oven rack to the top position and preheat the broiler. Place the whole peppers on a baking sheet and broil until their skins are blackened and the peppers are tender, turning them every few minutes to cook evenly.

If you are grilling the peppers (my preference): Place the peppers over the hottest part of the fire and blacken, turning as needed to cook evenly.

Place the blackened peppers from the broiler or grill in a bowl and cover with plastic wrap or a lid. This will trap the heat and steam the peppers, making it easier to remove their skins. Set aside until the peppers are cool enough to handle, then gently flake off the burned skin. It should slip right off, but if necessary, you can use a knife to gently scrape the peppers clean. Do not wash them! A little burned skin is better than washing away all the flavor. Remove the stem end and discard all the seeds from each pepper.

Cut the peppers into 1-inch strips and place them on a serving platter. Season lightly with salt. Arrange the mackerel pieces on top of the pepper strips. In a small bowl, toss the shallot, chile, and lemon juice to combine. Scatter over the peppers along with the mint and sprinkle with the mace. Drizzle the plate with oil and serve with the toasted baguette slices.

# Roasted Squash with Sun-Dried Shrimp

**SERVES 4**

Dried shrimp are funky and full of flavor and are fun to play around with. They can be found in Asian and Latin markets, though I'm partial to domestically produced products that are available online. These shelf-stable gems make a great addition to gumbos or can be added to pastas or stews to add a rich and deep umami flavor. I like to serve the skins on the squash, as it adds a nice textural contrast. They are fully edible, if a bit chewy, but that's a good thing given the textures in the salad. This dish is equally good without the shrimp. Simply omit the shrimp, and once the almonds are toasted, add 1 tablespoon fish sauce with the lime juice. In any case, it makes for a great starter or light lunch.

2 pounds winter squash, such as delicata or acorn, skins scrubbed under warm running water, cut into 1-inch wedges, seeds removed

¼ cup plus 1 tablespoon extra-virgin olive oil

2 garlic cloves, grated on a Microplane or minced

Salt

½ cup sliced or slivered almonds

½ cup dried tiny shrimp

Juice of 2 limes (about ¼ cup)

1 red onion, very thinly sliced (about 1 cup)

1 chile, such as jalapeño or serrano, thinly sliced

½ bunch cilantro, thick stems removed, leaves picked

½ bunch mint, leaves picked

Preheat the oven to 375°F.

In a large bowl, toss the squash with 1 tablespoon of the oil and the garlic and season with salt. Place the squash on a baking sheet in a single layer and roast until golden brown and fork tender, 20 to 25 minutes. Remove from the oven and reserve at room temperature.

In a medium skillet, toast the almonds in the remaining ¼ cup oil over medium heat until golden brown, about 3 minutes. Add the dried shrimp and continue to toast for 1 to 2 minutes, until the shrimp are aromatic and have taken on a little golden color. Stir in the lime juice, onion, and chile. Remove from the heat and let cool to room temperature.

Arrange the squash pieces on plates. Spoon the almond-shrimp sauce over the top. Top with the cilantro and mint.

# Fish and Chips, but Make It Salad

SERVES 4

Fish and chips go together so well. One day in London, I was in my favorite chippy and had the idea to make this salad, and it is now one of my favorites. That's right, I said salad. I had been eating Asian fish salads with fried shallots for decades, and I always added fried potato crisps to my steak salad . . . so why not do the same with smoked fish? I made it, and a star was born.

Instead of the thick fried potatoes seen in typical fish and chips, I make homemade potato chips—the salty crunch is the perfect crouton. And the sweet smoky trout is the perfect foil for the rest of the flavors in this superb dish. A word about the dressing: If you don't make your own and use a storebought dressing, take care not to overdress this salad.

2 quarts vegetable oil

2 russet potatoes (1 pound total)

**Salt**

12 to 16 ounces naturally smoked trout (get a good one—it will be less salty and better for you)

½ red onion, cut into thin strips (about ½ cup)

1 large European cucumber

1 head butter lettuce or red leaf lettuce

1 pint cherry tomatoes (about 10 ounces), halved

½ cup coarsely chopped dill

2 cups arugula

1 bunch scallions, thinly sliced at a 45-degree angle

1 fennel bulb, shaved (about 1½ cups)

1 recipe Honey-Dijon Dressing (recipe follows)

**Freshly cracked black pepper**

In a large pot (at least 6 quarts), heat the oil over medium heat to 375°F.

Cut the potatoes skin-on into about ⅛-inch-thick slices. I use a knife, but if you like you can use a mandoline. You need something sturdy to stand up to the salad tossing after they're fried. Slice them onto a paper towel (not into water) and immediately fry them, adding the slices 2 to 3 at a time so they don't stick together. When they are browned and toasty, about 5 minutes, remove them with a slotted spoon or spider and drain on paper towels. Season with salt.

While the potato chips are cooling, flake the trout and place it in a small bowl to reserve.

Soak the onion strips in a bowl of ice water for 20 minutes to soften the sharpness of their raw flavor. Drain well.

Halve the cucumber lengthwise and scoop out the seeds with a small spoon. Thinly slice the cucumber.

Pull the leaves from the lettuce and use them to line a platter. Slice the core and sprinkle the slices in the middle of the platter.

Combine the cherry tomatoes, half of the dill, the arugula, scallions, onion, cucumber, and fennel in a large bowl.

Toss the tomato mixture with half of the dressing, adding the potatoes at the end. Season with salt and pepper. Place the salad in the middle of the platter, scatter the flaked trout across the platter, garnish with the remaining dill, and drizzle with the remaining dressing.

# Honey-Dijon Dressing

**MAKES ABOUT ¾ CUP**

1 tablespoon honey
1 tablespoon dijon mustard
3 tablespoons aged sherry vinegar
Salt
⅓ cup extra-virgin olive oil
Zest and juice of 1 orange (about ¼ cup)

In a small bowl, whisk or blend together the honey, mustard, and vinegar and season with salt. Slowly whisk in the oil to incorporate and emulsify. Add the orange zest and stir it into the dressing. Slowly pour in the orange juice, in thirds, whisking as you go and tasting with each addition. When you have the balance of flavor you like, you're done. Refrigerate until ready to use.

The dressing will keep in an airtight container in the refrigerator for up to 1 week.

# A Modern Take on Caviar Service

CAVIAR! CAVIAR! CAVIAR! This food of peasants and of royals has a long history and offers a salacious tale of how tastes evolve over time, of greed, and near extinction. Its more modern chapter is being written as a product of sustainable farming. Because caviar is so valuable (and small), it's long been a staple in the black market, which has continued to drive unsustainable fishing of wild species. But worldwide farming practices of various species of sturgeon yields a product that can be outrageously good. And the best of these farms certainly have a story worth supporting.

Caviar was not always the preferred food of the elite. In fact, in France it was considered unfit for consumption at aristocratic tables until it slowly gained favor and began to accrue its reputation as the height of luxury and the associated formality of its traditional service. Often paired with **sour cream**, **red onion**, **grated boiled egg**, and little pancakes called **blinis**, this is certainly a nice way to eat it. But we entirely disagree that you can't step from tradition, even far away from tradition. It's time to see caviar as a platform for creative pairings.

**Caviar** is the salt-cured roe of sturgeon. But there are all sorts of other fish eggs that are cured and can be served with equal pomp and deliciousness. **Ikura (cured salmon roe)**, or satisfyingly poppy **trout eggs, tobiko/flying fish roe, bowfin**, and so on—each of these has its own character, and all are worth celebrating.

We insist on pairing **caviar** with something with a little crunch. A bag of **thick-cut, ruffled potato chips** gives just that. Additionally, because we are evangelists for fennel, some **toasted crunchy fennel seeds** on top combine with the **salty eggs** for a wonderful textural contrast. In place of sour cream, which is perfectly delicious, try serving caviar with **labneh**, the Middle Eastern strained yogurt, as this punches up the acidity level while keeping the same dairy creaminess that sour cream brings. Aromatic and elegant herbs like **mint** or **tarragon**, as well as a little **lemon zest**, bring freshness and a beautiful spike of color. A more-flavorful-than-spicy **chile flake**, such as **Aleppo** or **Urfa**, can add a wonderful earthy, smoky component.

What beverage to pair with caviar? Traditionally, it's luxury meets luxury, and only the finest **champagne** or top-shelf **vodka** will do. Is this tasty? Well, yeah. But so are a lot of other beverages. Try a smoky **mezcal**, a bright acidic white wine like **Sancerre**, or a hugely aromatic one like **sauvignon blanc** from New Zealand. An interesting pairing that plays on the ever-popular combination of sweet and salty is a great **dessert wine** with its unctuous sticky sweet savor. Plus, it's just a great excuse to drink more sweet wine. And **red wines,** yes, even RED WINES can pair well. We found that slightly aged **red Bordeaux**, especially those made of **merlot**, can very much flatter the subtle flavors of caviar.

However you do it, caviar can be sustainable, fantastic, and fun. Just because it's expensive doesn't mean you can't experiment a little bit: **BBQ potato chips,** anyone?

Too often caviar is served with stinky old red onion that's been cut with a dull knife. If you're serving caviar with red onion or shallot, it's worth seeking it out from the farmers market. There you're getting the highest quality and freshness. Cut them as small as you can with the sharpest knife you've got.

# Trout Roe on Toast with Soft-Boiled Egg and Fennel-Chile Crisp

**SERVES 4**

Trout roe is a perfect food. It's delightfully cheerful in color, and those spheres popping and giving up their flavor are so playful on the palate. Add eggs to this combo and the gooey oozy yolk gets all saucy with the crispy spicy oil. Hell yeah!

4 slices thick-cut sourdough bread

1/2 cup parsley leaves, torn

1/2 cup mint leaves, torn

4 scallions, thinly sliced

4 or 8 eggs, boiled for 6 minutes and peeled

2 to 3 ounces trout roe (smoked is great), or much more

Fennel-Chile Crisp (recipe follows)

Toast the bread and move it to plates.

In a medium bowl, mix the parsley, mint, and scallions. Divide among the toasts. Place 1 or 2 eggs on each piece and gently smash with a fork. Scatter the trout roe over the top and drizzle with a generous amount of Fennel-Chile Crisp.

## Fennel Chile Crisp

**MAKES ABOUT 1 1/2 CUPS**

Spicy, fennel, crunchy. Add mint, and you've got my epitaph.

1 cup neutral oil, such as peanut or vegetable

2 garlic cloves, grated on a Microplane or minced

1/4 cup fennel seeds

1/4 cup dried shallots

2 tablespoons red chile flakes, preferably gochugaru

Pinch of ground allspice

Pinch of ground mace or nutmeg

1 teaspoon salt

In a small pot, heat the oil with the garlic and fennel seeds over medium heat until the garlic is golden brown and the fennel seeds begin to pop, 3 to 4 minutes. Turn the heat off and add the shallots, chile flakes, allspice, mace, and salt. Stir to combine and cool to room temperature.

The chile crisp will keep in an airtight container for 1 to 2 weeks at room temperature.

# Pickled Herring with Dill and Fennel

**SERVES 4**

It couldn't be simpler to dress up
the already delicious-straight-from-
the-jar pickled herring (or smoked
herring or mackerel or sardines from
the can). The addition of a poached
or fried egg to this dish really
takes it over the top. This also
adds some heft to evolve the dish
from appetizer or hors d'oeuvre to
a light entree, perfect lunch, or
luxurious breakfast.

**1 red onion, sliced vertically ¼ inch thick (about
1 cup)**

**Salt**

**4 thick slices rye bread**

**1 cup labneh or crème fraîche**

**1 fennel bulb, shaved as thin as possible (about
1½ cups)**

**1 bunch dill, chopped**

**2 tablespoons butter**

**4 eggs**

**Freshly cracked Black Pepper–Fennel Blend
(page 53) or black pepper**

**One 12-ounce jar pickled herring in white wine,
drained**

Soak the red onion in a bowl of cold water with
a pinch of salt for 5 minutes. Drain and pat dry.

Lightly toast the bread and slather each slice
with labneh.

In a medium bowl, toss the onion, fennel, and dill
to combine. Place tufts of the vegetables on top of
the labneh.

Heat a large sauté pan over medium-high heat. Add
the butter and wait until it begins to foam. Crack
the eggs into the pan and season with salt and
pepper-fennel blend. As the edges begin to crisp,
spoon the butter over the top of the yolks and cook
to your desired doneness.

To serve, top the vegetable toast with pieces of
herring, fried eggs, and more pepper-fennel blend.

# Summer Tomato Salad with Pickled Eggplant and Smoked Sardines

**SERVES 4**

The pickled eggplant in this recipe is a delightful summer pantry staple. Make a big batch after the farmers market haul and keep it on hand for a week or two. Drape the slices over toast rubbed with garlic, shred them and add to a tuna salad, or simply toss them in with your salad greens. Any eggplant will do, but we prefer the smaller varieties, such as graffiti or Chinese, found at farmers markets and increasingly at supermarkets.

Smoked sardines can vary greatly from brand to brand in size, smokiness, strength of flavor, bone in or off, skin present or not. Find a brand you like and stick with it. At their best, the flavor of the sardines should be nuanced, not overpowering. The smoke should be well integrated and not acrid in any way, and the oil should be tasty on its own.

1 pound small eggplant, sliced lengthwise ¼ inch thick (about 1 to 3 eggplants)

Salt

½ cup extra-virgin olive oil

4 garlic cloves, sliced

1 tablespoon fennel seeds

1 teaspoon cumin seeds

1 teaspoon red chile flakes, such as Aleppo or gochugaru

1 teaspoon dried oregano

½ cup white wine vinegar

2 tablespoons sugar

¼ cup mint leaves, chopped

1½ pounds tomatoes, thickly sliced

4 ounces arugula

Two 4-ounce cans smoked sardines*

¼ baguette, sliced ½ inch thick, brushed with olive oil, and toasted

* I am a big fan of the Crown Prince brand brisling two-layer sardines.

Season the eggplant with salt and let it rest in a colander for 15 minutes. Pat it dry with a paper towel.

Heat the oil in a small pot over medium heat. Add the garlic and cook until golden brown, about 4 minutes. Add the fennel seeds, cumin seeds, chile flakes, and oregano and toast, stirring, for 30 seconds. Add the vinegar, sugar, and ½ cup water and bring to a simmer. Place the eggplant in a small container and pour the hot marinade over the eggplant. Stir gently to make sure the slices do not stick together and are equally coated in the brine. Let it cool to room temperature and add the mint leaves. Cover and let it rest in the refrigerator overnight.

Arrange the tomatoes on plates. Place the arugula in a serving bowl. Remove the eggplant from the marinade and toss with the arugula. Place tufts of the salad on top of the tomatoes. Flake the sardines around the plates and drizzle with a bit of the sardine oil. Crumble a few pieces of the toasted baguette over the top of each to serve.

# Salt-Cured Fish Fillets

I like to make my own salt-cured fish fillets. It's very easy, and I do it with sardines, anchovies, and every fish in between size-wise. I serve them laid over fire-charred roasted red peppers and parsley bagna cauda, literally translated as "warm bath." Served with some crusty bread, it's my favorite way to enjoy these stunning little fish.

*Andrew*

I eat lots of anchovies all year round, in sauces, salads, braises, and pastas, so I can't make enough to keep up. I buy large fat whole anchovies from gustiamo.com because they carry Nettuno anchovies from Italy, my favorites. They are salt-packed. I soak them in warm water for 30 minutes, then peel the fillets off the bone. Then I pat them dry and cover them in olive oil to use on the same day. By the way, the bones are great mashed up to a paste-I add them to my dogs' bowls, and they love them. I also buy Nardín or Nassari brand filleted anchovies from latienda.com.

Wash and dry your **sardines or anchovies**. Remove the heads and carefully clean the entrails out, rinse again, and pat dry. Dip in a **glass of white vinegar**, then set in a bowl set in a larger bowl of ice while you clean as many as you have.

Sprinkle some **large-grain sea salt** and **sugar** in a 2:1 ratio in the bottom of a sealable glass container. Lay the fish down in a single layer, then layer more salt mix, then more anchovies and so on. The final layer should be the salt mixture and gently weighed down with some square-ish nonporous flat stones. Refrigerate for 2 to 3 weeks. Remove, soak in warm water for 15 to 20 minutes, and pour off the water. Repeat and soak for 5 to 10 minutes and taste them. The fillets should peel off the bone and taste salty-delicious. Put the fillets in a small container, cover with olive oil, cover, and refrigerate. Use them up over the course of a week.

# Steelhead Trout Gravlax

**MAKES ABOUT 2 POUNDS**

Steelhead trout are undeniably unique. All wild steelhead are born and grow in gravel-bottomed, fast-flowing fresh water. Some live and die there-those are called rainbow trout. The fish we refer to as steelhead are trout that migrate to the saltier waters of the ocean to grow. They grow much bigger than their freshwater counterparts-some as big as fifty pounds! Those fish return to fresh water to spawn. Lately I have been buying steelhead trout from Riverence in Idaho. I think they are raising the best-tasting trout on the planet. I try to buy large fillets-14 to 16 ounces-or their largest whole fish, which are about 3 pounds.

This technique works for any member of the salmon family. Curing time varies depending on the size of the fillets: I cure large king salmon fillets for 3 days and dry them for 2 days before serving. I cure small, 9- to 12-ounce trout fillets for 18 to 24 hours and dry them for 1 day. Play around-the system works. Remember, curing is one of the most ancient forms of preservation, allowing salt and other seasonings to draw out moisture and kill harmful bacteria.

This gravlax is great on bagels or in salads.

1 bunch dill, chopped

1 bunch parsley, chopped

1 bunch tarragon, chopped

½ cup finely minced shallots (about 2 shallots)

1 tablespoon ground star anise or 5 star anise pods, well-crushed

1 tablespoon crushed fennel seeds

1 ounce aquavit or vodka

3 ounces sugar (weighing makes a difference here!)

3 ounces kosher salt (weighing makes a difference here!)

4 to 5 trout fillets, skin on, pin bones removed (about 3 pounds total weight)*

* I like to trim off the last 2 inches or so of the tail to make them uniform in thickness.

Combine the dill, parsley, tarragon, shallots, star anise, fennel seeds, aquavit, sugar, and salt in a large bowl.

Place the fillets skin-side down in a nonreactive pan and spread the cure mixture over the fish. Seal the container with plastic wrap. Let it rest for 18 to 24 hours in the refrigerator. You will notice a bit of liquid pulled from the fish.

Remove the fish fillets, wipe away the cure solids with a damp towel, and lay the fillets on a rack fitted into a pan. Place in the refrigerator, uncovered, for 24 hours to dry. It needs a day to really develop its texture. At this point you can wrap them in plastic wrap and store in a cold part of your refrigerator for up to a week or freeze for 3 months.

To serve, take the fish off the skin with a sharp knife, slice the flesh at a 45-degree angle—thin but not falling apart—and serve with buttered black bread, homemade crème fraîche, and cut lemons.

# Celery Root Remoulade with Smoked Mackerel

SERVES 4

Celery root, also known as celeriac, is not a commonly used ingredient in the American kitchen, but we'd love to change that. It certainly has a strong celery flavor, but it's more nuanced in that it also carries a root vegetable-like sweetness and is hugely aromatic. The recipe called *remoulade* is a classic French way to prepare celery root. Here we adapt it with a garnish of flaked hot-smoked mackerel, either from a can or in fillet form.

1 celery root bulb (about 1½ pounds)

Salt

Juice of 2 lemons (about ¼ cup)

1 cup Aioli (page 96) or mayonnaise

1 to 2 tablespoons dijon mustard (depending on how much you like mustard)

2 tablespoons capers, rinsed and patted dry

¼ cup chopped chives or scallions

1 teaspoon onion powder

½ teaspoon garlic powder

Two 7-ounce tins hot-smoked mackerel in water, drained, flaked into roughly 1-inch pieces

Freshly cracked Black Pepper–Fennel Blend (page 53) or black pepper

Cut off a small bit of the top and bottom of the celery root to give you a flat surface to stabilize for safety. Trim the skin off the celery root, starting at the top and curving the knife around the outside just underneath the skin. (The tough outer skin that is removed from celery root is great for including in stocks of all kinds!) Cut the celery root into manageable pieces and grate it through the large holes of a cheese grater or food processor with grater attachment.

Place the grated celery root in a colander, season well with salt and half of the lemon juice, toss to combine, and let it rest for 20 to 30 minutes to soften and shed moisture.

In a medium bowl, mix the aioli, the remaining lemon juice, the mustard, capers, chives, onion powder, and garlic powder and whisk to combine.

Remove the celery root from the colander and gently squeeze. Mix into the aioli mixture and let it rest for 10 minutes. Place the salad on serving plates or a platter. Flake the mackerel over the top and garnish with pepper-fennel blend.

# Acorn Squash with Smoked Salmon and Walnut-Herb Vinaigrette

**SERVES 4**

This supremely autumnal dish offers the warm flavors of roasted squash, kicked up with spice, and further sweetened with maple syrup. It's a luscious and perfect partner for flakes of hot-smoked salmon. Any salmon will do, but sockeye is particularly good, as it has a greater depth of flavor. The squash is cooked with the skin on, as it softens nicely and adds contrast to the silky texture.

1 large acorn squash, cut into 1-inch wedges, seeds removed

1/4 cup plus 1 tablespoon extra-virgin olive oil

2 garlic cloves, grated on a Microplane or minced

Salt

1/2 cup chopped walnuts

1 tablespoon fennel seeds

2 tablespoons sherry vinegar

1 tablespoon dijon mustard

1 small shallot, finely diced (2 to 3 tablespoons)

1 tablespoon maple syrup

Freshly cracked Black Pepper–Fennel Blend (page 53) or black pepper

8 ounces hot-smoked salmon, skin removed and discarded, flaked into small pieces

1/2 bunch parsley, leaves picked (about 1 cup)

1/2 bunch mint, leaves picked (about 1 cup)

3 ounces arugula

Preheat the oven to 400°F.

In a large bowl, toss the squash with 1 tablespoon of the oil and the garlic and season with salt. Place on a baking sheet and roast until caramelized on the outside and fork-tender throughout, 30 to 35 minutes total, flipping halfway for even color.

Heat the remaining 1/4 cup oil in a small sauté pan over medium heat. Add the walnuts and fennel seeds and toast until aromatic, 3 to 5 minutes. Meanwhile, in a medium bowl, combine the vinegar, mustard, shallot, maple syrup, and pepper-fennel blend. Slowly add the warmed olive oil–walnut mixture, whisking vigorously to combine. Season with salt.

In a medium bowl, toss the flaked salmon with half of the vinaigrette. In a separate bowl, combine the parsley, mint, and arugula and dress with the remaining vinaigrette.

Place the acorn squash pieces on plates and top with the dressed greens. Spoon on the salmon mixture and any remaining vinaigrette.

# Cream Chipped Smoked Sockeye Salmon over Texas Toast

**SERVES 4**

This recipe updates a classic American comfort food of creamed chipped beef, smothered in a rich creamy sauce. This construct provides a great platform for the smoke of the salmon. And the overall dish is a beautiful blend of textures and colors.

4 tablespoons (1/2 stick) butter

1 fennel bulb, cut into small dice (about 1 1/2 cups)

2 tablespoons fennel seeds

1 bay leaf

Pinch of ground mace or freshly grated nutmeg

1/3 cup all-purpose flour

3 cups whole milk, plus more if needed

10 ounces hot-smoked sockeye salmon, skin removed and discarded

4 slices Texas toast or thick-sliced sourdough bread

2 tablespoons chopped scallions or chives

Red chile flakes, such as Aleppo or gochugaru

Melt the butter in a medium pot over medium heat. Add the fennel, fennel seeds, and bay leaf. Cook until the fennel begins to soften, 6 minutes. Remove the bay leaf and discard. Add the mace and flour and cook for 2 minutes, stirring constantly to ensure no clumps of flour remain. Whisk in the milk and cook for 10 minutes, or until the sauce is thickened. Flake the salmon into the sauce. Toast the bread and serve arrange the warm salmon mixture over the top, and garnish with the scallions and chile flakes.

# Barton's Tuna Salad

Tuna salad is a choose-your-own-adventure. Sometimes I just want a classic **mayonnaise**-y mashed-up tuna on toasted **whole grain bread**. Sometimes I'm in more of a bruschetta mood with ripe summer **tomatoes**. Other times I treat it like a heavy tapas dish. A couple things I always include are something crunchy and something spicy, such as chopped up **giardiniera**, the Italian chile-pickled vegetable condiment. Another great crunchy-spicy option is the **Fennel-Chile Crisp** (page 175) or store-bought chile crisp. If using mayonnaise, it's absolutely worth it to make your own **Aioli** (page 96). I like this best because it avoids the sweetness that can be overwhelming in store-bought brands. I always use **oil-packed tuna**, as it is richer in texture but also in flavor. And the oil itself is useful when whisked into the aioli or mayonnaise or used as part of a vinaigrette for an accompanying salad.

# Andrew's Tuna Noodle Casserole

**SERVES 6**

I could write a book about this dish. Is there a recipe more polarizing than one for hot tuna mixed with noodles and baked? I don't think so. Hot Tuna is one of my favorite bands, so maybe I am biased. In the Midwest, where I live, casseroles and hot dishes are a religion in the kitchen. Casseroles are mixed and baked, hot dishes are layered. You're welcome. This one is so creamy, vegetal, and addictive that even tuna haters will love it. Topped with crunchy crumbs and loaded with fresh herbs, this casserole eats fancy despite its humble roots.

## THE BREADCRUMBS

1/2 bunch parsley, chopped (1/2 cup)
2 shallots, diced (about 1/4 cup)
Zest of 1 lemon
3 garlic cloves, grated on a Microplane or minced
Several pinches of cayenne pepper
Salt and freshly cracked black pepper to taste
4 cups torn day-old bread
4 tablespoons (1/2 stick) butter, melted

## THE CASSEROLE

Salt
1 pound extra-large egg noodles
5 tablespoons butter
1/4 cup all-purpose flour
A few pinches of freshly grated nutmeg
2 carrots, finely diced (about 1 cup)
2 celery stalks, thinly sliced (about 1 cup)
2 medium yellow onions, minced (about 2 cups)

1 cup Chicken Stock (page 90)
2 cups whole milk
1/4 cup chopped parsley
1/4 cup chopped dill
2 tablespoons instant chicken bouillon powder (I like Wyler's brand)
8 ounces frozen peas, rinsed in hot water to thaw
8 ounces aged white cheddar cheese, grated
1/3 cup grated parmesan cheese
Three 5-ounce cans tuna, drained and gently "crushed" to separate
Freshly ground white pepper

Make the breadcrumbs: Preheat the oven to 350°F.

Place all of the ingredients in a food processor and pulse to create large coarse breadcrumbs. Spread out on a baking sheet and bake for 20 to 25 minutes, until crisp and golden brown. Reserve for topping the casserole. Keep the oven at 350°F.

Fill a large pot with water and heavily salt it. Add the noodles and cook about halfway to al dente following the package instructions. Drain and reserve.

Melt the butter in a large skillet with high sides over medium heat. Add the flour and cook, stirring, for 3 to 4 minutes to create a blond roux. Stir in the nutmeg. Add the carrots, celery, and onions and cook until softened.

Add the stock and milk in batches, stirring until it simmers. Add the parsley, dill, and bouillon powder and stir until the mixture thickens.

Add the peas and cheeses and stir well to incorporate. Remove from the heat, fold in the tuna, and season with salt and white pepper.

Add the noodles to the tuna mixture and transfer to a lasagna pan. Cover with aluminum foil and bake for 35 to 40 minutes, until bubbly.

Remove the foil and cover with the breadcrumbs.
Slide back into the oven and bake for a few minutes
to warm through and slightly toast the breadcrumbs.

# Pink Salmon Cakes with Pomegranate-Jalapeño Relish

The ingredients in this recipe are a perfect combo for the demure flavored pink salmon, but also just about any seafood. The Worcestershire sauce in particular brings depth of flavor. The pomegranate-jalapeño relish is a perfect topping for any roasted or grilled fish, and here it's a beautiful and colorful way to elevate this into a classy entree. Pomegranate arils are commonly available in prepared form in the produce aisle and also frozen, but fresh is best if available. Top these cakes with a poached or fried egg and you have a charming brunch dish.

*J.t.*

This recipe works for any leftover fish you have. I'll often cook extra fish for dinner so that I have more on hand to make cakes for my sons' lunches the next day.

1 cup panko breadcrumbs

¼ cup mayonnaise

1 tablespoon whole grain mustard

2 tablespoons chopped tarragon

2 scallions, thinly sliced

1 teaspoon Worcestershire sauce

Zest and juice of 1 lemon (2 to 3 tablespoons juice)

Pinch of red chile flakes, such as Aleppo or gochugaru

Salt

One 15-ounce can pink or red salmon, drained (or leftover slow-roasted salmon, chilled)

2 tablespoons butter

1 recipe Pomegranate-Jalapeño Relish (recipe follows)

Preheat the broiler.

Combine the panko, mayonnaise, mustard, tarragon, scallions, Worcestershire, lemon zest and juice, and chile flakes in a bowl. Season with salt and mix to combine. Add the salmon and gently mix to combine, taking care to not break up too much.

Divide the mixture into 4 equal portions, gently forming them into patties. They should be packed just tightly enough so they will hold together during cooking but not so hard as to crush the fish.

Heat the butter in a large sauté pan over medium heat until foaming. Place the cakes in the pan and cook until the bottom and edges begin to brown, about 4 minutes. Spoon the butter from the pan over the tops of the cakes, then place the pan under the broiler and broil until the tops have browned, 5 to 8 minutes. Serve with the Pomegranate-Jalapeño Relish.

## Pomegranate-Jalapeño Relish

### MAKES ABOUT 1½ CUPS

2 tablespoons extra-virgin olive oil

1 tablespoon maple syrup

Juice of 1 lime (about 2 tablespoons)

1 cup pomegranate arils

1 jalapeño or serrano chile, grated on a Microplane

2 tablespoons chopped cilantro

1 tablespoon fennel seeds, toasted

Salt

In a medium bowl, combine all the ingredients. Let rest for 5 minutes before using.

Keep in an airtight container in the refrigerator for a day or two, but it's best the day it's made.

# 4.05

# Seaweed and Sea Vegetables

SEAWEED HAS LONG been a part of our cuisine, an underpinning of flavor and complexity that we've not known to attribute to the glorious array and variety of what green (but also red and brown) grows under water. Seaweed, both harvested from the wild and farmed, is a giant industry that has grown to over $7 billion annually. Most of it is produced in Asia, where seaweeds have a prominent place in cuisine. It's been a wonderful addition to Western seafood economies so that lately kelp farming in particular is now seen as a booming opportunity to bring environmentally restorative and delicious, nutritious foods to our table from our own shores.

What is seaweed? Well, it's algae, typically macro algae—meaning we can see it with our naked eye—that's grown in salt and fresh water. For culinary purposes, most of it comes from salt water. Seaweed has some bad connotations. Why? It's what Bart's brother tortured him with on beach vacations when he was a young child. It's what brings a less than pleasant smell perhaps to low tide on sandy shores. This is not to turn you off from the category, but to acknowledge that most Americans aren't starting out from a positive vantage point. So, let's not call them seaweeds. Let's call them sea vegetables or seagreens. This isn't obfuscating any truth—it's a helpful way to think of them from a use perspective. Sea vegetable: It's a vegetable that comes from the sea. Done. Your culinary mind has already taken seaweeds all the way to the plate.

# Forms of Sea Vegetables

The market for sea vegetables has for a long time focused on dried product, which has been readily available in health food and grocery stores. There is a range of different species, which we'll get into a bit later. This shelf-stable, oft-sold-in-bags variety is easy to use, convenient to have on hand, and incredibly versatile in terms of application. Like herbs, when

sea vegetables go from fresh to dried, some vivacity and character is lost, but some qualities and depth of flavor are gained as well. And to be certain, the flavor is amplified. A little can go a long way. This dried product can be used as is as a seasoning rub (see page 42), or a light sprinkling can add a nice flavor punctuation to soups, stews, salads, you name it. We usually rehydrate them in some way before using to reanimate not only their flavor but to bring them into balance and meld with the rest of the dish. You can soak sea vegetables in vinegar, wine, stock, citrus, or just water. As they hydrate, they will become a bit more voluminous, pulling in the flavor of whatever liquid is used. Try adding aromatics and spices such as star anise, cardamom pods, or arbol chiles for added dimension. Once rehydrated, sea vegetables are perfect to add to sweet-but-savory autumn squash salads or sautéed zucchini and garlic, tossed in at the last moment.

The most well-known use of dried sea vegetables is the nori wrapper for sushi, or simmered into stocks, such as a dashi (see pages 83 and 84), to form the base of miso soup. But seagreens don't have to be relegated to dishes with Asian flavor. Are you making a summer-fresh dish of minestrone? Fabulous. Throw a sheet of dried sugar kelp in there. Check out our recipe for gigante beans slowly simmered in a flavorful broth, the kelp then removed and minced with herbs to form a sauce to be served over the beans (page 201). Simmer a bit of smoked dulse into your butternut squash soup for added charisma and depth of flavor.

# Fresh-Frozen

Sea vegetables are highly perishable and so, unless you are on the coast, gather your own, or know a sea farmer, it's unlikely that you'll have straight-from-the-water product. But you're not missing out. Sea vegetables freeze so well that they lose absolutely nothing of their flavor or texture. In fact, in climates like the Gulf of Maine, where sugar kelp and other species are at the fore of innovative blue economies, the waters there, and thus the species that grow there, freeze regularly. Sea vegetables don't pull in nutrients using a root system like land plants do but draw nutrients directly through the cells on their surface. Those cells are adapted to freezing and thawing repeatedly. When we pull them from the water and freeze them, it's just another day at the beach for them. Think about it this way. Take a pound of fresh spinach and freeze it. Once thawed, you have significantly less volume. When you freeze and thaw sugar kelp, you start with 100 percent and end up with 100 percent. Another benefit here is cost and yield. You might pay $8 a pound for spinach, and you might pay twice that much for a pound of kelp. When you cook that pound of spinach, you go from a gallon-sized bag to about 2 cups. Kelp? When you cook it, it doesn't lose anything. So, the value-to-volume ratio is very high. And from a flavor and nutrition perspective, you really don't need much of this power-packed superfood to make a big difference.

Frozen sea vegetables are ready to use and can be taken straight from the bag to the plate. We suggest passing them through a marinade first (see the Seaweed Salad on page 196) or scattering a bit through your land greens. Chop them up and toss them in a vinaigrette so their flavor is evenly distributed. Combine sea vegetables with cooking greens such as kale, collards, or escarole (see page 203).

Imagine a comforting, hearty lasagna with silken ricotta and funky parmesan and sweet-tangy tomato sauce, all boosted with the umami depth of sea vegetables layered in. Smoked dulse is a particularly interesting ingredient in that it performs as a spice (think smoked sweet paprika), a seasoning (think MSG), and an herb/vegetable to add volume and color. How cool is that?!

*Fresh frozen sea vegetables* and rehydrated-from-dried are virtually interchangeable in recipes.

There are thousands of species of aquatic plants/seaweed/algae. Of these there are a handful that have long been appreciated and cultivated. And yet there is a whole culinary realm we've yet to explore. We certainly hope and expect to find new varieties emerging into the market in the coming years. The following species can be found at high-end grocery stores, online, and, increasingly, everywhere.

## Sugar Kelp, *Saccharina latissima* / Bull Kelp, *Nereocystis luetkeana*

Kelp has become the darling and focus of production on the East Coast and beyond. There are a handful of species, including sugar kelp, bull kelp, and ribbon kelp, among others, that for culinary reasons are treated the same and are generally equal, and all of which can be sold under the Japanese name, *kombu*. Like most sea vegetables, it is beautiful and somewhat otherworldly in its undulating sheets and dream-tone green color. It is more subtly—though still confidently—flavored than other sea vegetables and is a great gateway ingredient (and a destination in its own) for cooks new to the category to use and learn to love the flavor that sea vegetables bring.

Called sugar kelp because of its high natural sugars, it has a decidedly herbal, even fruity aroma to it. It's available frozen, fermented, and dried. When it reaches a larger size (and it grows very quickly, up to a meter a week in the winter in Maine!), it can retain a wonderful crunch and pleasant texture, similar to a perfectly blanched green bean. Kelp has a particular affinity for raw onion—the two combine in a most elegant way. Pureed sugar kelp is a very convenient product relatively new to the market. It can be found in frozen cubes, perfectly easy to pop into your smoothie, marinade, or vinaigrette.

> Kombu is superb on its own, softened in hot water, and served with mirin (Japanese sweet rice wine) and soy sauce. I also put a square of it in a pot of rice to perfume it.
>
> *Andrew*

# Winged Kelp, *Alaria esculenta*

Also known as alaria, Atlantic wakame, and the charming moniker of lady kelp, this beautiful thick-ribbed variety coaxes a boldness from and summons the character of any ingredients it's paired with. When rehydrated, its still-snappy texture provides a nice counterpoint to softer land greens. When rehydrating, try adding a bit of quality wine vinegar, as the jolt of acidity will accentuate its sea-brine tang.

# Wakame, *Undaria pinnatifida*

You've likely had the bright/neon green seaweed salad introduced to us at sushi joints that is now firmly embedded in America's culinary culture. The glowing hues of salted and blanched blades are often enhanced with a bit of food coloring. It has a delightful snap and resilient texture. It pairs particularly well with warm, heady spices such as ginger and star anise as well as cool flavors such as tarragon, lime juice, and mint. Try it dressed up with a little smoked sweet paprika that's been bloomed in warm olive oil with a bit of sizzled garlic and a dash of sherry vinegar and you've got a delightful Iberian-style seaweed salad.

# Dulse, *Palmaria palmata*

While most of the sea vegetables we use and write of here are green or brown algaes, dulse belongs to the red algae category. It has a lovely burgundy/violet-hued matte color. Its texture is more toothsome, pleasantly leathery even, than most other sea vegetables. And as its deep, brooding color suggests, its rustic flavor is also of the same mood. It certainly has the umami/briny/tidal zip, but not the herbal notes of other sea vegetables, though it offers a unique, meaty, spiced, even dark chocolate temperament. Dulse is commonly sold in sheets and flakes, both as is and smoked. It crisps nicely when roasted or sautéed with a bit of oil and has a particular affinity for and willingness to get along with butter. Try adding some, especially the smoked, to your next beef stew or lentil soup. Puree some with lemon juice, garlic, and olive oil as a marinade for lamb. Or roast up some smoked sheets to serve as a replacement for the bacon in a BLT (page 198).

# Laver, *Porphyra umbilicalis*

This is what we know of as nori, the dried sheets of sea vegetables used to make maki sushi and dried snack chips. Though there are a couple of different species that we call nori, they are all interchangeable. While all sea vegetables are a powerhouse of vitamins and minerals, the nutritional profile of this species is particularly impressive.

Beyond its function in the sushi roll, nori has a gentle personality as well as a very delicate texture that softens quickly when exposed to liquid. You can enhance the flavor of nori by toasting it gently in a low oven or pan, not to cook it but just to bloom its flavors briefly to bring out a welcome sweet nuttiness. And on the topic of sweet, nori is a particularly good partner to sweet ingredients, such as fruit. Peaches, nori, mint, and thin shaved red onion and perhaps some chile flakes is a revelation. Watermelon, lime, and nori is an equally delicious pairing.

## Sea Lettuce, *Ulva lactuca*

This most delicate sea vegetable has the biggest flavor and briniest bite. Its color is glowing green, with broad, beautiful, undulating leaves. Most often sold dried as flakes or a powder, this sea vegetable is a flavor to be used sparingly. We think of sea lettuce as we do dried oregano, a charismatic ingredient, though it can be a bit brash. And it has some of the same flavor qualities as oregano, with a somewhat resiny, piney, hoppy-marijuana funk. When dried, this sea vegetable should be used for seasoning, not volume. Try adding it to some of your favorite spice blends, such as Creole, Montreal steak blend, or anywhere you'd use oregano.

## Additional Species

**Hijiki** is a brown seaweed that turns black when dried. It is found off the coasts of China, Japan, and Korea. Try it in stir-fries or served on its own seasoned with sweet soy sauce and sesame seeds, especially good pairings to finned fish.

**Sea Grape** *Caulerpa lentillifera* is a species from coastal regions in the Asia-Pacific. This seaweed has a soft and succulent texture. In Japan it is called *umibudo*.

# Seaweed and Livestock Feed

In addition to the burgeoning and exciting new economy of sea vegetables for human consumption, there is great interest in looking to marine and freshwater algae as part of a climate solution. This ranges from biofuels to novel ingredients in aquaculture feeds. There is even the possibility of using some species to sequester carbon, sinking it to the bottom of the ocean where, over eons, it will become fossil fuel.

Also of note: Ranchers and scientists have found that feeding algae to livestock can improve their digestive process and significantly reduce methane emissions, a greenhouse gas exponentially more powerful than $CO_2$. As the old adage goes, you are what you eat. Our environment is also a reflection of what we eat, and of what we eat eats.

> The challenge is huge. Corn and soy are massively subsidized for animal feed. And while this helps keep meat cheap at the counter, it comes at great cost to the planet and the well-being of the animals. We would all be better off if we subsidized the seaweed farmer with as much zeal as we do the farm-to-freighter economy.
>
> *Andrew*

# Kelp Tabouleh

**SERVES 4**

This coastal variation on a traditional tabouleh salad is a great way to introduce kelp into your diet via a familiar favorite. The flavor of this dish requires a heavy hand with salt and a firm punch of acidity, so don't skimp on the lemon juice. Keep tasting as you go and add more until it tastes really good to you.

*[signature]*

This is the only recipe I use curly parsley in. I think curly parsley is a fine ingredient-it's just that I usually prefer the more nuanced flavor of flat-leaf parsley. Here curly parsley adds volume as well as a bright, aromatic quality that gives the dish lift.

½ cup fine bulgur wheat

1 shallot, minced (about 3 tablespoons)

½ cup extra-virgin olive oil

2 garlic cloves, grated on a Microplane or minced

¼ cup lemon juice (about 2 lemons), plus more if needed

Pinch of ground allspice

Red chile flakes, such as Aleppo or Urfa

2 tablespoons smoked dulse flakes

Salt

2 bunches curly parsley, thick stems discarded, finely chopped

1 bunch mint, leaves picked, finely chopped

6 ounces fresh or frozen shredded kelp

1 cup ¼-inch diced European cucumber (about ½ cucumber), no need to peel, but remove seeds from large cucumbers

2 cups ¼-inch diced Roma tomatoes (about 3 tomatoes)

Freshly cracked Black Pepper–Fennel Blend (page 53) or black pepper

In a large bowl, cover the bulgur with 2 to 3 inches of tepid water and soak for 20 to 30 minutes.

In a large bowl, stir together the shallot, oil, garlic, lemon juice, allspice, chile flakes, and dulse. Season well with salt and let rest while you prepare the other ingredients.

Add the parsley, mint, kelp, cucumber, and tomatoes and season with pepper-fennel blend. Let rest for 10 minutes to allow flavors to meld. Mix, taste, and add more lemon juice and/or salt, if needed.

# Seaweed Salad

Soaking dry seaweed in cold water for 10 to 15 minutes is all it typically takes to rehydrate. If you have access to fresh dulse, you can fry the leaves in vegetable oil until crisp like potato chips, sprinkle with salt as they drain on a paper towel, and garnish the salad with them. I love to serve this salad as is, with cold poached fish, leftover grilled seafood, sliced chicken, or even sliced leftover cold charred beef from the grill.

**1 head tender cabbage***

**1 tablespoon sesame oil (not the toasted version!)**

**Salt**

**1/2 ounce dried wakame**

**1/2 ounce dried hijiki**

**1 square piece of kombu (roughly 6 x 6 inches)**

**1 head green butter lettuce**

**8 ounces mixed fresh sea lettuce and sea grapes**

**2 Persian cucumbers, thinly sliced**

**1 red Fresno chile, thinly sliced, seeds discarded**

**2 tablespoons toasted sesame seeds**

**4 scallions, thinly sliced at a 45-degree angle, I use the whole scallion**

**1 recipe Seaweed Salad Dressing (recipe follows)**

**4 cilantro sprigs, optional**

* I love using Chinese flat head cabbage from my local Asian markets or arrowhead cabbage from the farmers market. Ask for arrowhead-shaped varietals where you shop. They are small and delicious beyond measure.

Preheat the oven to 450°F.

Brush the cabbage head with the oil. (I usually roast 4 heads, about 2.5 pounds, at a time and reserve the rest in my refrigerator for another use.) Season well with salt and place in a pie tin or small baking pan. Place in the oven and roast for 45 minutes until tender. Remove and let cool.

While all that is going on, rehydrate the wakame and hijiki in a bowl with cold water to cover until tender, about 10 minutes. Place the kombu in a small pot, add water to cover, and bring to a simmer over medium-high heat. Cook for 10 minutes, then turn off the heat and allow the kombu to cool for 45 minutes in the water.

Take the 4 largest leaves from the head of lettuce and reserve them for plating. Discard the core and thinly slice the remaining leaves. Thinly slice the cooled cabbage, discarding the core.

Drain and pat dry the seaweeds you refreshed. Rinse and pat dry the fresh seaweeds. Remove the kombu from the water, cut it in half, stack the pieces, and slice into strips as thinly as you can.

In a medium bowl, combine the cucumbers, chiles, sesame seeds, and scallions. In a separate bowl, combine the lettuce, cabbage, wakame, kombu, sea lettuce and sea grapes, and hijiki. Place in the refrigerator along with 4 large low bowls or plates for 1 hour.

To serve, place a lettuce leaf in each bowl or on each plate, off center. Build your salad just to the side of the leaf, as if the salad was pouring out of it. Dress the seaweed mixture with one-third of the dressing and place a small spoonful against the base of the lettuce leaf. Dress the cucumber mixture with another third of the dressing and place a smaller spoonful against the seaweed. Brush or spoon the remaining dressing along the top of the lettuce leaf. Garnish each with a cilantro sprig.

I wrap any leftover seaweed well and refrigerate it. I stir-fry it with sliced garlic and Chinese or Savoy cabbage and season it with really good aged soy sauce when I spill it from the wok. Heavenly.

For fried dulse I take handfuls of the "leaves" and fry them in 375°F vegetable oil, in batches, for just a minute or two, draining on a paper towel and seasoning with sea salt. Fresh dulse can be treated like frying basil leaves or sage for crispy garnishes.

You can toast some nori over an oven burner for a second and crush some on top of the salad, or use kizami nori, a pre-sliced nori that I throw on top of everything.

# Seaweed Salad Dressing

**MAKES ABOUT 1 CUP**

1/4 cup rice wine vinegar

Juice of 1 lemon (2 to 3 tablespoons)

1 tablespoon brown sugar

1/4 teaspoon salt

1 teaspoon gently crushed shichimi togarashi (Japanese seven-spice)

2-inch knob fresh ginger, grated (about 1 tablespoon)

2 tablespoons soy sauce

2 tablespoons toasted sesame oil

1/2 cup grapeseed, peanut, or untoasted sesame oil

In a large bowl, whisk the vinegar, lemon juice, brown sugar, salt, shichimi togarashi, ginger, and soy sauce. Gradually whisk in the oils. I like about a scant 1/3 cup or so, but everyone has a different acidity level they are comfy with. Once you taste the balance you like, you are done.

# Smoky DLT

**SERVES 4**

Smoked dulse has a prominent personality with an umami richness that makes it a sultry partner to ripe tomatoes that rivals bacon. Toasting the dulse brings out its smokiness and accentuates its chewy texture. To further deepen its appeal, we add a bit of tahini with the aioli/mayonnaise, a trick recommended for any sandwich that uses mayonnaise. Of course, a good BLT, or *DLT*, is more about the quality of the tomato than anything else. So, treat this as a seasonal dish for when tomatoes are at their peak.

2 ounces smoked dulse pieces (not flakes)

2 tablespoons extra-virgin olive oil

1 to 1½ pounds tomatoes

8 thick slices crusty bread, toasted

⅓ cup Aioli (page 96) or mayonnaise

¼ cup tahini

Juice of 1 lemon (2 to 3 tablespoons)

1 ounce arugula

Salt

Freshly cracked Black Pepper–Fennel Blend (page 53) or black pepper

Preheat the oven to 350°F.

Place the dulse strips on a baking sheet and spray or brush them with the oil. Bake until crisp, about 10 minutes.

Slice the tomatoes ⅓ inch thick.

In a small bowl, whisk together the aioli, tahini, and lemon juice. Add a bit of water if needed to get it to mayonnaise consistency.

Slather 4 slices of toast with the aioli mixture. Evenly divide the arugula among the slices of bread, top with the tomato slices, and season with salt and pepper-fennel blend. Top with the dulse and the remaining slices of bread and squish just a bit.

# Gigante Beans with Seaweed Salmoriglio

**SERVES 6**

Salmoriglio is a Mediterranean sauce
with herbs, garlic, and olive oil.
In this version, after simmering its
umami goodness into a pot of creamy
beans, kelp is used as the base of
the sauce. There's a lot of olive oil
in this recipe. The oil first simmers
with the beans and is then skimmed off
to be used in the sauce to ensure all
the flavors are perfectly integrated.

3/4 cup extra-virgin olive oil

1 fennel bulb, cut into 1/2-inch dice (about 1 1/2 cups)

3 celery stalks, sliced 1/2 inch thick on a bias (about 2 cups)

3 carrots, cut into roughly 1/2-inch pieces (about 1 1/2 cups)

1 onion, cut into 1/2-inch dice (about 1 cup)

4 garlic cloves, roughly chopped

1 pound dried gigante or cannellini beans, soaked overnight in cool water and drained

2 tablespoons fennel seeds

1/2 ounce dried kelp (4 x 6-inch piece)*

2 bay leaves

Salt

1 recipe Seaweed Salmoriglio (recipe follows)

*Or try substituting 1 tablespoon smoked dulse flakes.

Heat the oil in a heavy-bottom stockpot over medium-high heat. Add the fennel, celery, carrots, onion, and garlic and cook for 3 to 5 minutes, until the vegetables are beginning to brown. Add the beans, fennel seeds, kelp, bay leaves, and enough water to cover by 2 inches. Bring to a simmer and cook until the beans are soft but not falling apart, 1 1/2 to 2 hours. Season with salt and cool to room temperature, about 1 hour. Discard the bay leaves.

Skim off any oil from the surface and remove the kelp (reserving both for the Seaweed Salmoriglio).

Serve the beans room temperature or warm with the Seaweed Salmoriglio drizzled over the top.

## Seaweed Salmoriglio

**MAKES ABOUT 2 CUPS**

1/2 teaspoon dried oregano leaves

1 cup chopped parsley

1/4 cup chopped mint

1 garlic clove, grated on a Microplane or minced

Zest and juice of 1 lemon (2 to 3 tablespoons juice)

1/2 ounce dried kelp, rehydrated in 1 cup water (best if you use the kelp from cooking the beans), chopped

1 cup extra-virgin olive oil (use the oil skimmed from the beans and add more oil as needed to make 1 cup)

Salt

1 teaspoon red chile flakes, such as Aleppo

Combine the oregano, parsley, mint, garlic, lemon zest and juice, kelp, and 1/4 cup bean cooking liquid (if you're making this without the beans, use 1/4 cup kelp rehydrating liquid) in the bowl of a food processor and pulse until it forms a chunky paste. If you prefer a smoother texture, continue to process until it's to your liking. Remove the herb paste to a bowl and whisk in the oil. Season with salt and the chile flakes.

The sauce will keep in an airtight container in the refrigerator for up to 3 days.

# Braised Kelp and Escarole with Almonds and Dates

SERVES 4

When raw, escarole can be bitter and fibrous. But when braised, it develops a unique sweetness and depth of flavor. That flavor is given additional contour by umami-rich kelp. Dates add little punctuations of sweet and almonds of course add nutty flavor but also textural interest.

6 tablespoons extra-virgin olive oil

4 garlic cloves, sliced

1 tablespoon fennel seeds

8 dates, pitted and roughly chopped

½ cup slivered or chopped almonds

1 pound escarole, cut into 1- to 2-inch pieces

6 ounces ready-to-eat kelp

Salt

Juice of 1 lemon (2 to 3 tablespoons)

¼ cup chopped parsley

Heat the oil in a dutch oven over medium heat. Add the garlic, fennel seeds, dates, and almonds and cook until the garlic is soft but not browned, 3 to 4 minutes. Add the escarole, kelp, and ½ cup water. Season with a good pinch of salt and stir to combine. Cover and bring to a simmer, then reduce the heat to medium-low (or transfer to a preheated 325°F oven) and cook for about 30 minutes, until tender and fragrant and the liquid is reduced to a light syrup consistency, neither dry nor soupy. Stir in the lemon juice and parsley. Taste and adjust the seasoning as needed.

# Pasta with Kale-Kelp Pesto

**SERVES 4**

We include two versions of kelp pesto here—one with kale and almonds and the other with cilantro and pecans. The cilantro pesto is particularly good over simple roasted sweet potatoes as a lunch, appetizer, or side dish. The kale pesto is a deeply savory and full-flavored combination. Try a spoonful or two stirred into butternut squash or chicken noodle soup as a garnish.

A key step in this dish is to finish cooking the pasta by simmering it with the pesto and a bit of the cooking water. This ensures that you get a rich, integrated sauce and the rawness of the pesto is tamed. The pickled ginger provides a nice punch of punctuation.

Salt

1 pound linguine

1 recipe Kale-Kelp Pesto (recipe follows) or Cilantro-Pecan-Kelp Pesto (recipe follows)—take your pick!

¼ cup pickled ginger, sliced into very thin threads

Bring a large pot of heavily salted water to a boil, add the linguine, and cook according to the package instructions to just below al dente. Drain and reserve 1 cup cooking water. Return the pasta to the pot with ½ cup cooking water and the pesto. Stir until the sauce is thickened and coats the pasta evenly. Add more of the cooking water if needed. Divide among 4 plates and top with the pickled ginger threads.

## Kale-Kelp Pesto

**MAKES ABOUT 1½ CUPS**

6 ounces shredded fresh kelp
2 cups firmly packed (stems included) lacinato kale
¾ cup extra-virgin olive oil
2 garlic cloves
Juice of ½ lemon (about 1 tablespoon)
¼ cup almonds
Salt

Combine the kelp, kale, oil, garlic, and lemon juice in a food processor and process until smooth. Add the almonds and pulse a few times until well combined and chunky. Season with salt.

This will keep in the refrigerator for 3 to 4 days. This freezes well—it will keep frozen in an airtight container for up to 3 months.

## Cilantro-Pecan-Kelp Pesto

**MAKES ABOUT 1½ CUPS**

2 garlic cloves
1 bunch cilantro, including stems
6 ounces shredded fresh kelp
Juice of 1 lime (about 2 tablespoons)
Salt
½ cup vegetable oil
¼ cup pecans, toasted
**Red chile flakes, such as Aleppo or gochugaru, optional**

Combine the garlic, cilantro, kelp, lime juice, a pinch of salt, and the oil in a blender and blend on high speed until smooth. If needed, add more oil to get the mixture to the consistency of pancake batter. With the machine running, add the pecans and process until the pesto thickens. Season again with salt and chile flakes, if using.

This will keep in the refrigerator for 3 to 4 days. This freezes well—it will keep frozen an airtight container for up to 3 months.

# Lasagna with Seaweed and Herbs

**SERVES 6 TO 8**

In this twist on a classic dish, kelp adds a marine tang to an otherwise entirely familiar dish. The umami that the kelp brings draws out the flavor of the cheese. The sprinkle of mace in the spinach lends a very savory touch.

**1 pound lasagna noodles**

**2 tablespoons extra-virgin olive oil**

**2 garlic cloves, grated on a Microplane or minced**

**10 ounces spinach**

**Pinch of ground mace or freshly grated nutmeg**

**Red chile flakes, such as Aleppo or gochugaru**

**Salt**

**12 ounces fresh or frozen shredded kelp**

**1 pound ricotta cheese**

**2 eggs, beaten**

**One 28-ounce jar marinara sauce***

**4 ounces grated parmesan cheese**

**4 ounces grated cheddar cheese**

\* You can make a double batch of Andrew's Tomato Sauce (page 123), but note that you'll have about 2 cups remaining.

Bring a large pot of well-salted water to a boil, add the lasagna noodles, and cook according to the package instructions. Drain and reserve. Preheat the oven to 350°F.

Meanwhile, heat the oil in a large sauté pan over medium-high heat. Add the garlic and spinach and season with the mace, chile flakes, and salt and cook until the spinach is wilted. Remove to a colander. Gently press with a ladle or spoon to remove some of the moisture. Move the spinach to a cutting board, combine with the kelp, and roughly chop.

Combine the ricotta and eggs in a large bowl. Add a pinch of salt and reserve.

Assemble the lasagna in a baking dish, starting with a layer of the tomato sauce, then noodles, ricotta mixture, and greens. Repeat, alternating ingredients as you build upward. Finish with a top layer of tomato sauce. Scatter the parmesan and cheddar cheeses over the top. Bake until hot all the way through and bubbling, about 20 minutes. If desired, place the dish under the broiler for a few minutes to brown the cheese.

# Dessert

Seafood for dessert? What?! Well yeah, why not. I mean a fish fillet, probably not, even for us with our robust and diverse love of all things seafood. But hey, carrot cake, zucchini bread, kelp crisp, all of these belong in the same category, which is delicious. With the infusion of a little smoked dulse or the delicious umami bomb of kelp, these ingredients can greatly augment the sweet experience, not by tacking toward savory but by adding color, contrast, and depth of flavor. And, of course, it also adds a boost of nutrition. The dessert recipes included here are not gimmicks, nor do they include seafood just because. They are interesting culinary compositions in and of themselves.

> . . . although there was that time I ordered oysters for dessert in NOLA.
> See page 104.

# Chocolate Chip Dulse Brownies

**MAKES ABOUT 24 BARS**

This recipe comes from our dear friend Jennifer Bushman. The addition of the sustainable seaweed imparts a richness to the brownies in a way that cocoa alone cannot achieve. In this recipe, we used dulse, a crimson-colored seaweed that tastes a bit fruity and salty-SO yummy! Using smoked dulse is extra sexy.

1/2 cup (1 stick) butter, at room temperature

3 cups (18 ounces) semisweet chocolate chips

2 cups sugar

1 1/3 cups all-purpose flour

1/4 cup dried dulse flakes

1 teaspoon vanilla extract

1/2 teaspoon baking powder

3/4 teaspoon salt

6 large eggs, at room temperature

3/4 cup heavy cream

Preheat the oven to 350°F. Grease a 9 x 13-inch glass baking dish.

In a medium saucepan, melt the butter and 2 cups of the chocolate chips over medium-low heat. Pour the mixture into a large bowl. Add 1 2/3 cups of the sugar, the flour, dulse, vanilla, baking powder, 1/2 teaspoon of the salt, and 3 of the eggs and beat until well mixed. Spread the mixture in the prepared pan.

Heat the heavy cream in a small saucepan over medium heat until it starts to simmer, but don't let it boil. Add the remaining 1 cup chocolate chips and stir until the chocolate is melted. Cool slightly.

Combine the 3 remaining eggs, 1/3 cup sugar, and 1/4 teaspoon salt in the bowl of an electric mixer and mix at medium speed until foamy. Add the chocolate and cream mixture and stir until combined. Pour this over the batter in the pan.

Bake for 45 minutes, or until a toothpick inserted in the middle comes out surrounded with gooey crumbs. Cool on a wire cooling rack and then cut into 2-inch squares.

# Warm Cranberry Apple Crisp with Kelp Crumble

**SERVES 6**

Here is a great example of how kelp brings a savory touch to the sweet course. Blending it with apples brings out a nuanced flavor. Leave the skins on the apples for greater flavor and nutrition as well as visual appeal and textural contrast.

### FILLING

1/2 cup dried cranberries

4 medium firm apples, such as Granny Smith (about 6 cups sliced)

Juice of 1/2 lemon (about 1 tablespoon)

1/4 cup dark brown sugar

1 teaspoon ground cinnamon

1/4 teaspoon freshly grated nutmeg

1 teaspoon vanilla extract

1 tablespoon cornstarch

### TOPPING

4 tablespoons (1/2 stick) butter, melted

2 tablespoons dried kelp, sea lettuce, or wakame, chopped (or you can use premade seaweed sprinkles)

1/4 cup dark brown sugar

1 teaspoon ground cinnamon

1/4 teaspoon salt

1/2 cup all-purpose flour

1/2 cup rolled oats

1/2 toasted nuts, such as pecans or almonds, chopped

Preheat the oven to 325°F.

In a large bowl, cover the cranberries in hot water and plump for 5 minutes. Drain the water and pat the cranberries dry. Return the cranberries to the bowl, add the apples, lemon juice, brown sugar, cinnamon, nutmeg, vanilla, and cornstarch, and toss to combine. Transfer the mixture to a 2-quart baking dish.

To make the topping, in a medium bowl, combine the butter, kelp, brown sugar, cinnamon, and salt until fully incorporated. Stir in the flour, oats, and nuts until the mixture is well mixed and crumbly. Sprinkle the oat topping evenly over the top of the apple mixture.

Bake for 40 to 45 minutes, until the topping is golden brown and the filling is hot.

Serve warm, with a scoop of vanilla ice cream or yogurt, if desired.

# 4.06

# Flaky White Fish

# Fluke and California Sea Urchin Ceviche

**SERVES 4 TO 6**

I think my friend Diego Oka, the
brilliant chef from La Mar in Miami,
is one of the best chefs in America.
Full stop. His ceviche is the gold
standard against which I measure
all others; there is none better. I
have adapted his recipe for the last
few years after eating it and making
it with him several times. And, of
course, I had to slowly squeeze his
secrets out of him. Here I add lots
of sea urchin for a truly decadent
chilled seafood course. Put your
serving bowls in the freezer to chill
while you make the ceviche-the colder
this dish is the better. Make sure
the urchin stays on top of the fish
for flavor and textural contrast.

Diego garnishes his ceviche in the
classic way, and so do I. Use boiled
and sliced pieces of sweet potato,
just one or two per serving, as well
as boiled fresh starchy oversized
Peruvian sweet-corn kernels called
*choclo*, which you can find at Latin
markets canned under the Amigos brand
if you don't have access to the fresh
stuff. Or you can use corn nuts, the
Peruvian cancha, Inca's brand, which
is available online. The crunchy,
salty contrast is authentic, honest,
and, above all, scrumptious.

*Andrew*

Salt

One 15-ounce can choclo (sweet corn), rinsed and drained

1 red onion, thinly sliced (about 1 cup)

12 ounces fluke or flounder, skin off, cut into ½-inch cubes

1 Thai red chile or ½ habanero chile, very thinly sliced

Juice of 1 lime (about 2 tablespoons), plus some more if need be

½ cup Leche de Tigre (page 214)

1 sweet potato, peeled, boiled until just tender, cooled, and sliced

1 cup cancha (corn nuts)

6 ounces Santa Barbara, Maine, or Hokkaido sea urchin tongues

4 cilantro sprigs

Place a medium bowl in the refrigerator to chill.
Place 4 to 6 individual bowls in the refrigerator
or freezer.

Bring a small pot of salted water to a boil. Add the
choclo and blanch for about 30 seconds, until slightly
tender. Drain and transfer to an ice water bath to
chill. Drain well.

Soak the onion in a bowl of ice water for about
10 minutes. Drain well.

Mix the fish, chile, lime juice, and Leche de Tigre in
the chilled bowl. Add the onions and season with
salt. Toss and plate the mixture right away in piles
right in the middle of the chilled or frozen bowls.
Place the sweet potato slices, choclo, and cancha
around the fish. Top the piles of ceviche with the sea
urchin. Place a cilantro sprig over each portion.

# Leche de Tigre

**MAKES ABOUT 2 CUPS**

Juice of 10 limes (about 1¼ cups)

Juice of 1 orange (about ¼ cup)

¼ cup cold Basic Fish Stock (page 85)

A few ice cubes

1 celery stalk, chopped (about ½ cup)

4 ounces fluke or flounder, skin off (use whatever white fish you use for the ceviche)

1 small shallot

1 small red Thai chile or ½ habanero chile, stemmed

3 or 4 cilantro sprigs

½ garlic clove, peeled

Salt

Combine the lime juice, orange juice, fish stock, ice, and celery in a blender and blend until smooth. Add the fish and pulse to combine. Add the shallot, chile, cilantro, and garlic and season with salt. Blend for 10 seconds until homogenous. Strain and discard the solids. Keep ice cold and use right away.

# Safety Tips for Eating Raw Seafood

The proliferation of sushi in this country has tempered our cultural taboos against raw seafood, but we still need to maintain some vigilance to mitigate the risk of foodborne illness. First precaution, as with all seafood: Always, always, always buy the freshest, most pristine, most beautiful seafood you can, from the most trusted fishmonger you can find. Avoiding bacteria is mostly about proper handling of seafood throughout the supply chain. Seafood-borne parasites pose another risk, and these can be a little harder to identify. Ask your fishmonger about any potential dangers from parasites, and seek out seafood that has been properly frozen to kill parasites.

# Barton's Ceviche with Crunchy Almonds and Raisins

SERVES 4

Ceviche is always a bit of a choose-your-own-adventure type of dish, the basis of which is a bath of fresh citrus juice, salt, and chiles. From there you can add whatever you want. Toasted almonds, with their slight bitterness and crunchy texture, meet sweet raisins that plump in the dressing and the cool clean flavor of fresh herbs to create a memorable pairing.

*Barton*

**1 pound white fish, such as flounder or halibut, cut into ¹/₃-inch pieces**

**Salt**

**6 limes, juiced (³/₄ cup)**

**2 tablespoons extra-virgin olive oil**

**¹/₄ cup sliced almonds, toasted and roughly chopped**

**3 tablespoons raisins**

**1 Fresno or serrano chile, very thinly sliced**

**1 red onion, very thinly sliced (about 1 cup), rinsed briefly under cold water and patted dry**

**¹/₂ cup loosely packed chervil or cilantro leaves**

**¹/₄ cup mint leaves, torn**

**Pita chips or crostini**

Season the fish with salt and let it rest for 10 minutes.

In a large bowl, combine the lime juice, oil, almonds, raisins, and chile. Stir gently and let rest for 5 minutes. Add the fish and stir to combine, taking care not to break up the fish. Let rest in the refrigerator for 15 minutes. Add the onion, chervil, and mint and toss to combine.

Divide among individual dishes and spoon any remaining marinade over the ceviche. Serve with pita chips or crostini.

I find the individually wrapped Cryovac frozen portions of seafood at my local Asian markets particularly good for ceviche. When you find a great resource for frozen fish, take advantage of it.

*Andrew*

# Cobia Ceviche with Herbs and Chiles

**SERVES 4**

This is kind of a mashup dish between a South American-style ceviche and a French tartare. The labneh or sour cream mixed with mustard provides a cooling and fatty aspect to the dish. It's a wonderful blend of textures and bright colors.

¼ cup labneh or sour cream

¼ cup extra-virgin olive oil, plus more for drizzling

1½ teaspoons whole grain mustard

Pinch of ground mace or freshly grated nutmeg

Salt

1 large sweet potato (about 1 pound), sliced into ¼-inch rounds

12 ounces cobia, cut into ⅓-inch dice

1 small shallot, sliced as thinly as possible (about 2 tablespoons)

4 radishes, finely diced or very thinly sliced

1 chile, such as serrano or Fresno, thinly sliced on a mandoline

¼ cup walnut pieces, toasted and roughly chopped

1 orange, preferably blood orange, peeled and cut into segments

Juice of 2 limes (about ¼ cup)

2 tablespoons cilantro leaves, torn

1 tablespoon chopped basil

2 tablespoons chopped mint

In a small bowl, thin the labneh with a bit of water to make it a mayonnaise-like consistency. Whisk in the oil, mustard, and mace, season with salt, and reserve.

Bring a medium pot of salted water to a boil. Drop the sweet potato rounds into the water, taking care that they don't stick together. Cook until barely tender, about 4 minutes. Strain and cool.

In a large bowl, combine the cobia, shallot, radishes, chile, walnut pieces, orange segments, lime juice, and sweet potatoes. Season with salt and toss to combine. Let the mixture rest for 5 minutes.

Spread the labneh mixture across the bottom of 4 plates. Add the cilantro, basil, and mint to the fish mixture and toss to combine. Arrange the fish mixture over the top and drizzle with additional oil.

# Brandade de Morue

Salt preservation is as old as the sea, as it were, and salt cod is the king of salt-preserved fish. For thousands of years, cod had been fished the world over, salted, and preserved for years. Salt cod in its dried form has been both food and a form of currency, and as such was essential for our exploration of the world over the past three thousand years. Today, salt cod is typically refreshed in the fridge for a few days in changes of cold water. Then you can poach it and puree or mash it, braise it, and sauce it as is commonly done in Portugal and Spain. You could also batter and fry it. Here we combine it with potatoes and dairy and then bake it to make brandade. *Morue* is the French word for cod, and it's one of the great edible pieces of history that delights our senses.

Andrew

1 pound salt cod

1 pound russet potatoes

1/2 cup white wine

1 teaspoon black peppercorns

Bouquet garni of a few sprigs each thyme and parsley and 2 fresh bay leaves

4 tablespoons (1/2 stick) butter

1/2 cup milk

1/4 cup crème fraîche

4 garlic cloves, thinly sliced

Salt and freshly ground black pepper

1/2 bunch chives, minced, optional

1 baguette, sliced 1/2 inch thick, brushed with extra-virgin olive oil, and toasted

Place the salt cod in a large dish and cover with a couple inches of cold water. Soak for about 8 hours in the refrigerator. Rinse and repeat twice more over a 24-hour period.

Preheat the oven to 375°F. Place the potatoes on a baking sheet, prick with a fork, and bake for 45 minutes to 1 hour until tender and cooked through.

Meanwhile, drain the cod and place it in a low, straight-sided 4-quart pot or pan with fresh cool water to cover, then remove the cod. You are simply measuring so you don't overflow the pan later. Add the wine, peppercorns, and bouquet garni to the pan.

Place the pan over medium heat and bring to a simmer. Cover and simmer for 15 minutes. Add the cod, and when the water returns to a strong simmer, cook for 3 to 5 more minutes, until the thickest pieces of cod start to flake apart. Turn off the heat. Remove the cod and allow it to cool on a plate. Discard the cooking liquid.

In the same pan, heat the butter over medium-low heat until it browns, stirring to make sure you get all the browned bits loose from the bottom and sides of the pan. Pour into a bowl and set aside.

When the potatoes are done baking, remove them from the oven and turn the oven temperature up to 425°F. Carefully holding the potatoes using a hand towel, split them in half and scoop out the flesh. Pass through a ricer or food mill into a large bowl. Add the butter, milk, crème fraîche, and garlic to the bowl.

Pulse the fish in a food processor. Do not puree it; you are simply trying to uniformly flake it into small pieces.

Add the cod to the potato mixture and season with salt and pepper. Your mixture should be the consistency of perfect mashed potatoes. Place the mixture in a medium baking dish and place in the oven. Roast for 10 to 15 minutes, then arrange an oven rack 7 to 8 inches from the heating element and turn the oven to broil. Place the baking dish under the broiler and broil until the top is browned. Top with chives, if using. Serve immediately with the toasted baguette slices for dipping.

# Fish Stick "Panzanella"

**SERVES 4**

Fish sticks, like any other frozen, breaded product, conjure up visions of a utilitarian meal. But there's no reason fish sticks, which really can be very tasty, can't be lent a little class by pairing them with marquee ingredients, such as fresh-from-the-vine heirloom tomatoes. Panzanella, a rustic Italian salad of chunks of yesterday's bread brought back to life with the juice of fresh tomatoes, herbs, and crunchy sweet onions, is a perfect starting point for changing one's mind about fish sticks.

In this recipe, crunchy, just-cooked fish sticks replace the bread and perform their task marvelously.

12 ounces prepared breaded fish sticks
2 tablespoons whole grain mustard
1/2 cup extra-virgin olive oil
1/4 cup red wine vinegar
Salt
1 1/2 pounds heirloom tomatoes, cut into 1-inch pieces
1 red onion, thinly sliced (about 1 cup)
1 fennel bulb, thinly sliced (about 1 1/2 cups)
4 cups arugula
Freshly cracked Black Pepper–Fennel Blend (page 53) or black pepper

Prepare the fish sticks according to the package instructions, adding a minute or two additional cooking time so they are extra crispy.

Whisk the mustard, oil, vinegar, and salt to taste in a large bowl to make a vinaigrette. Place the tomatoes in a separate bowl, drizzle with a few spoonfuls of the vinaigrette, and season with salt.

Combine the onion, fennel, and arugula in the bowl with the vinaigrette and toss. Remove the fish sticks from the oven. Cut or tear each stick into pieces roughly the size of croutons (about 3 pieces per fish stick). To serve, place the fennel-arugula mixture onto a platter or plates and top with the seasoned tomatoes and the warm fish stick pieces. Sprinkle with pepper-fennel blend.

# Deep-Poached Halibut with Green Goddess Dressing

**SERVES 4**

Deep-poaching seafood is a great way to prepare a dish for serving cold or at room temperature, especially if it is chilled in the broth to fully develop the flavor before serving. Deep-poaching requires seafood to be fully submerged in a flavorful liquid to cook. An accompanying sauce is typically made separately, although the poaching liquid can be strained and saved to flavor soups and stews. Or it can be frozen and used again later as a poaching broth.

1¼ pounds halibut fillets
**Salt**
**1 cup white or red wine, optional**
**½ cup white wine or red wine vinegar**
**2 thyme sprigs**
**2 garlic cloves, smashed**
**Zest of 1 orange**
**2 juniper berries**
**1 bay leaf**
**½ apple, very thinly sliced (about 1 cup)**
**1 fennel bulb, very thinly sliced (about 1½ cups)**
**4 radishes, very thinly sliced (about ¼ cup)**
**2 tablespoons torn parsley leaves**
**Juice of ½ lemon (about 1 tablespoon)**
**1 tablespoon extra-virgin olive oil**
**Green Goddess Dressing (recipe follows)**

Season the fish with salt and let it rest for 15 minutes.

Combine the wine, if using, the vinegar, and 3 cups water in a medium pan with high sides. Add the thyme, garlic, orange zest, juniper berries, and bay leaf and season with salt. Heat over medium-high heat until the liquid reaches 175°F. Add the fish to the pan and reduce the heat to low. Use a thermometer to maintain the poaching liquid between 160°F and 170°F and cook for 8 to 10 minutes per inch of thickness. The fish is done when a toothpick pierces the fish with no resistance. If serving immediately, remove from the cooking liquid and pat dry. If the skin has been left on, gently remove it by using a fish spatula and discard. We recommend cooling in the cooking liquid at room temperature or in the refrigerator overnight to be served room temperature or chilled.

In a medium bowl, toss together the apple, fennel, radishes, and parsley. Dress with the lemon juice, oil, and a pinch of salt. Spread Green Goddess Dressing on each plate. Place a piece of fish onto each plate and top with the salad. If you like, garnish with a few leaves of watercress reserved from making the dressing.

# Green Goddess Dressing

**MAKES ABOUT 2 CUPS**

The best of both worlds—creamy and bright with herbs—this dressing is wonderful over vegetables or as an accompaniment to grilled, broiled, slow-roasted, or deep-poached seafoods.

1 cup Aioli (page 96) or mayonnaise
One 2-ounce can oil-packed anchovies
1 bunch watercress, thick stems trimmed
1 bunch tarragon, leaves picked
½ bunch parsley, leaves picked
Juice of 1 lemon (2 to 3 tablespoons)
Salt

Combine the aioli, anchovies with their oil, watercress, tarragon, parsley, and lemon juice in a food processor and process until mostly smooth and bright green. Season with salt. Transfer to a container, cover, and let rest for at least 1 hour and up to overnight in the refrigerator to allow flavors to meld. It will keep in the refrigerator up to a week.

# Seared Cobia with Cherry Tomato and Garlic Pan Sauce

**SERVES 4**

Sweet-tart, summer-ripe cherry tomatoes, especially the culinary wonder that is the sungold variety, make for a perfect cooking medium and sauce for this one pot-dish. Starting garlic in a good amount of olive oil provides a deep, nutty flavor in which tomatoes then blister, and the fish is nestled into the sauce-in-the-making. Then it's all simmered together for the flavors to meld, with the tomato juice reducing and emulsifying with the heady oil. All in, this is a perfect method for nearly any type of fish.

1¼ pounds cobia fillets

Salt

⅓ cup extra-virgin olive oil

4 garlic cloves, sliced

1 shallot, diced (about 3 tablespoons)

1 pint cherry tomatoes

2 tablespoons chopped mixed herbs, such as parsley, chives, cilantro, and mint

Season the fish with salt and let it rest for 15 minutes.

Heat 1 tablespoon of the oil in a large sauté pan over medium-high heat until it shimmers. Add the fish and sear on one side until golden, about 4 minutes. Remove from the heat and reserve.

Add the rest of the oil to the same pan, then add the garlic and shallot and sauté for 3 to 4 minutes, until the garlic is a golden, nutty brown. Add the tomatoes, season with salt, and toss to combine. Cook until the tomatoes just begin to burst, then cook for another 5 minutes to reduce the sauce slightly.

Nestle the fish into the tomato mixture, uncooked-side down. Reduce the heat to low and simmer for 3 to 5 minutes. Remove the fish to plates. Add the herbs to the sauce and toss vigorously to emulsify and combine. Pour the sauce over the fish.

# Basque Cod al Pil Pil

**SERVES 4**

In this classic Spanish dish, the natural gelatin in flaky white-fleshed fish is coaxed from the fillet through gentle low, slow heat in a generous bath of olive oil. Once the fish is cooked, it only takes a bit of elbow grease to emulsify the pan juices and olive oil, spiked with fresh herbs and garlic, into a thick, rich sauce.

1¼ **pounds cod fillets**
**Salt**
¾ **cup extra-virgin olive oil**
**4 garlic cloves, grated on a Microplane or minced**
½ **teaspoon red chile flakes, such as Aleppo or gochugaru**
**1 tablespoon dijon mustard**
**Juice of ½ lemon (about 1 tablespoon)**
**2 tablespoons chopped parsley or chives**
**Crusty bread**

Season the fish with salt and let it rest for at least 1 hour, and as long as overnight, loosely covered in the refrigerator, to firm up and slightly dry the fish.

Heat the oil with the garlic in a pan with a lid just large enough to fit all the fish over medium-low heat. Cook until the garlic has a nutty smell, 6 to 8 minutes. Place the fish in the pan along with the chile flakes, cover, and turn the heat down to low so there is barely a bubble around the fish as it cooks. Cover and cook for 10 to 15 minutes depending on the thickness of your fish. The fish is done when it flakes under gentle pressure. Turn off the heat and remove the fish to a plate. Add the mustard, lemon juice, and parsley to a bowl and, while whisking vigorously, add the cooking oil and any juices in the pan to emulsify into a loose but creamy sauce. Taste for seasoning and adjust with salt as desired. Spoon the sauce over the fish and serve with plenty of crusty bread.

# Nashville Hot–Inspired Catfish

This "new classic" dish takes its
inspiration from the now-named
Prince's Hot Chicken, a legendary
shop in Nashville, Tennessee, where
the Prince family has been slinging
Nashville hot chicken for nearing
a century. In this recipe, catfish
replaces the original chicken, which
is fried, then bathed in a potent
cayenne pepper paste and garnished
with the crisp bite of pickles.

4 portions catfish, about 1¼ pounds total

Salt

¼ cup roughly chopped dill pickles (reserve ¼ cup brine)

2 quarts plus ¼ cup vegetable oil

1 tablespoon cayenne pepper

1 tablespoon smoked sweet paprika

1 teaspoon dried oregano

½ teaspoon garlic powder

1 teaspoon onion powder

¼ teaspoon ground allspice

Pinch of ground cinnamon

1½ teaspoons brown sugar

1 cup sifted flour

2 tablespoons sifted cornstarch

1½ cups seltzer water

4 slices white bread, toasted

Juice of 1 lemon (2 to 3 tablespoons)

In a small bowl or zip-top bag, combine the catfish,
a few pinches of salt, and the reserved pickle brine
and let rest for 20 minutes.

Heat the ¼ cup oil in a small pot over medium heat
until it is just shimmering. Turn off the heat and
stir in the cayenne, paprika, oregano, garlic powder,
onion powder, allspice, cinnamon, and brown sugar,
and reserve.

In a large, tall-sided pot, heat the remaining 2 quarts
of oil to 375°F. Line a large platter with newspaper
or paper towels. Make the batter by combining the
flour, cornstarch, and seltzer water. Whisk until
smooth and use within 10 minutes.

One piece at a time, dip the fish into the batter
and place immediately in the hot oil, holding it for
5 seconds before releasing. Cook until golden and
crispy, about 5 minutes. Turn with a slotted spoon if
necessary to evenly cook both sides.

Remove the fish from the oil and place it on a paper
towel–lined plate for 30 seconds. Transfer the fish to
a bowl and toss to coat with the spice oil.

Serve each portion of fried fish on a piece of
toasted white bread. In the same bowl, combine
the chopped pickles with the lemon juice and add
generous spoonful to each piece of fish to finish the
open-face sandwich.

# Poisson en Papillote Provençale

SERVES 4

Cooking fish in a relatively airtight environment, letting it "stew" in paper sealed with egg whites, is one of the best ways I know of to preserve the saline purity of fresh seafood. Paired with the flavors of Provence-tomatoes, herbs, garlic, and fennel-it takes on a whole new level of edible excellence. This preparation is a classic and one I learned when I first went to France to cook in my late teens. If there is a better fish dish, I am not aware of it. And opening these pouches with a scissor at the table, allowing everyone to smell the burst of aromatic steam that wafts out of each pouch, is truly a showstopper no matter how many times you've enjoyed it. A word about economics: This dish is a great way to use up little odds and ends of fish pieces, a few shrimp, a few mussels and clams. That makes it a real value as the cost of our seafood goes up, seemingly every time we go shopping.

*Andrew*

2 large tomatoes

$^1/_3$ cup extra-virgin olive oil

1 small shallot, thinly sliced (about 2 tablespoons)

2 garlic cloves, grated on a Microplane or minced

$^1/_2$ fennel bulb, thinly sliced (about $^3/_4$ cup)

1 tablespoon herbs de Provence

8 basil leaves

$^1/_4$ cup tarragon leaves

2 tablespoons parsley leaves

12 threads saffron

$^1/_2$ cup white wine

Four 3-ounce pieces firm saltwater fish (such as pollock, halibut, snapper, monkfish, or bass)

16 mussels

8 clams

8 shrimp, peeled and deveined

8 dry-pack scallops

Juice of $^1/_2$ lemon (about 1 tablespoon)

Salt and freshly cracked black pepper

1 egg white, lightly beaten

**Special equipment: 4 large circles of parchment paper, about 18 inches in diameter. If you like, use large rectangles, but I prefer circles because ultimately these pouches will go on a circular plate.**

Preheat the oven to 400°F and grease a baking sheet.

Bring a large pot of water to a boil and set up a bowl of ice water for an ice bath. Score the tomatoes and dip them in the boiling water for about 20 seconds. Remove to the ice bath and slip the skins off. Remove the cores and seeds from the tomatoes and dice the tomatoes. Reserve.

Heat the oil in a large sauté pan over high heat. Add the shallot, garlic, fennel, herbs de Provence, basil, tarragon, parsley, and saffron. Sauté until shallot is glassy, about 2 minutes. Add the tomatoes and wine, bring to a boil, and cook for 1 minute. Remove from the heat and set aside in the refrigerator to chill.

Lay out the circles of parchment. Working in the center of one half of the paper circles, so that it's one-quarter of the way from an edge, arrange the fish, mussels, clams, shrimp, and scallops among the 4 papers. Divide the chilled tomato mixture on top of the fish. Drizzle with the lemon juice and season with salt and pepper.

Seal the pouches by folding the unused half over the half you have just worked on. Now you have 4 large

Recipe continues >

half-moons. Brush the inside and outside of the round edge with egg white, using the egg white like glue, and, working from one pointy end to the other, fold in 3-inch sections to seal in a pleated fashion. It's like sealing a dumpling or edging an empanada. Brush the tops of the packages with egg whites to shine them up.

Place the 4 packages on the prepared baking sheet (make sure there is no rack directly above them, as they will inflate) and bake for 14 minutes.

To serve, cut each pouch open while it sits in front of each guest. The first whiff of steam is what it's all about.

# Seafood Potpie

## SERVES 4

Because its flavors are so fresh and light, this potpie works just as well for a summery lunch as it does for a wintry supper. Though we specify a few types of vegetables, feel free to make use of whatever is on hand, including potatoes, butternut squash, celery root, even golden beets. Color is a good thing! This dish is excellent served with chilled red wine, such as Beaujolais, and a green salad full of fresh herbs and lightly dressed with olive oil and lemon.

### PASTRY

2 cups all-purpose flour, plus extra for rolling

1 tablespoon sugar

2 teaspoons salt

Pinch of cayenne pepper

1 cup (2 sticks) cold butter, cut into cubes

2 tablespoons vodka

### FILLING

4 tablespoons (½ stick) butter

¼ cup all-purpose flour

3 garlic cloves, grated on a Microplane or minced

4 thyme sprigs, leaves picked

2 bay leaves

1 tablespoon onion powder

½ teaspoon ground mace or freshly grated nutmeg

1 quart milk

Salt

1 fennel bulb, cut into ½-inch dice (about 1½ cups)

1 carrot, cut into ½-inch pieces (about ½ cup)

1 yellow onion, cut into ½-inch dice (about 1 cup)

8 radishes, quartered

2 tablespoons extra-virgin olive oil

12 ounces mixed white fish, skin-off and cut into bite-size pieces

5 ounces scallops, cut into ½-inch pieces

1 tablespoon sherry, such as amontillado (page 000), optional

½ bunch parsley, leaves chopped

2 teaspoons smoked sweet paprika

To make the pastry: Combine the flour, sugar, salt, cayenne, and butter in the bowl of a food processor and pulse until it begins to form large clumps. Add the vodka and pulse as you add cold water 1 tablespoon at a time just until the dough comes together. Remove from the bowl and form into a loose ball with your hands. Wrap in plastic wrap and refrigerate for at least 1 hour or up to 2 days.

To make the filling: Preheat the oven to 400°F. Line a baking sheet with parchment paper.

Melt the butter in a large saucepan over medium heat. Add the flour and garlic and cook, stirring, until smooth and pale gold in color, 7 to 8 minutes. Add the thyme, bay leaves, onion powder, and mace. Whisk in the milk, season with salt, and bring to a simmer. Lower the heat to low and cook gently until thickened, 10 to 15 minutes. Remove from the heat and pluck out and discard the bay leaves.

Meanwhile, toss the fennel, carrot, onion, and radishes with the oil on a large baking sheet and season with salt. Roast until tender, about 15 minutes. Keep the oven on.

Season the fish and scallops with salt and let rest for 10 minutes.

Remove the pastry from the refrigerator and roll it out on a lightly floured work surface to ¼ inch thick. Cut the pastry so that it is roughly the same size as the single serving dish or into multiple pieces to fit the bowls that the potpie will be served in. Transfer the pastry to the prepared baking sheet and bake until golden brown, 15 to 20 minutes. Add the fish and roasted vegetables to the milk sauce and stir to combine. Cook over medium heat until the fish is cooked through, about 10 minutes. Remove from the heat and stir in the sherry, if using.

Ladle into bowls or a serving dish. Lay the crust over the stew and sprinkle with the parsley and paprika.

# Tilapia with Masala Tomato Sauce

**SERVES 4**

This recipe combines two techniques.
First a quick sear in butter and the
tilapia takes on a hint of color
and depth of flavor. The fish then
finishes cooking as it simmers in
the heady-spiced tomato and coconut
sauce. Make this as fiery as you wish
with more chile flakes. Coconut has a
way of coaxing out and carrying the
flavors of spices while taming heat.
This is perfect served atop rice
pilaf (see page 287), and is made
better if left to rest overnight and
gently rewarmed before serving.

**1¼ pounds tilapia fillets**

**Salt**

**1 teaspoon red chile flakes, such as Aleppo or gochugaru**

**1 tablespoon garam masala**

**1½ tablespoons smoked sweet paprika**

**1 teaspoon ground cumin**

**1 teaspoon ground turmeric**

**5 tablespoons butter**

**2 garlic cloves, grated on a Microplane or minced**

**1 tablespoon grated fresh ginger**

**½ cup slivered almonds**

**One 28-ounce can peeled diced tomatoes**

**One 14-ounce can unsweetened coconut milk**

**1 cup cilantro leaves**

**¼ cup parsley leaves**

**¼ cup mint leaves**

**1 small shallot, sliced as thinly as possible (about 2 tablespoons)**

**Juice of 1 lime (about 2 tablespoons)**

**Cilantro-Almond Rice Pilaf (page 287)**

Season the fish with salt and let it rest for 15 minutes.

Place the red chile flakes, garam masala, paprika, cumin, and turmeric in a small bowl and stir to combine. (*Combine your spices first. Otherwise, in the time it takes to measure them, the spice you added first will have burned.*)

Melt 4 tablespoons of the butter in a medium pot over medium heat. Add the garlic, ginger, and almonds and toast until golden brown, about 5 minutes. Add the mixed spices to the pan and toast for 15 seconds. Add the tomatoes, season with salt, and bring to a simmer. Cook until the liquid has reduced by half, about 10 minutes. Add the coconut milk and stir to combine. Simmer until thick and the tomatoes are mostly broken down, about 10 minutes.

Meanwhile, melt the remaining 1 tablespoon butter in a large sauté pan over high heat. When it begins to bubble, add the tilapia and cook on one side until lightly browned, about 3 minutes. Flip the tilapia and turn the heat down to low. Pour the sauce over the fish and simmer for 3 minutes. Turn off the heat and let it rest for 10 minutes. In a small bowl, toss the cilantro, parsley, mint, shallot, and lime juice and season with salt. Spoon the fish and its sauce onto plates and top with herb salad and rice pilaf alongside.

# Broiled Tilapia with Lemon-Parmesan Mayonnaise

**SERVES 4**

Didn't plan dinner and were
wondering about what to make? Here
you go! Couldn't be easier. Totally
delicious. Add some dried herbs if
you'd like. Oregano would be great!

1¼ pounds tilapia fillets
**Salt**
¼ cup mayonnaise or Aioli (page 96)
**Zest of 1 lemon**
2 tablespoons grated parmesan cheese

Preheat your oven or toaster oven's broiler to low.

Season the fish with salt and let it rest for
15 minutes.

In a small bowl, mix together the mayonnaise,
lemon zest, and cheese.

Place the tilapia on a broiler-safe baking tray. Spread
the mayonnaise-cheese mixture evenly over the fish.
Broil until the crust is browned and the fish is done,
about 7 minutes.

# Almond-Crusted Hake with Pea Puree

**SERVES 4**

You know what goes really great with seafood? Mayonnaise! This technique of slathering fish with a flavorful mayonnaise then broiling until crisp is an easy way to surely impress. This version includes crushed almonds for added texture and lemon zest to help cut the richness and add a delightful aroma. A nice variation would be adding grated garlic and parmesan to the mayonnaise mixture.

1¼ pounds hake fillets
Salt
⅓ cup crushed almonds
Zest and juice of 1 lemon (2 to 3 tablespoons juice)
2 tablespoons mayonnaise
½ cup torn mint leaves
½ cup chervil or parsley leaves
1 recipe Pea Puree (recipe follows)

Season the fish with salt and let it rest for 15 minutes.

Set an oven rack in the position closest to the heat and preheat the broiler to medium.

In a small bowl, combine the almonds, lemon zest, and mayonnaise. Divide the mixture among the tops of the fillets. Place the fish on a baking sheet crust-side up and slide under the broiler. Cook until the crust is browned and the fish flakes under gentle pressure, about 8 minutes.

In a small bowl, toss the mint and chervil with the lemon juice. Spread the pea puree across a platter or plates and place the fish over the top. Top with the herb salad and serve.

## Pea Puree

**MAKES ABOUT 3 CUPS**

¼ cup extra-virgin olive oil
1 shallot, minced (about 3 tablespoons)
2 garlic cloves, grated on a Microplane or minced
4 cups fresh shelled fresh peas or frozen peas
Salt
Juice of 1 lemon (2 to 3 tablespoons)

Heat the oil in a medium saucepan over medium-low heat. Add the shallot and garlic and cook for 2 to 3 minutes, until fragrant. Add the peas and ½ cup water and season with salt. Increase the heat to medium-high and bring to a simmer. Reduce the heat to medium-low, cover, and cook until the peas are tender, 5 to 8 minutes. Transfer the mixture to a blender, add the lemon juice, season with salt, and blend to a smooth consistency. Adjust the seasoning with salt as needed. This will keep in the refrigerator for up to 4 days.

# Bouillabaisse

**SERVES 8**

This is a dish that requires attention and intention. It's a complex layering of flavors, ingredient by ingredient, each one cooking at its own pace. The shellfish, cooked in the already-very-tasty stock, add their liquors to the brew. Both butter and olive oil add their personalities to the mix. The last step is to nestle in the fish fillets and let the heat of the broth gently cook them through while the flavors all rest for a spell and meld together. You'll end up with an outrageously delicious "wow" dish, and any so lucky to have scored an invite to your table will know that you love them.

There's a lot of liquid in this recipe. I like a very brothy bowl with lots of bread. But if you don't serve all the broth, great! You've now got an extra-fortified broth to strain and save/freeze for another use.

3 quarts Barton's Rich Fish Stock (page 87)

2 pounds mussels

2 pounds littleneck clams

1 pound shrimp, head on, peeled and deveined

6 tablespoons extra-virgin olive oil

3 tablespoons butter

2 celery stalks, finely diced (about 1 cup)

4 shallots, finely diced (about ¾ cup)

1 fennel bulb, finely diced (about 1½ cups)

2 tablespoons fennel seeds

4 garlic cloves, sliced

1 lemon, zested in wide strips

1 orange, zested in wide strips

1 pound red potatoes, cut into bite-size pieces

2 cups white wine*

Salt

1 pound mixed fish fillets, skin-off, cut into roughly 2-ounce pieces (try monkfish or another meaty dense fish)

8 ounces small scallops

1 baguette, sliced ½ inch thick, brushed with olive oil, and toasted

2 cups Aioli (page 96)

2 tablespoons Pernod, pastis, or Herbsaint, optional

¼ cup chopped herbs (try chives, mint, and/or parsley)

* If you prefer no alcohol, use 2 tablespoons white or red wine vinegar and skip the reduction step.

Pour 2 cups of the stock into a large pot and bring to a boil over high heat. Add the mussels, cover, and cook, shaking the pot, until they have opened, 5 to 7 minutes. Remove from the liquid and reserve, discarding any shells that didn't open. Repeat with clams, cooking for 7 to 8 minutes. Add the shrimp and cook for 3 to 4 minutes. Keep the seafood at room temperature, as it will be rewarmed just prior to serving. Strain the broth through a fine-mesh strainer lined with a paper towel and reserve.

Heat the oil and butter in a pot large enough to hold all the ingredients (ideally the pot you will serve from) over medium-high heat. Add the celery, shallots, fennel, fennel seeds, and garlic and sauté until the vegetables are soft, about 5 minutes. Add the lemon and orange zest, the potatoes, and wine. Bring to a simmer, then lower the heat to maintain a simmer and cook until the wine is reduced by half and the alcohol smell has dissipated, about 4 minutes.

Add the reserved shellfish cooking stock and remaining fish stock, season with salt, and bring to a simmer. Maintain a simmer until the potatoes are barely cooked, 6 to 8 minutes. Remove the citrus zests. Nestle the fish and scallops into the broth and cook for 1 minute. Add the cooked shellfish, cover the pot, and turn off the heat. Let it rest for at least 10 minutes and up to an hour for the fish to gently cook through and flavors to meld.

To serve, place a couple toasted baguette slices on the bottom of bowls and ladle the soup over them. Dollop with aioli, drizzle with Pernod, if using, and sprinkle the herbs over the top. Serve with additional slices of toasted bread.

# 4.07

# Salmon Family

# Arctic Char in the Style of Porchetta

**SERVES 4 TO 6**

In this stunning recipe, Arctic char is prepared in the style of porchetta, an Italian dish made of pork belly/loin with a potent marinade of fennel, garlic, and herbs. In our recipe, the fillet is sliced in half horizontally to maximize the amount of surface area and integration of the toasty-tasty marinade. This preparation is equally good with a fillet of salmon-just increase the quantity of the marinade recipe for larger fillets. It's key to fully develop the flavors of the marinade before rolling it inside: toasting the nuts, cooking the garlic, and blooming the spices and herbs so they don't retain any of their brash, raw quality.

Because it cooks so quickly, this is a great dish to serve when entertaining, especially for its wow factor. We would suggest doing all the prep work and getting it rolled and tied as much as a day before. The flavor is only going to get better. Remove it from the refrigerator about an hour before cooking, as the broiling/roasting process is a delicate balance of cooking through in the same time as it takes to crisp and char the skin. So having the flesh at room temperature is a big plus.

1/4 cup extra-virgin olive oil

1/4 cup almonds, roughly chopped

4 garlic cloves, grated on a Microplane or minced*

2 tablespoons fennel seeds

1 teaspoon (or more) red chile flakes, such as Aleppo or gochugaru

1/2 bunch parsley, chopped

2 rosemary sprigs, leaves finely chopped (plus more for nesting around the fish while it roasts, if desired)

Freshly cracked black pepper

1 large Arctic char fillet (about 1 1/2 pounds), skin-on, pin bones removed

Salt

1 lemon, cut into wedges

* Or much more!

Heat the oil in a small sauté pan over medium heat. Add the almonds, garlic, and fennel seeds and cook until the garlic is browned and the nuts are toasted, 3 to 5 minutes. Stir in the chile flakes, parsley, and rosemary and season with pepper. Remove from the heat and let cool.

Slice the fillet in half horizontally. Start at the tail end and slice your way toward the head, aiming to have two pieces of even thickness. *(I find it helpful to have a guide for this, so I place the handle of a wooden spoon on either side so my knife stays at the level of the spoons while I'm slicing through the fish. The spoons must be of the same thickness.)* On the skin-on side, make 4 or 5 shallow furrows through the flesh down to, but not through, the skin, running parallel to the fillet. This is so you can massage the marinade in so it integrates into the dish as best as possible.

Cut the other side of the fillet into 3 or 4 long strips. Season all the flesh lightly with salt.

Spread half of the marinade into the furrows, rubbing it into the cuts in the fillets and slathering it across the surface. Toss the strips with the remaining marinade to coat, then lay them onto the flesh side of the skin-on piece, so there is roughly even thickness from the head to tail section. There will be an inch or two near the tail where you don't have any overlaying strips, and that's fine.

Form the fish into a roll with the skin on the outside and the seam on the bottom. Tuck the last few inches of the tail under the roll to give it uniform thickness. Using butcher's twine, tie the roll to secure every few inches, as you would a roast, so it maintains its shape and the filling is compact.

Arrange the oven rack close to the heat source. Preheat the oven to 450°F. Then turn the broiler to high. This is to ensure your oven is at the right temperature as you are cooking both under the direct heat and using the ambient temperature.

Place the fish on a roasting pan. Arrange the lemon wedges, and if using, the additional rosemary sprigs, around the roll. These will char and likely burn a little, adding perfume to the dish. (They look good but are not necessary.) Roast the fish for 9 to 10 minutes, rotating as needed so the skin crisps and chars evenly. Some black and burned bits are okay. The fish is done when it reads 125°F to 130°F on an instant-read thermometer. Remove from the oven and let it rest for 5 minutes or so. Snip the twine off and discard it. Using a very thin knife, slice on a bias into about 1-inch-thick slices. Serve with the roasted lemon wedges.

# Poached Salmon with Hollandaise

**SERVES 6 TO 8**

This salmon is a superb dish, a classic, and my no-fail hollandaise is the one you will make again and again. Every cook should know how to make this dish. I love slicing cucumbers paper thin to create scales to decorate the fish or cover in a mixture of minced herbs and citrus zest. I even love serving this with a mountain of potato crisps on top. Garnish the platter with a medley of spring vegetables, cooked asparagus, herb sprigs, or all of the above. This is a show-off dish, so show off!

One 2- to 3-pound salmon fillet, skin-off, pin bones removed, tail trimmed off

Salt

3 cups dry white wine

1 onion, chopped (about 1 cup)

3 celery stalks, chopped (about 1½ cups)

1 tablespoon whole black peppercorns

3 parsley sprigs

3 dill sprigs

3 tarragon sprigs

1 recipe No-Fail Hollandaise (recipe follows)

Season the fish with salt and set it aside.

Make the poaching liquid (*court bouillon* in French) by combining the wine, onion, celery, peppercorns, parsley, dill, tarragon, and salt to taste in a fish poacher or deep rectangular pan large enough to hold the salmon. Add 3 to 4 inches of water and bring to a boil. Place the salmon fillet on an oiled piece of butcher paper with edges that stick out over the sides of the pan, or on a large piece of cheesecloth. (This is so you can remove the fillet without it breaking if you don't have the specialized pan called a salmon poacher.) Lower the salmon fillet into the liquid and bring the court bouillon back to a simmer. Lower the heat to maintain the barest simmer possible, cover, and cook gently until the salmon is just cooked through, 12 to 16 minutes, depending on the thickness. Turn off the heat and let the fish rest in the liquid for 2 to 3 minutes.

Lay a towel next to a platter. Using the paper or cheesecloth, remove the fish from the liquid and place on the towel. Dab the fish dry as best as possible. Carefully transfer the salmon to a platter. Garnish with any accoutrements you'd like, such as cucumber slices or herbs and citrus.

Serve the salmon warm with the No-Fail Hollandaise.

Recipe continues >

# No-Fail Hollandaise

**MAKES ABOUT 1½ CUPS**

Juice of 1 lemon (2 to 3 tablespoons)
1 teaspoon dijon mustard
2 tablespoons freshly minced fresh tarragon leaves
⅛ teaspoon cayenne pepper
5 egg yolks
1 cup (2 sticks) butter, cut into ¼-inch pieces
Salt

Set up a pot of gently simmering water over which you can rest a stainless-steel bowl. In that bowl, whisk together 1½ tablespoons water, the lemon juice, mustard, tarragon, cayenne, and egg yolks until thickened, 2 to 3 minutes. Whisk continuously, removing the pan from the heat source briefly if it gets too hot. Add the butter, whisking constantly until the butter is fully incorporated, about 2 minutes. Season with salt. Whisk over the heat to make sure the sauce is warm. Your yolks are already cooked and stabilized!

If the sauce is too thick, whisk in warm water, 1 teaspoon or so at a time, until the sauce is just pourable.

This sauce can be made ahead by about an hour if kept stored in a plastic quart container in a pot of hot water. You can store leftovers in an airtight container in the refrigerator for up to a week and reheat in a double boiler over low heat.

# Rosemary Teriyaki-Style Glazed Salmon with Vegetables

**SERVES 4**

The smoky-sultry-sweet personality of true teriyaki sauce is a perfect foil for seafood. So often bottled versions of teriyaki lack nuance and the beauty of what originally made this sauce globally famous. We take a little liberty here to add in the woodsy flavor of rosemary and a slight jolt of chile flakes for further distinction. Once the sauce is made, the salmon is combined with vegetables and/or rice and broiled to a sticky glaze.

**4 portions salmon fillet, about 1¼ pounds total**

**1 recipe Rosemary Teriyaki-Style Sauce (recipe follows) or 8 ounces store-bought teriyaki sauce**

**2 rosemary sprigs**

**1 pound steamed vegetables, such as carrots, bok choy, broccoli, and/or cauliflower florets**

**Cooked rice, optional**

Place the salmon fillets in a zip-top bag and add half of the sauce. Seal the bag and let marinate for at least 30 minutes and up to overnight in the refrigerator.

Preheat the broiler to medium. Heat a baking dish in the broiler. (*This will help cook the salmon from both sides.*)

Place the vegetables and rice, if using, in the preheated baking dish. Place the salmon skin-side up (if the skin is present) over the top, leaving plenty of space between the fillets. Drizzle any remaining marinade from the bag over the salmon. Place under the broiler and broil for 3 to 4 minutes. Remove from the broiler and, using rosemary stems as a brush, glaze the fish with additional sauce. Broil for another 3 to 5 minutes, depending on the thickness of your fillet. If the glaze is becoming a bit too dark, move the fish farther from the heat source. The fish is done when it flakes under gentle pressure. Drizzle with the remaining sauce and serve.

# Rosemary Teriyaki-Style Sauce

**MAKES ABOUT 1 CUP**

This sauce is great for any dish you can imagine. If rosemary isn't your bag, simply omit it from the recipe or try another herb, such as tarragon, thyme, or mint.

Note that this recipe calls for half a lemon to be steeped in the sauce as it reduces. This adds a much more nuanced perfume/flavor than would straight lemon juice. Once the sauce is made, that lemon will be delicious, so you'll find a use for it.

**¹/₂ cup soy sauce**

**¹/₄ cup aji-mirin (sweet wine vinegar)**

**¹/₄ cup sugar**

**1 tablespoon rice wine vinegar**

**One 1-inch knob fresh ginger, thinly sliced**

**1 garlic clove, grated on a Microplane or minced**

**¹/₂ lemon**

**Red chile flakes, preferably something smoky like morita or Urfa chile**

**2 rosemary sprigs**

Combine all the ingredients in a small saucepan and bring to a simmer over medium-low heat. Cook until the sauce reduces by half, about 10 minutes. Remove the pan from the heat and discard the lemon, ginger, and rosemary before using. Keeps up to 2 weeks in the refrigerator.

# Pan-Roasted Salmon with Horseradish Gremolata

**SERVES 4**

Gremolata is classically a blend of lemon zest, parsley, olive oil, and garlic and is used to add brightness to rich braised dishes, such as osso buco. Our version is more of a global mash-up, introducing more acidity with sherry vinegar and potent horseradish and, of course, copious herbs.

1 1/4 pounds salmon fillets, skin-on
Salt
2 tablespoons extra-virgin olive oil or butter
2 lemons, cut in half
1 recipe Horseradish Gremolata (recipe follows)

Preheat the oven to 325°F.

Scrape the skin of the salmon with the back of a knife to remove any excess moisture and pat dry with a paper towel. Lay the fish skin-side down on paper towels. Season the flesh with salt and let it rest for 15 minutes.

Heat the oil in a large sauté pan over medium-high heat until it begins to shimmer. Add the fish to the pan, skin-side down. Gently press the fillets into the pan and move them around just a bit to ensure they do not stick. Add the lemons, cut-side down. Sear the fish and lemons until the fish skin begins to crisp, 2 to 3 minutes. Place the entire pan in the oven without flipping and cook for 6 to 8 minutes more, until cooked through.

Remove the fish from the pan and serve skin-side up with the caramelized lemons and a generous spoonful of gremolata over the top.

## Horseradish Gremolata

**MAKES ABOUT 2 CUPS**

1 bunch parsley or chervil, chopped (about 1 cup)
1/2 bunch dill, chopped (about 1/2 cup)
2 tablespoons grated fresh horseradish or 3 tablespoons prepared horseradish
1 tablespoon maple syrup or honey
Zest and juice of 1 lemon (2 to 3 tablespoons juice)
1 tablespoon sherry vinegar
1/4 cup extra-virgin olive oil
Pinch of ground mace or freshly grated nutmeg
Salt to taste

Combine all the ingredients in a medium bowl. The gremolata will keep in an airtight container in the refrigerator for up to 1 week.

# Slow-Roasted Salmon with Dulse Butter

**SERVES 4**

Slow-roasting is as easy as fish cooking gets. In my house, it's what I turn to many weeknights. And it's my toaster oven that is my most used appliance, because it's a small environment compared to a traditional oven, and so it heats up and maintains its temperature quickly and easily.

This technique doesn't create the stark color change we're used to seeing between raw and cooked fish. Slow-roasted salmon can look raw even when fully cooked, though it will flake under gentle pressure from the thumb. This technique is so easy and surefire that I often use it to cook seafood directly from the freezer, adding 10 to 15 minutes to the cooking time.

Because the roasting is so slow and low, there's no vaporizing of the oils in the fish and there is no aroma to spread. And as it takes a long time to go from raw to cooked, it also takes a long time to go from cooked to overcooked, so you have a lot of leeway in the time and attention that this dish requires.

One 1¼ pounds salmon fillets, skin on
**Salt**
**2 tablespoons extra-virgin olive oil**
**Dulse Butter (page 254)\***

\* Because slow-roasted fish never gets hot (130°F is not that hot), the butter should be at room temperature before being served over the fish.

Preheat the oven to 275°F.

Season the fish with salt and let it rest for 15 minutes. (If using frozen seafood, proceed without this step.)

Brush the fish with the oil. Arrange the fish skin-side down in a baking pan and place in the oven. Remove from the oven when just done, 20 to 25 minutes per inch of thickness. The flesh will flake under gentle pressure, but the color will not change much. Alternatively, use an instant-read thermometer, reading 125°F to 130°F when done. Remove from the oven and remove the skin by sliding a spatula between the skin and flesh. Carefully transfer the fish to a platter and discard the skin. Dot the fish with thin pats of Dulse Butter.

Recipe continues >

# Dulse Butter

**MAKES ABOUT ½ CUP**

6 tablespoons butter, softened

1 garlic clove, grated on a Microplane or minced

1 tablespoon smoked dulse flakes or flaked dried kelp

¼ teaspoon ground mace or freshly grated nutmeg

½ teaspoon onion powder

½ teaspoon red chile flakes, such as Aleppo or gochugaru

1 tablespoon chopped tarragon or chives

1 teaspoon Pernod or other anise-flavored liquor, optional

Salt

In a small sauté pan, combine 2 tablespoons of the butter, the garlic, and dulse. Place over medium heat and cook until the garlic is no longer raw, about 3 minutes. Add the mace, onion powder, and chile flakes and stir to combine. Remove from the heat. Let cool slightly. Add the remaining 4 tablespoons butter, the tarragon, and Pernod, if using. Season with salt and stir to combine. Keeps for up to a week in the refrigerator.

# Sockeye Salmon–White Bean Crostini

**SERVES 4 TO 6 AS AN APPETIZER,
2 AS MAIN COURSE**

This is really a bean dish in which
sockeye salmon is a flavoring rather
than the focus. It's great served
warm, room temperature, or cold.
Don't skimp on the herbs, as they're
what keeps the flavors bright.

2 tablespoons butter

2 garlic cloves, grated on a Microplane or minced

2 tablespoons capers, rinsed and patted dry

1/4 cup chopped almonds

One 15-ounce can cannellini beans, liquid reserved

5 ounces sockeye salmon, skin off, cut into 1-inch sections

2 tablespoons chopped tarragon

1 jalapeño chile, thinly sliced

1 shallot, very thinly sliced (about 3 tablespoons)

Salt

Juice of 1/2 lemon (about 1 tablespoon)

1 baguette, sliced 1/2 inch thick, brushed with extra-virgin olive oil, and toasted

Heat the butter in a medium sauté pan over medium heat. Add the garlic, capers, and almonds and cook until the garlic and almonds are toasted and aromatic, about 5 minutes. Add the beans and their liquid and bring to a simmer. Use the back of a spoon or spatula to lightly crush about half of the beans. Simmer until the mixture begins to thicken, about 3 minutes.

Nestle the salmon into the beans, reduce the heat, cover, and simmer for 3 to 5 minutes, until the salmon is just cooked through. Add the tarragon and gently stir, trying to break the salmon into small pieces (approximately the size of the beans). Taste and season with salt as needed. Depending on the saltiness of the canned beans, this recipe may or may not need additional salt.

In a small bowl, toss the chile and shallot with a pinch of salt and the lemon juice. Spoon the bean-salmon mixture over the toasted baguette slices, top with the jalapeño-shallot mixture, and serve.

# Campfire-Style Trout with Bacon and Italian Dressing

**SERVES 4**

I was on an epic trip with my friend Paul Greenberg, author of *Four Fish* and *American Catch*, way up in the headlands of Bristol Bay watershed in Alaska. As we floated down the Stuyahok River, we would catch our dinner, to be accompanied by whatever ingredients we still had on hand, which were diminishing by the day. As is my nature, I was doing most of the cooking. And one day, after running out of fresh herbs and olive oil to accompany the catch, I was left with just a bottle of store-bought Italian dressing. So, fish grilled over alderwood doused with Italian dressing became our go-to meal. Ever since, I've been a proponent of the glory that is Italian dressing, even the cheap stuff you can buy by the gallon. It's a perfectly delightful combination. The heady herbs, especially oregano, that serve as its backbone, flatter every seafood I can think of. And what could be easier than popping open a bottle of Newman's Own (or whatever brand you prefer), drizzling it over the fish of the day, and calling dinner done? Of course, homemade is better, and the recipe included here will last in the refrigerator (and even improve over the course of) a week or more. Oh yeah, it's also good on salad.

4 steelhead or rainbow trout, butterflied (this is how trout are most commonly available)
Salt
Freshly cracked Black Pepper–Fennel Blend (page 53) or black pepper
12 strips smoked bacon
1 lemon, sliced as thin as possible on a mandoline
Italian Dressing (recipe follows) or about ¾ cup store-bought

Preheat the oven to 325°F.

Season the trout on the inside with salt and pepper-fennel blend and let it rest for 15 minutes.

Place the bacon on a baking sheet and bake for about 10 minutes for most of the fat to render out but so it is still pliable. Remove from the oven and set on paper towels to drain.

Place the lemon slices on one side of the trout. Use 3 strips of bacon per fish to wrap the lemons and trout. Use toothpicks to secure.

Preheat a charcoal or gas grill to a medium-high heat. Grill the trout for about 5 minutes per side, until the bacon is crisp and the lemons are slightly charred. The bacon fat will drip into the fire, causing flare-ups (which is why we rendered most of the fat off ahead of time). If this becomes an issue, simply move the fish to a cooler part of the grill. Pry open one of the fish to make sure it's cooked through. Or use an instant-read thermometer. The thickest part of the fish will read 125°F to 130°F when fully cooked. If they need more time, simply cover the grill and cook for another couple minutes.

Serve with Italian dressing drizzled over the top.

## Italian Dressing

**MAKES ABOUT ¾ CUP**

¼ cup extra-virgin olive oil

2 tablespoons red wine vinegar

2 tablespoons dijon mustard

Zest of 1 lemon

2 teaspoons maple syrup or brown sugar

1 teaspoon dried oregano

½ teaspoon dried thyme

1 teaspoon garlic powder

1 teaspoon onion powder

1 tablespoon chopped parsley

1 tablespoon chopped mint

Salt to taste

Freshly cracked Black Pepper–Fennel Blend (page 53) or black pepper to taste

In a small bowl, whisk all the ingredients together. The dressing will keep in an airtight container in the refrigerator for at least 1 week.

# Sockeye Salmon Enchiladas

We developed this recipe to serve six to eight people because enchiladas are a party food in our minds. They also make great leftovers themselves, as they are easily reheated. This recipe is a great use for leftover fish of any kind, so much so that it's worth it to plan to cook enough fish one night with the intention of having leftovers for this dish later in the week. We claim no authenticity for this recipe, but rather it's a creative combination of delicious ingredients in the style of a dish that so many people know and love. For any seafood-averse eaters you might have in your house, this is a great way to meet them where they are, by making the dish, not the fish, the centerpiece.

The ingredients here are particularly autumnal in profile, and the addition of goat cheese is a brightly acidic way to explore how all these unexpected flavors can merge in such a lovely way.

Note that we call for jarred or canned enchilada sauce here. Sure, you can make your own, and there are plenty of recipes online, but you know what? What's available off the shelf can be quite good. Especially our buddy Rick Bayless's Frontera brand.

1 pound butternut squash, peeled and cut into ½-inch sticks

2 tablespoons extra-virgin olive oil

1 teaspoon ground cumin

1 teaspoon garlic powder

1 teaspoon smoked sweet paprika

1 teaspoon onion powder

Salt

1 red onion, sliced (about 1 cup)

1 pound (or more) previously cooked salmon fillets, skin-off, flaked into thumb-sized pieces

Zest and juice of 1 lime (about 2 tablespoons)

Two 15-ounce jars enchilada sauce

24 corn tortillas

4 ounces goat cheese, queso fresco, or queso blanco (or 1 cup shredded cheddar cheese)

4 scallions, thinly sliced

¼ cup chopped cilantro

Preheat the oven to 350°F.

In a large bowl, toss the squash with the oil, cumin, garlic powder, paprika, and onion powder and season with salt. Place on a roasting pan and roast until tender, about 25 minutes. Remove from the oven and let cool. Keep the oven on.

While the squash cooks, heat a large heavy-bottom pan over high heat until very hot. Add the onions to the dry pan and cook for 2 to 3 minutes, until slightly charred, stirring frequently so they don't burn. Add the onions to the roasting pan with the squash and add the salmon and lime zest and juice.

Pour a thin layer of enchilada sauce into a casserole dish. Heat your tortillas gently in the microwave or on a skillet. Keep them warm, stacked in a clean kitchen towel, while you work. Place one layer of tortillas in the sauce at the bottom of the dish. Place half of the salmon-squash mixture on top. Cover with another layer of tortillas and sauce. Repeat with the remaining salmon-squash mixture, tortillas, and sauce. Pour the remaining enchilada sauce over the top and dot with the cheese.

Roast in the oven for 10 to 15 minutes, until the sauce is bubbling and the cheese is melted and just lightly browned. Remove from the oven and serve garnished with scallions and cilantro.

We've structured this recipe as a casserole. (Mexican-ish lasagna?) But feel free to build these in the traditional way of rolling the filling within individual tortillas and coating with the sauce before roasting.

# 4.08

# Meaty Dense Fish

# Braised Seafood for Entertaining

Braised seafood, such as Shakshuka Monkfish (page 270), are wonderful dishes for entertaining. Like all braised dishes (think beef stew), seafood improves if given a chance to rest overnight in the refrigerator and is reheated prior to serving. There's some chemistry stuff that happens during this process that greatly accentuates and brings harmony to the combined flavors that have been layered through the braise process. Braising is also one of the most fun ways to cook, in that technique upon technique is applied to ingredient upon ingredient, building flavor and making the dish far more than the sum of its parts and developing an intricate flavor all its own.

Given the flavor benefits of cooking such a dish the day before, there's also the benefit that serving it is as easy as heating it over low heat until warm. There's no more technical aspect than that requiring our attention and diverting us from our company. Everybody wins!

# Grilled Amberjack and Summer Vegetables in Adobo

**SERVES 4**

Adobo is a marinade or sauce that originated in Spain and is now popular throughout Latin America and all the way to the Philippines, each region having its own unique variation. Ours takes a global approach and includes smoked sweet paprika, cumin, and a host of other spices, all mixed together in a garlicky blend of sweet-sour lime and orange juice. All of this is then spiked with the piquant tang of ancho chiles, adding a smoky, rich backbone of flavor that helps to draw out the meaty characteristics of amberjack and other like fish.

**6 dried ancho chiles**

**3 tablespoons extra-virgin olive oil**

**8 garlic cloves, roughly chopped**

**1 tablespoon smoked sweet paprika**

**1 teaspoon onion powder**

**1 teaspoon dried oregano**

**1 teaspoon ground cumin**

**1 teaspoon brown sugar**

**½ cup orange juice (about 2 oranges)**

**½ cup lime juice (about 4 limes)**

**Salt**

**1¼ pounds amberjack fillet***

**2 zucchini and/or summer squash, cut into 1-inch chunks**

**1 bunch spring onions or 1 red onion, cut into 1-inch pieces (about 1 cup)**

**1 pint cherry tomatoes**

**1 cup Aioli (page 96)**

**½ bunch cilantro, leaves picked**

\* Given the fillet we call for is just about a pound, it is manageable to grill as one piece, which we find easier than 4 individual pieces.

Toast the chiles in a dry pan over medium heat until fragrant and warm, turning as needed, 3 to 4 minutes. Remove from the heat and discard the stem and seeds. Roughly chop the chiles and reserve. Add 2 tablespoons of the oil and the garlic to the same pan and cook until the garlic is golden brown, about 5 minutes. Add the paprika, onion powder, oregano, and cumin and toast, stirring, for 15 seconds. Add the chiles, brown sugar, orange and lime juices, and ¼ cup water. Bring to a simmer and reduce by half. Transfer to a blender, add a pinch of salt, and blend until smooth.

Preheat your grill with a medium-high heat.

Divide the marinade in half. Place half the marinade and the fish in a zip-top bag and let it rest for 30 minutes.

Season the zucchini, spring onions, and cherry tomatoes with salt and drizzle with the remaining 1 tablespoon oil. Grill on skewers or in a grill basket until cooked through and lightly charred, 8 to 10 minutes.

Remove the fish from the marinade and grill, flipping after 5 to 7 minutes, when it is about three-quarters done. Grill for another 2 to 3 minutes, until cooked through.

Place the grilled vegetables on a platter and place the fish over the top. Drizzle with the remaining adobo and top with the aioli and cilantro.

# On Underutilized Fish

I have received a lot of mail over the years asking about the many varieties of Atlantic Coast fish that vacationing Minnesotans have been seeing on menus for the first time. Even the maligned bluefish seems to be getting its star turn. New and different fish are being cooked all over the country, especially on the East Coast, utilizing oddball species that had never really been of much interest here in America. Blood cockles, spiny dogfish, tautog, carp, and sea robins all grace hometown seafood restaurant menus from Maine to the Carolinas.

You see the same thing in Houston, where my pal PJ Stoops made a career out of selling the by-catch from the Gulf's larger fishing vessels to local chef-owned restaurants. And he's not alone. In fact, some of the best chefs in the country are making a big deal out of featuring both invasive species and the sadly mischaracterized "trash fish" on their menus. There is tremendous community benefit to becoming a sustainable eater. In our fisheries, deep cuts have taken place, limiting the catch of a number of species that have been recklessly overfished. Back East, even cod, the state fish of Massachusetts, is less available these days and therefore more expensive. Gulf of Maine cod fisheries alone are paring down cod hauls, in some cases more than 70 percent.

Inversely, there is a different narrative playing out. Closer to home, we find a different story. Bighead, silver, and several other carp species are multiplying faster than we can fish or hunt them recreationally. They are now in the Mississippi and in our Great Lakes, after being imported from China in the 1970s to improve water quality in Midwestern ponds because they voraciously devour plankton. The problem arose when floods washed them into the Mississippi. These carp have no predator fish to devour them, they eat the food that supports other native species, and they destroy larval habitat. Here in Minnesota, I see lots of education and efforts to raise awareness with control efforts and field surveys, but I think we need to do more. The good news is that there is a processing plant built where the Ohio and Mississippi rivers meet in Kentucky, and its goal is to process and freeze the fish and ship it to Asia to meet the high demand for human consumption.

Here's a more radical idea: I say eat it here.

According to a recent report from the USDA, the number of Minnesotans suffering from food insecurity, or not having access to enough food, is at a twenty-year high. Fifteen percent of Minnesota households don't have enough access to food. I have eaten many species of carp that are just awful-tasting, but the silvers and bigheads I've taken from the Mississippi have been delicious, firm, white, and sweet: a perfect eating fish. Local processing should be encouraged everywhere, and restrictions should be eased, allowing fishermen to donate edible species to the communities that need them most.

But the tide won't turn until there is demand from the consumer. Mississippi River commercial fishing is almost nonexistent because consumer demand for carp and other non-game species has declined over the last forty years after research showed that many fatty river fish carry contaminants such as mercury and PCBs, making them unfit for consumption. Our state waterways are cleaner than they have been for generations, and it's time to reengage how we feed ourselves from our local waterways. Consuming even a small percentage of fish from local rivers and lakes would ease pressure on other overstressed food systems, disengage our overreliance on factory farms, and aid in decentralizing our food system.

The model is already in place. Go check out your local Asian markets. Head to the fish counter and grab some carp or other local fish from a river system. It probably came from a small-time commercial fisherman who works the river pulling carp, buffalo, sheepshead, suckers, and catfish for the growing ethnic communities in our towns and cities.

I am not asking anyone to eat something unhealthy or unpalatable. These fish taste good, and local chefs could do more to work with native and invasive species, but they need customer buy-in, literally. It's working out East, and it can work everywhere. Cultural, economic, and environmental sustainability is of paramount importance, and so is feeding our most vulnerable populations in schools, senior centers, hospitals, and prisons. So many Americans live with food insecurity, but I think that because of the stigma associated with the issue, many go hungry and don't ask for help. Giving someone a fish would help. Reminding a culture how we should be fishing would help to do so much more.

# Miso Broiled Carp

**SERVES 4**

Miso-glazed anything is one of the most popular treatments for fish or poultry thanks to the famous globe-trotting chef Nobu Matsuhisa. His Miso-Glazed Black Cod is one of the most famous dishes of the last sixty years, right up there with the Blackened Redfish that Paul Prudhomme made so popular. The curing process is incredibly easy, and the amount of water loss to the fish is small, but it works wonders removing muddy or off flavors from species like carp that have taken a real beating reputationally. Some people don't even think it's edible! Guess what, it's delicious-you just need to cook it in ways that optimize its assets and negate its undesirable qualities.

Note: Part of this recipe is a multiday curing process.

2 tablespoons salt

3 pounds carp fillet, cut into 8 pieces at a 45-degree angle

1 pound kasu*

¹/₂ cup brown sugar

2 to 3 tablespoons white miso

¹/₄ cup aji-mirin

Cooked Japanese short-grain rice

Japanese vegetable pickles**

* Fermented sake lees (sediment from rice wine production and available online from many resources)

** Japanese vegetable pickles, like daikon, turnip, cucumber or cabbage. Varieties of them are almost endless and they are available at any Asian market or online. Pickled daikon radish is very common and readily available even in conventional supermarkets

In a small, nonreactive baking tray, dissolve the salt in 1 quart water. Add the carp and let it rest in the refrigerator for 1 hour. Remove the fish, discard the water, and fully dry the fish.

In a large bowl, mix the kasu, brown sugar, miso, and aji-mirin and whisk to combine. Add the fish to the marinade, cover, and refrigerate for 2 days. You can transfer to a zip-top bag if space is at a premium in your fridge.

Arrange an oven rack 4 to 5 inches from the heat source and preheat the broiler. Remove the fish from the marinade. Discard the marinade.

Place the fish on a nonstick liner (like a Silpat or parchment paper) laid into a broiler tray. Let the fish come to room temperature, then broil the fish on high for about 7 minutes until caramelized and cooked through. You want the fish to flake.

Serve with rice and vegetable pickles.

# Catfish Braised in Black-Eyed Peas

**SERVES 4**

In many cuisines, there are a few ingredients that form the foundation of flavor. In French cooking, it is mirepoix: carrot, celery, and onion. In Cajun cuisine, it's the trinity: green bell pepper, celery, and onion that are all sautéed down together. This is the building block of flavor for stews, soups, and braises. Here, I replace the green bell pepper with red bell pepper, because I've never really loved green bell pepper. It just tastes unripe to me. And the red bell pepper not only adds striking color, but also a nice sweetness to round out the luscious creamy beans and catfish simmered in a delicious broth.

1¼ pounds catfish fillets
Salt
2 tablespoons neutral oil or butter
1 red bell pepper, seeds and stem removed, cut into thin strips
1 red onion, sliced super thin (about 1 cup)
3 celery stalks, thinly sliced (about 1½ cups)
2 garlic cloves, sliced
Two 15-ounce cans black-eyed peas with liquid
4 scallions, thinly sliced
Hot sauce, preferably vinegar-based, such as Crystal or Tabasco
Cooked rice, optional

Season the fish with salt and let it rest for 10 minutes.

In a large heavy-bottom pot or dutch oven, heat the oil or melt the butter over medium-high heat. Add the catfish and sear on one side for 3 to 4 minutes, until lightly colored. Remove it from the pan. Add the bell pepper, onion, celery, and garlic to the same pan and cook for 3 to 5 minutes, until they begin to soften. Add the black-eyed peas and their liquid and stir to combine. Reduce the heat to medium, cover, and simmer for 5 minutes. Nestle the catfish seared-side up into the bean-vegetable mixture and add about ¼ cup water to achieve a thin stew consistency. Cover and simmer for another 5 minutes, or until the fish is cooked through.

Divide among 4 bowls and sprinkle with the scallions and a dash (or more) of hot sauce and rice.

# Shakshuka Monkfish with Cilantro-Almond Rice Pilaf

**SERVES 4**

Monkfish provides a confident platform for the heady North African spice blend in this preparation. Its texture retains its integrity, while slowly braising in a tangy tomato sauce, wholly yielding its flavor into the dish. It's a perfect make-ahead meal to be reheated for company, as its flavor and texture improve overnight.

- 2 teaspoons ground coriander
- 1 teaspoon ground cumin
- 1 teaspoon ground turmeric
- 2 teaspoons smoked sweet paprika
- 1/2 teaspoon ground ginger
- 2 tablespoons salt
- 1 1/4 pounds monkfish loins, cut into 2- to 3-ounce pieces
- 8 tablespoons extra-virgin olive oil
- 1 red bell pepper, seeds and stem removed, cut into 1/2-inch dice
- 1 onion, finely diced (about 1 cup)
- 4 garlic cloves, grated on a Microplane or minced
- One 28-ounce can San Marzano peeled tomatoes, juice drained and reserved, tomatoes roughly chopped
- 2 teaspoons brown sugar
- Juice of 1 lime (about 2 tablespoons)
- 1/4 cup chopped cilantro
- 2 tablespoons chopped mint leaves
- 1 recipe Cilantro-Almond Rice Pilaf (page 287), or steamed rice or crostini

In a small bowl, mix the coriander, cumin, turmeric, paprika, ginger, and salt together. Use half of the spice mixture to season the fish all over and let it rest for 15 minutes.

Heat 2 tablespoons of the oil in a large ovenproof pan or dutch oven over medium-high heat. When the oil is shimmering, add the fish pieces and sear lightly on all sides. You're not cooking the fish through, just getting a little sear and blooming the flavor of the spices. Remove the fish from the pan and reserve.

To the same pan, add 4 tablespoons of the remaining oil, the bell pepper, onion, and garlic. Cook for 4 to 5 minutes, until the peppers are wilted and the garlic begins to brown. Add the remaining spice mixture and cook for 30 seconds, stirring to incorporate. Add the tomato pieces and cook for 3 to 5 minutes, until they begin to break down and no longer smell raw. Add the tomato juice and brown sugar and bring to a simmer. Lower the heat to medium-low and cook for 15 to 20 minutes, until the sauce has thickened and reduced by one-quarter to one-third. Add water, 1/2 cup at a time, if the sauce gets too dry before the vegetables are fully cooked and the flavors have developed.

Taste and adjust the seasoning if needed. Nestle the fish pieces into the sauce, leaving the top of the fish showing.

Preheat the broiler to high.

Place the whole pan, uncovered, under the broiler and broil for 5 to 7 minutes, until the sauce is thick and bubbling and the fish is browned. Remove from the broiler and rest for 5 minutes.

Drizzle the dish with lime juice and scatter the herbs over the top. Drizzle with the remaining 2 tablespoons oil.

Serve with rice pilaf, steamed rice, or crostini.

Add some heat with diced fresh hot pepper cooked with the onion and garlic, or throw in as much dried chile flakes as you'd like as part of the spice blend.

# Monkfish Piccata

This recipe borrows a page from the seemingly infinite canon of chicken recipes. Monkfish, with its meaty-yet-yielding texture, is pounded out, then crisply fried, and drenched in a delicious lemony pan sauce. Given the broad surface area of this dish, the cooking needs to be done in batches. This is particularly delightful served with arugula dressed with anchovy vinaigrette. You could add some shaved fennel and celery to the salad for texture.

1¼ pounds monkfish loins, cut into 4 pieces

**Salt**

**Zest and juice of 2 lemons (about ¼ cup juice)**

**¼ cup all-purpose flour**

**1 egg**

**1 teaspoon anise-flavored liquor, such as Pernod or Herbsaint, optional**

**1 cup panko breadcrumbs**

**8 tablespoons (1 stick) butter**

**4 tablespoons extra-virgin olive oil**

**¼ cup capers, rinsed and patted dry**

**¼ cup Basic Fish Stock (page 85), Chicken Stock (page 90) or either Dashi (page 83 or 84)**

**¼ bunch parsley, leaves chopped**

Season the fish with salt and the lemon zest.

Working in batches, place one piece of monkfish between two pieces of plastic wrap and pound with a rolling pin or wine bottle until it is a uniform ¼-inch thickness. Repeat with the remaining pieces.

Dust each piece with flour and shake off excess.

In a small bowl, whisk the egg with 1 tablespoon water and the anise-flavored liquor, if using, and brush onto one side of each piece.

Spread ¼ cup panko onto a plate in a thin layer. Press the first piece of fish egg-side down evenly over the panko to coat. Brush the other side with the egg mixture and flip to coat with panko. Press the panko into the flesh to make sure it adheres. Repeat with the remaining pieces. Allow to rest for 10 minutes.

Melt 1 tablespoon of the butter in 1 tablespoon of the oil in a large pan over medium-high heat. When the butter and oil start to foam and brown, add one piece of fish and cook for about 4 minutes, until browned. Flip and cook for another 3 to 4 minutes, until cooked through and golden brown. Remove from the heat and keep warm as you cook the remaining pieces, adding 1 tablespoon of butter and oil each to the pan per piece.

After all fish has been cooked, add 2 tablespoons of the remaining butter and the capers to the same pan. Cook over medium-high heat for 3 to 4 minutes, until the butter browns and the capers begin to crisp. Add the lemon juice and stock and bring to a simmer. Add the remaining 2 tablespoons butter and the parsley and whisk to combine. Season with a pinch of salt, pour the sauce over the fish, and serve.

# Tomato-Confit Braised Sturgeon

**SERVES 4**

Oven-dried tomatoes, here called *confit*, are among life's great pleasures. So easy. So incredible. So very hard to resist eating as is with a spoon. They make for an intensely flavorful partner to meaty dense fish. The acidity in the sauce helps to break down the tough meat into a silken texture. And that oil! Don't miss a drop of it. Make sure to scrape every last molecule out of the pan to mix with the beans. The whole dish is a hearty, easy, low-stress, long-cook winner.

*Josh*

12 plum tomatoes

Salt

3/4 cup extra-virgin olive oil

6 garlic cloves, grated on a Microplane or minced

6 thyme sprigs or 1 to 2 rosemary stalks

2 bay leaves

1 1/4 pounds sturgeon fillet

One 15.5-ounce can cannellini beans, drained, liquid reserved

Juice of 1 lemon (2 to 3 tablespoons)

1 baguette, sliced 1/2 inch thick, brushed with extra-virgin olive oil, and toasted

1/2 cup torn mint leaves or picked chervil

Try this with halibut or salt cod in place of the sturgeon.

Preheat the oven to 300°F.

Bring a large pot of water to a boil. Score the tomatoes and dip them in the boiling water for about 20 seconds. Use a slotted spoon to remove to a bowl of ice water, slip off the skins, and discard the skins. Cut the tomatoes into quarters and place in a baking dish just large enough to hold them. Season with salt. In a small bowl, mix the oil with the garlic and drizzle over the tomatoes. Place the thyme and bay leaves in the dish. Bake uncovered for 1 1/2 hours.

Season the sturgeon with salt and let it rest for the last 15 minutes that the tomatoes are in the oven.

Remove the tomatoes from the oven. Nestle the fish into the tomatoes and spoon the oil over the top of the fish to coat. Cover with aluminum foil and return to the oven. Roast for another 20 to 25 minutes, until the fish flakes under gentle pressure. Remove from the oven, uncover, discard the herbs, and let cool.

When ready to serve, in a small saucepan, combine the beans, lemon juice, and most of the oil from the tomatoes. Place over medium heat and gently mash the beans, adding a tablespoon or two of the reserved bean liquid if needed to form a chunky paste. Spread the bean mixture on the toasted baguette slices. Top the pieces with tomatoes and a few flakes of fish. Garnish with mint and drizzle with any remaining oil.

# Seafood "Cassoulet" with Dulse and Fennel

**SERVES 4**

Cassoulet here is in quotes, as the inspiration for this recipe is among the great dishes of southern France, where white beans are cooked with fatty pork, bacon, and sausage, slowly simmered to a melting texture. As this dish has no meat in it, the smoky flavor from bacon is gained here through smoked dulse flakes. And the hours-long process of slowly cooking is instead accomplished in just a few minutes because we're using canned beans and the rich liquid they are packed in. Like most braised dishes, this one improves if left overnight to be reheated for serving the next day.

*Though I most often make this with meaty dense fish, salmon, scallops, or any flaky white-fleshed fish are all good options. Or try a mixture of several!*

1 baguette, sliced ½ inch thick, brushed with extra-virgin olive oil, and toasted

2 garlic cloves, sliced in half

1¼ pounds meaty dense fish, such as swordfish, amberjack, or monkfish

Salt

¼ cup extra-virgin olive oil

2 onions, sliced vertically ¼ inch thick (about 2 cups)

2 carrots, cut into ½-inch pieces (about 2 cups)

1 celery stalk, cut into ½-inch pieces (about 1 cup)

1 tablespoon fennel seeds

4 thyme sprigs

2 bay leaves

1 tablespoon smoked dulse flakes

½ teaspoon ground mace or freshly grated nutmeg

Two 15.5-ounce cans cannellini beans with their liquid

1 cup Basic Fish Stock (see page 85) or Andrew's or Barton's Dashi (page 83 or 84)

¼ cup chopped parsley

While the toasted baguette slices are still warm, rub them with the cut side of the garlic cloves. Reserve.

Season the fish with salt and let it rest for 15 minutes.

Heat the oil in a large pot over medium heat. Add the onions, carrots, celery, and fennel seeds and cook until the onions are caramelized, about 30 minutes. Add the thyme, bay leaves, dulse, and mace and stir to combine. Add the beans with their liquid and the stock to the pot. Bring to a simmer and cook until slightly thickened, about 5 minutes. Nestle the fish into the beans, cover, and reduce the heat to low. Cook until the fish is done, 8 to 10 minutes. Remove from the heat, discard the thyme stems and bay leaf, and stir in the parsley, lightly breaking up the fish. You don't want to pulverize it, but you want it well integrated. Serve with the toasted baguette slices.

# 4.09
# Steak Fish

# Oil-Poached Swordfish Nicoise

**SERVES 4 TO 6**

Confit is a method to slowly cook something submerged in oil or fat. This low and slow approach helps retain moisture and infuses flavor and richness. The first step is to lightly cure the fish in salt and sugar. This takes a couple hours, better yet overnight, so plan accordingly. It will still be delicious without the full cure time, but you'll sacrifice the uniquely silken texture that is gained only by time.

The salad is a choose-your-own-adventure dish, so if any of the ingredients below aren't to your liking, then leave them out. Yes, there are a lot of ingredients, but it's not complicated, and the result is a satisfying assemblage of colors and textures, a perfect dish for a picnic or leisurely lunch.

This confit method is also perfect for tuna.

1¼ pounds swordfish steak

1 tablespoon Pernod, Herbsaint, vodka, or gin, optional

1 teaspoon sugar

2 teaspoons salt

About 2 cups neutral oil, enough to cover

1 bay leaf

8 ounces green beans, blanched and cut into bite-sized pieces

4 cups lettuce, a fluffy variety such as frisée or curly endive

4 medium-boiled eggs, peeled and quartered

One 15.5-ounce can cannellini beans, drained and rinsed

One 12-ounce jar oil-packed artichoke hearts, drained and cut into quarters*

¼ cup green olives, such as picholine, pitted and sliced

¼ cup capers, rinsed and patted dry

12 ounces new potatoes, cut into 1-inch pieces, simmered in heavily salted water until tender

1 pint cherry tomatoes, cut in half

1 recipe Lemon Vinaigrette (recipe follows) or 1½ cups store-bought

Freshly cracked Black Pepper–Fennel Blend (page 53) or black pepper

* The oil from the artichokes can be added to the oil the swordfish is cooked in.

Brush the swordfish with the Pernod, if using, to coat and season with the sugar and salt. Let it rest uncovered in the refrigerator for at least 2 hours and up to 1 day.

Preheat the oven to 250°F.

Remove the fish from the refrigerator and place it in the smallest baking dish that it will fit in. Add oil to cover. Add the bay leaf and cover the dish with

Recipe continues >

aluminum foil. Place dish in the oven and cook for 1 hour. Remove the dish from the oven and do not uncover. Allow to cool to room temperature. If the skin is present, remove and discard it.

The fish will keep for up to 1 week in the refrigerator if kept fully submerged in the cooking oil.

Build the salads on serving plates, starting with a bed of lettuce. Divide the remaining ingredients among the plates. Flake the swordfish over the top and drizzle with the Lemon Vinaigrette. Garnish with pepper-fennel blend.

# Lemon Vinaigrette

## MAKES ABOUT 1½ CUPS

Make this lemon vinaigrette with the confit oil in the Oil-Poached Swordfish Nicoise to further enhance the flavors in the salad. The remaining oil can be used to make aioli or to sauté vegetables like zucchini. Or drizzle it over just-cooked pasta!

3 to 4 lemons, preferably Meyer, juiced (about ½ cup)

2 garlic cloves, grated on a Microplane or minced

4 teaspoons dijon mustard

2 teaspoons brown sugar or maple syrup

½ cup extra-virgin olive oil (or use the swordfish cooking oil)

Salt to taste

3 tablespoons chopped parsley

1 tablespoon chopped mint

In a bowl, whisk all the ingredients. If making it ahead of time, add the herbs just before serving. The vinaigrette will keep in an airtight container in the refrigerator for up to 1 week.

# Tuna Tonnato

SERVES 4

This recipe is inspired by vitello tonnato, a classic Italian veal dish that is beloved in our home. Traditionally cold poached rosy slices of veal were paired with a puree of tuna, anchovies, and olive oil. I rarely make this dish with veal-instead I substitute cold poached fish, raw tuna, or leftover sliced poached chicken or even sliced raw beef in place of the rosy poached veal. The earthy tuna sauce is spiked with capers, citrus, and anchovies.

These days I most often make it the simplest way. Tuna on tuna for the win, every time.

*Andrew*

**1¼ pounds center-cut line-caught bluefin tuna, trimmed of all skin and bloodline***

**1 recipe Tonnato Sauce (recipe follows)**

**3 tablespoons thinly sliced pitted black Cerignola or Nicoise olives**

**2 Meyer lemons, cut into segments**

**3 tablespoons thinly sliced chives**

**Crispy Shallots (recipe follows)**

\* I prefer to use a rectangular piece so I can slice it at an angle and make 20 to 24 uniform slices about ⅓ inch thick or a smidge less.

Slice the tuna into uniform slices and keep in the refrigerator until ready to serve, which should be as quickly as you can.

When ready to serve, spread several tablespoons of the Tonnato Sauce on 4 plates. Arrange the tuna slices in the middle of each plate. Garnish with a scattering of the olives, lemon segments, chives, and Crispy Shallots. Serve right away.

## Tonnato Sauce

**MAKES ABOUT 1½ CUPS**

**One 6-ounce jar Italian, Spanish, or Portuguese olive oil–packed tuna, drained, oil reserved**

**6 anchovy fillets**

**2 tablespoons capers, rinsed and patted dry**

**Juice of ½ lemon (about 1 tablespoon)**

**½ cup extra-virgin olive oil (start your measuring with the reserved tuna oil)**

**¼ cup Hellmann's or Duke's mayonnaise**

**Salt and freshly cracked black pepper**

Combine the tuna, anchovies, capers, and lemon juice in the bowl of a food processor. Process until finely chopped. Add the oil and mayonnaise and process until smooth and thick. Season with salt and pepper. Scrape the sauce into a bowl, cover, and refrigerate until well chilled, about 2 hours or overnight. It will keep for a week if need be.

## Crispy Shallots

**6 whole peeled shallots, thinly sliced on a mandoline (about 1¼ cups)**

**3 cups vegetable oil**

**Salt**

Place the shallots and oil in a medium pot and place over medium-low heat. Cook, stirring occasionally, until the oil reaches 300°F. Increase the heat to medium, stirring as it rises to 350°F to 360°F. By this time the shallots will have started to turn light brown and crispy. When they are a half shade darker, immediately take them out of the oil using a small strainer and drain on paper towels. Season with salt. I have never been able to have leftovers of these, they are addictive. But they will keep in an airtight container for a day or so.

# Swordfish Involtini

Swordfish is a wonderfully versatile fish in the ways that it can be cut and used. It's great as a steak on the grill, cut into kebabs, or sliced into slivers for a stir-fry. Or try as we do here, thinly sliced into sheets that are then rolled around a crunchy and well-flavored stuffing. The tubes of swordfish are then nestled amid zucchini and the whole dish is broiled. Finish it off with mint and you've got a delicious meal redolent of a Mediterranean summer.

1¼ pounds swordfish loin, skin-off

**Salt**

5 tablespoons extra-virgin olive oil

2 garlic cloves, grated on a Microplane or minced

1 shallot, minced (about 3 tablespoons)

1 tablespoon fennel seeds

3 tablespoons chopped pistachios

1 tablespoon chopped raisins

1 teaspoon red chile flakes, such as Aleppo or gochugaru

½ cup panko or other breadcrumbs

Zest and juice of 1 lemon (2 to 3 tablespoons juice)

2 tablespoons chopped mint

2 small zucchinis, halved lengthwise and cut into ½-inch slices

Cut the swordfish loin into two pieces and remove and discard most of the dark red bloodline tissue. Place the swordfish broadside-down on a cutting board. Place chopsticks along the sides to use as a thickness guide, slicing horizontally with your knife on the chopsticks to make thin sheets of the fish.

Lay the swordfish slices out flat. Season the fish lightly with salt and let it rest for 5 minutes.

Heat 3 tablespoons of the oil in a large sauté pan over medium heat. Add the garlic, shallot, fennel seeds, pistachios, and raisins and cook until the pistachios are toasted and the garlic is soft, about 5 minutes. Add the chile flakes, breadcrumbs, and lemon zest. Cook until the breadcrumbs have absorbed the oil and are lightly browned, 2 to 3 minutes. Season with salt (unless the pistachios you are using are salted). Add the lemon juice and mint and stir to combine. Remove to a plate and allow to cool to room temperature.

Add 1 tablespoon of the remaining oil to the same pan and increase the heat to medium-high. Add the zucchini and cook until lightly colored, 2 to 3 minutes. Remove from the pan and set aside to come to room temperature. Once cooled, arrange in a baking dish large enough to hold the zucchini in a single layer.

Preheat the broiler to high. Divide the breadcrumb mixture among the swordfish pieces and spread across each slice. Roll each slice with the filling in the center. Nestle the rolls seam-side down in amid the zucchini. Drizzle with the remaining 1 tablespoon oil and sprinkle any remaining breadcrumb mixture over the top of the dish. Place under the broiler and broil for 5 to 7 minutes, until the fish is opaque and flakes under gentle pressure.

# Seared Albacore with Black Olive Oil, Pickled Raisins, and Herb Salad

**SERVES 4**

The intense flavor of kalamata olives is made even more so by drying them in an oven until they crumble into powder. This is then mixed with extra-virgin olive oil to make a striking black oil that is powerfully flavorful and stands in beautiful contrast to the rosy tuna. Sweet-sour raisins cut the salty tang of the oil and provide the acid component to the herb salad, resulting in a delightfully exciting balance.

4 ounces dry-cured kalamata olives, pitted

1/2 cup plus 1 tablespoon extra-virgin olive oil

2 tablespoons raisins (golden are best)

2 tablespoons red wine vinegar

1 1/4 pounds albacore loin or other tuna steak

Salt

1/2 cup mint leaves

1/2 cup parsley leaves

1/2 cup basil leaves (purple basil offers even more color)

1 shallot, shaved into very thin rounds (about 3 tablespoons)

1 tablespoon pink peppercorns, crushed*

* Though I am not usually a fan, this dish is wonderfully accentuated by pink peppercorns, which lend their floral/fruity character.

Preheat the oven to 300°F.

Place the olives on a baking sheet, place in the oven, and let dry for about 1 hour, until they crumble easily. Using the flat side of a knife, mortar and pestle, or spice grinder, crush the olives into a powder. Transfer to a small bowl and whisk in 1/2 cup of the oil.

In a small bowl, combine the raisins, vinegar, and a few tablespoons hot water. Let rest for 20 minutes to plump the raisins. Drain and discard the liquid.

While the raisins are plumping, season the tuna with salt and let it rest for 15 minutes.

Heat a large, heavy sauté pan over high heat until the pan is screaming hot. Add the remaining 1 tablespoon oil and the tuna. Sear for 2 to 3 minutes, then flip and cook for about 1 minute more. Depending on the thickness of the fish, you may need to cook for a few minutes longer to achieve the desired doneness. Remove from the pan and let rest for a few minutes.

In a medium bowl, combine the raisins, mint, parsley, basil, and shallot. Thinly slice the fish on a bias and place on a platter. Top the fish with the raisin-herb salad and pink peppercorns and drizzle with the black olive oil.

# Grilled Tuna Steaks with Walnut-Raisin Salsa

SERVES 4

The cooking time of this dish depends on the size of your tuna steak. If you're using bigeye or yellowfin, there is a relatively high surface area compared to volume. Smaller blackfin or wahoo is going to be more like a loin. The point here is to grill until well colored on the outside and to medium-rare to medium doneness. It only takes a few minutes on each side to achieve this. Make sure your fire is nice and hot to get the right color and caramelization quickly. This recipe works very well with one very large steak. The greater volume of a single steak allows for greater coloration while attaining the desired internal doneness. Also, it looks wonderfully generous to fan out the slices of a big, beautiful steak to serve family style.

3 garlic cloves, grated on a Microplane or minced

1 tablespoon chopped thyme leaves

1 teaspoon ground coriander

2 tablespoons extra-virgin olive oil

1 tablespoon red wine vinegar

1 tablespoon Pernod or Herbsaint, optional

Salt

Freshly cracked Black Pepper–Fennel Blend (page 53) or black pepper

1 tuna steak or loin (about 1¼ pounds)

1 recipe Walnut-Raisin Salsa (recipe follows)

In a container or zip-top bag, mix together the garlic, thyme, coriander, oil, vinegar, and Pernod, if using, and season with salt and pepper-fennel blend. Coat the tuna steak with the marinade and let it rest for at least 20 minutes or up to 2 hours.

Prepare a grill with a very hot fire. Grill each side of the fish until well colored and medium-rare to medium doneness, about 3 minutes per side, depending on thickness. Baste with any remaining marinade as it cooks. Allow to rest for a couple of minutes, then thinly slice on a bias. Serve with the Walnut-Raisin Salsa spooned over the top.

## Walnut-Raisin Salsa

MAKES ABOUT 1½ CUPS

I'm a huge fan of partnering raisins with fish, especially meaty fish such as tuna. By plumping the raisins in lemon juice, they take on a brilliant sweet-sour component that accentuates the mineral briny flavor of the fish.

¼ cup golden raisins, roughly chopped (black raisins or currants are fine too)

Zest and juice of 1 lemon (2 to 3 tablespoons juice)

1 cup walnut pieces

1 garlic clove, grated on a Microplane or minced

½ cup plus 2 tablespoons extra-virgin olive oil

½ bunch mint, leaves chopped

Salt

Freshly cracked Black Pepper–Fennel Blend (page 53) or black pepper

In a small bowl, combine the raisins with lemon juice and a few tablespoons hot water. Let rest for 20 minutes to plump the raisins. Drain and discard the liquid.

Toast the walnut pieces in a small dry sauté pan over medium heat until fragrant, about 3 minutes. Place them in a small bowl. While the walnuts are still warm, toss them with the lemon zest, garlic, and oil. When the mixture has cooled to room temperature, add the drained raisins and mint. Season with salt and pepper-fennel blend.

This is best used the day it's made, but it will keep in an airtight container in the refrigerator for up to 2 days.

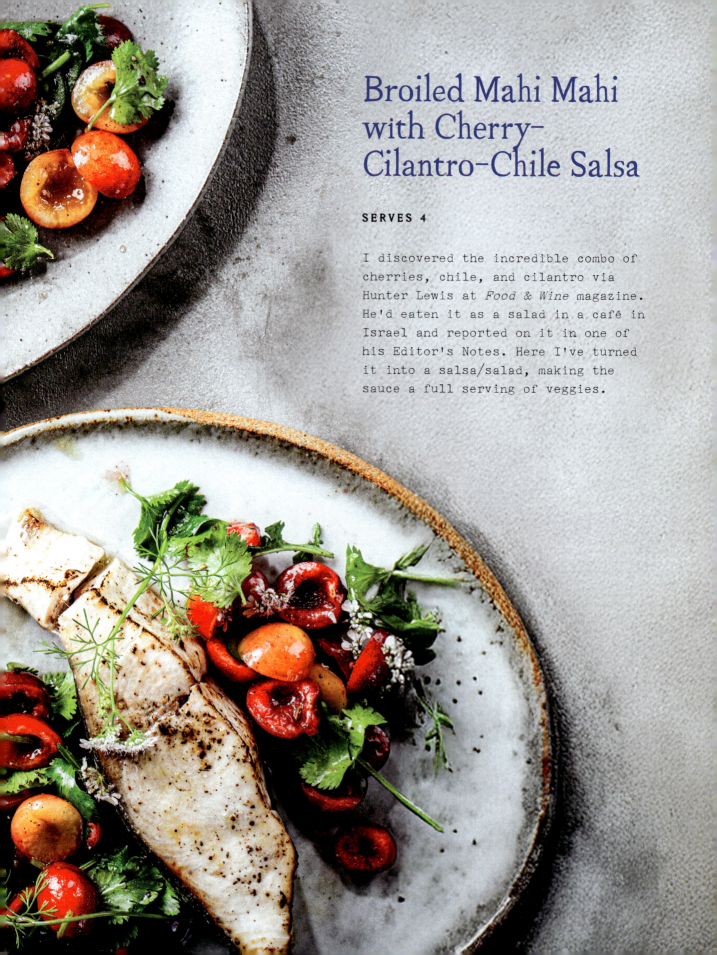

# Broiled Mahi Mahi with Cherry-Cilantro-Chile Salsa

**SERVES 4**

I discovered the incredible combo of cherries, chile, and cilantro via Hunter Lewis at *Food & Wine* magazine. He'd eaten it as a salad in a café in Israel and reported on it in one of his Editor's Notes. Here I've turned it into a salsa/salad, making the sauce a full serving of veggies.

The cooking method on the mahi combines a high and low approach. It starts under a searing hot broiler to color the fillet, then it's transferred to a lower rack and the heat is turned off. The residual heat in the oven is enough to gently finish cooking the fish while freeing the cook's attention with little risk of overcooking the fish.

cooking time should be 10 to 15 minutes, depending on the thickness of the fillet.

While the fish cooks, in a medium bowl, combine the cherries, cilantro, mint, chile, the remaining oil, and vinegar. Season with salt and pepper-fennel blend. Take the fish from the oven and spoon the cherry salsa over the top, allowing the heat of the fish to gently warm it.

1¹/₄ pounds mahi mahi fillet

Salt

¹/₄ cup extra-virgin olive oil

2 cups cherries, cut in half and pits removed

1 bunch cilantro, leaves and tender stems cut into 1-inch pieces

4 mint sprigs, leaves picked and chopped

1 serrano chile, very thinly sliced on the bias

2 tablespoons sherry vinegar

Freshly cracked Black Pepper–Fennel Blend (page 53) or black pepper

Season the fish with salt and let it rest for 15 minutes.

Arrange one of the oven racks as close to the heat as possible and another at the bottom of the oven. Preheat the broiler to high.

Place the mahi on a baking sheet and brush with just enough oil to give it a sheen. Broil on the upper rack for 4 minutes. Move the baking sheet to the bottom rack and turn the heat off. There should be enough heat in the oven to continue to cook the fish gently as you prepare the rest of the meal. If the oven does not feel hot (or your broiling unit is not part of your oven), then warm it to 275°F. Total

## Cilantro-Almond Rice Pilaf

**MAKES ABOUT 4 CUPS**

3 tablespoons butter or extra-virgin olive oil

¹/₂ cup orzo

2 garlic cloves, grated on a Microplane or minced

1 cup basmati rice

¹/₂ cup sliced or slivered almonds

2 bay leaves

Salt

¹/₄ cup chopped cilantro or mint

Zest and juice of 1 lemon (2 to 3 tablespoons juice)

Melt the butter or heat the oil in a large saucepan with a lid over medium heat. Add the orzo and garlic and cook, stirring, until golden brown, about 5 minutes. Add the rice, almonds, and bay leaves and stir to combine. Cook for another 2 minutes, or until the rice becomes translucent. Add 3 cups water and season with salt. Cover and bring to a boil. Reduce the heat to low and cook until all the liquid is absorbed and the rice and orzo are cooked, 12 to 14 minutes. Remove from the heat, fluff with a fork, and add the cilantro and lemon zest and juice.

# Vadouvan-Spiced Grilled Sturgeon

**SERVES 4**

Vadouvan is a French version of curry powder, combining many spices, bringing heat with chiles and mustard and sultry tones with cumin, turmeric, nutmeg, cloves, and more. Vadouvan spice blends can be found in specialty retail stores and online. Marinating thick fillets of fish in spiced yogurt tenderizes the meat and infuses flavor throughout. The marinade also acts as a brine, helping the fish to retain moisture when cooked. This technique is borrowed from the popular Indian dish tandoori chicken. This marinade can also firm up flaky fish like halibut or cod, making them easier to grill.

This requires an overnight marinade, so plan ahead.

½ cup plain labneh
1 tablespoon sherry vinegar or red wine vinegar
2 tablespoons extra-virgin olive oil
1 tablespoon vadouvan spice
1 shallot, finely diced (about 3 tablespoons)
2 garlic cloves, grated on a Microplane or minced
Salt
1¼ pounds sturgeon fillet, skin-off
1 recipe Cilantro-Almond Rice Pilaf (page 287) or 4 cups cooked white rice

In a small bowl, whisk together the labneh, vinegar, oil, vadouvan, shallot, and garlic and season with salt. Place the sturgeon fillet and labneh marinade in a large zip-top bag or baking dish. Massage to evenly coat the fish. Seal the bag or cover the baking dish and refrigerate for 12 to 24 hours.

Prepare a grill to medium heat with the coals on one side. If using a gas grill, heat one area to medium and an adjacent area to low. Remove the sturgeon from the marinade and place on the hottest part of the grill. Grill for 5 minutes, or until a deeply colored crust forms. Without flipping, move to the cooler part of the grill, cover the grill, and cook for 10 to 15 minutes, depending on thickness.

The fish is done when it flakes under gentle pressure or reads 130°F in the thickest part of the fillet. Serve with Cilantro-Almond Rice Pilaf.

# 4.10

# Fillet Fish

# Striped Bass Crudo with Cilantro and Lime

**SERVES 4**

The Mexican style of aguachile served underneath strips of pristinely fresh fish has always been one of my favorite ways to start a meal. However, I often am left wanting some way to sop up that delicious sauce once the fish is gone. I've embarrassed myself too many times trying to drink the remaining aguachile from the bowl or plate, dripping it onto my shirt. So, I make my herb and pepper puree a bit thicker so it clings to the fish. This also provides a nice textural contrast and flavor punch.

In a small sauté pan over medium-high heat, combine the oil with the garlic and jalapeño chile. Heat over medium-high heat until the chile skin is blistering or the garlic is golden brown. Transfer to a blender and add the cilantro leaves, mint, lime juice, and a large pinch of kosher salt. Add ¼ cup water and blend until smooth. Remove from the blender and refrigerate to chill.

To prepare the bass, pat it with a paper towel to dry well. Lay flat on a cutting board. Using a sharp knife angled at 45 degrees to the cutting board, cut slices on a bias about ¼ inch thick.

To serve, spoon the herb puree on plates and layer the fish over the top. Season each piece of fish with flaky salt. Garnish with the shallot and Fresno chile slices (about one slice each per bite) and cilantro sprigs.

1 tablespoon extra-virgin olive oil

4 garlic cloves, thinly sliced

1 jalapeño chile, cut in half lengthwise, seeds and stem removed

¾ cup cilantro leaves, plus 8 sprigs

¼ cup mint leaves

Juice of 4 limes (about ¼ cup)

Kosher salt

1¼ pounds striped bass fillet, skin-off

Flaky salt, such as Maldon

1 small shallot, very thinly sliced (about 2 tablespoons)

1 Fresno or red jalapeño chile, sliced razor thin

# Kingfish Tartare with Smoky Eggplant and Candied Red Onions

**SERVES 4**

The flavors here offer a tour of the Mediterranean with the smoky/bitter eggplant puree balanced by the sweet/sour onions.

If you have any sexy salt, such as Maldon or Jacobson flaky salt, this is the dish you've been waiting for. It adds a nice pop of texture.

1 pound kingfish fillets, trimmed of any bloodline and cut into ¼- to ⅓-inch cubes*

Salt

½ cup plus 2 tablespoons extra-virgin olive oil

1 medium eggplant, cut in half lengthwise

4 large basil leaves

¼ cup Candied Red Onion (recipe follows)

Freshly cracked Black Pepper–Fennel Blend (page 53) or black pepper

1 baguette, sliced ½ inch thick, brushed with olive oil, and toasted

* Though we use kingfish here, it's closely related to and sometimes called variously: yellowtail, kanpachi, kampachi, hiramasa. Any of these will work perfectly for this dish.

Preheat the oven to 400°F.

Season the fish with salt and let it rest for 15 minutes in the refrigerator to keep cold.

Pour ½ cup of the oil into a small baking dish just large enough to hold the eggplant and swirl it around to coat the bottom. Place the eggplant in the oil cut-side down. Roast until charred and tender throughout, about 35 minutes. Remove and let cool. Scoop the flesh, getting all the caramelized bits where it touched the baking dish. Discard the skin. Place the eggplant in the bowl of a food processor or blender. Scrape the pan to get all the oil and bits and process until it is silken smooth. Season with salt and chill.

Roll the basil leaves like a cigar and then slice them as thin as possible across the roll. Mix the basil with the fish and the remaining 2 tablespoons oil.

Spoon the eggplant puree onto plates. Place a scoop of fish over the top followed by a small dollop of candied onion. Sprinkle pepper-fennel blend over the top. Serve with the toasted baguette slices.

## Candied Red Onion

**MAKES ABOUT 1 CUP**

This is a great condiment to make in bulk, as it stores well in the refrigerator for a couple weeks and is wonderful served with cheese or charcuterie or tossed into a salad. Or just eat it by the spoonful.

1 red onion, finely diced (about 1 cup)

½ cup sugar

1 cup red wine vinegar

1 bay leaf

Combine all the ingredients in a small saucepan, place over medium-low heat, and cook, stirring frequently, for about 15 minutes, until the liquid reduces to a thick, coating syrup and the onions are fully cooked but still retain a snappy texture. Remove from the heat and let cool. The candied red onion will keep in an airtight container in the refrigerator for up to 2 weeks.

# Minnesota Fish Fry

The most traditional meal in Minnesota is the shore lunch and the most traditional shore lunch is a fish fry. And it's not just for Friday nights! At the cabin on the lake, this is a regular meal anytime someone pulls the boat up with some lake fish, especially walleye, our state fish. Absent walleye, use any mild, tender white-fleshed fish.

If you can, make the coleslaw the day before you're serving. Bake your potatoes the day before as well. Cool and refrigerate unwrapped. Make the tartar sauce the day of, keeping it in the refrigerator until you're ready to use it. You can fry the potatoes at the same time you fry the fish if your pot is large enough.

3 quarts vegetable oil

2 cups all-purpose flour

Salt and freshly ground white pepper

3 eggs, beaten

2 sleeves Ritz crackers, pulsed in food processor until finely crushed (about 2 cups)

2 to 3 pounds walleye fillets, trimmed and cut into 3- to 5-ounce pieces

4 russet potatoes, washed, dried, pricked with a fork, and baked for 90 minutes in a 350°F oven or until tender. Then cooled, and then refrigerated overnight unwrapped.

1 recipe Chopped Coleslaw (recipe follows)*

1 recipe Tartar Sauce (recipe follows)**

Lemon wedges

* If you are using store-bought, you will need about a cup or so for each diner.

** You can use store-bought, but I beg you to make your own.

Heat the oil in a deep pot or dutch oven over medium heat to 375°F.

Spread the flour out onto a plate and season very well with salt and white pepper. Beat the eggs in a wide bowl. Place the crushed crackers in another bowl. Season the fish with salt and white pepper. Dredge the fish in the flour mixture. Dip into the beaten egg, coating well, and then into the cracker crumbs. Working in batches, fry the fish pieces until golden brown, about 5 minutes. As the fish come out of the fryer, place on paper towels to drain and season with salt.

Return the frying oil to 375°F. Break the cold baked potatoes with your hand for a rustic look. Add the potatoes to the frying oil and fry until golden brown and very crispy, about 6 minutes. Drain on paper towels and season with salt.

Serve the walleye and potatoes with the coleslaw, tartar sauce, and lemon wedges.

# Chopped Coleslaw

MAKES ABOUT 2 QUARTS

2½ cups Hellmann's or Duke's mayonnaise

1½ tablespoons sugar

Salt

5 tablespoons sweet pickle relish

3 tablespoons apple cider vinegar

1 teaspoon red chile flakes

2 teaspoons celery seeds

2 teaspoons fennel seeds, toasted and crushed

1 head green cabbage

3 carrots, trimmed

1 red onion, minced (about 1 cup)

In a large bowl, whisk together the mayonnaise, sugar, salt, pickle relish, vinegar, chile flakes, celery seeds, and fennel seeds. Cover and chill in the refrigerator.

Cut the cabbage into wedges and put through the food processor with the grating attachment (alternatively, you can hand shred on a box grater or mandoline). Next, pass the carrots through the food processor with the grating attachment or shred on a box grater. Place the shredded carrots and cabbage in a large bowl and add the onion. Toss well. Add the dressing and stir to combine. Taste and adjust the seasoning. Cover and chill for at least 6 hours before serving.

# Tartar Sauce

MAKES ABOUT 2 CUPS

3 egg yolks

2 tablespoons white distilled vinegar

1 teaspoon dijon mustard

¾ cup canola oil

¾ cup extra-virgin olive oil

Salt

Zest and juice of 1 lemon (2 to 3 tablespoons juice)

6 tarragon sprigs, chopped (2 tablespoons)

¼ cup sweet pickle relish

3 tablespoons brined capers, rinsed and patted dry

3 tablespoons minced parsley

2 tablespoons minced dill

Put the yolks, vinegar, and mustard in a food processor and pulse to combine (or use an immersion wand fitted with a blade attachment and make it in a 4- or 6-cup Pyrex measuring cup).

With the machine running, add the canola oil in a thin stream to emulsify. Next, add the olive oil in a thin stream to emulsify into mayonnaise. Remove the mixture to a medium bowl and add the salt, lemon zest and juice, the tarragon, pickle relish, capers, parsley, and dill. Refrigerate until chilled. The tartar sauce will keep in an airtight container in the refrigerator for up to 1 week.

# Seared Snapper and Spicy Mango Basil Salad

**SERVES 4**

Both of us lived and cooked through the heyday of fruit salsas, when they were on menus everywhere, often an uncompelling combination of unripe fruit and too-big-chopped peppers. Sure, deliciously ripe fruit with aromatics can be a fantastic pairing with seafood, but the inspiration for such must come from having perfect fruit, more so than just a belief in the concept. Here with spicy greens, peppers, and ginger, the sweetness of the fruit is far more balanced and integrated with the dish. And the colors are simply striking.

1¼ pounds snapper fillets, skin-on
**Salt**
2 tablespoons vegetable or peanut oil
1 recipe Spicy Mango-Basil Salad (recipe follows)

Scrape the skin of the fish with the back of a knife to remove excess moisture and pat dry with a paper towel. Score the skin with shallow incisions, taking care not to cut too deeply into the flesh. Season the flesh side of the fish with salt and let it rest for 10 minutes.

Heat the oil in a large nonstick pan over high heat until it just begins to shimmer. Add the fish to the pan, skin-side down. Gently press the fillets into the pans, as they will try to curl up. This ensures even cooking/browning. Reduce the heat to medium and cook until skin begins to crisp, 5 to 7 minutes. Turn the heat off, flip the fish, and cook through, 1 to 2 minutes. Remove from the pan and serve with Spicy Mango-Basil Salad.

## Spicy Mango-Basil Salad

**SERVES 4**

2 tablespoons grated (on a Microplane) or minced fresh ginger
1 garlic clove, grated on a Microplane or minced
1 serrano chile, finely diced
¼ cup fresh lime juice (about 2 limes)
2 teaspoons dijon mustard
2 tablespoons extra-virgin olive oil
6 large basil leaves
2 ripe Champagne mangos, peeled and sliced (about 2 cups)
1 red bell pepper, seeds removed, very thinly sliced
3 cups arugula
**Salt**

Combine the ginger, garlic, chile, and lime juice in a large bowl. Season with salt and let it rest for 10 minutes for the flavors to meld. Stir in the mustard and oil. Roll the basil leaves like a cigar and slice across the roll as thinly as possible. Add the basil, mangos, bell pepper, and arugula to the bowl with the dressing. Season with salt.

# Steamed Black Bass with Ginger, Garlic, and Scallions

**SERVES 4 TO 6**

I'm not sure there is a nicer method and presentation than steaming a fish and plating it on an oval platter or serving it in the dish it was steamed in. This dish is also my poster child for simple food: It's made with just a few ingredients and it delivers spectacular results. Whole fish tastes better, but if you don't have access to whole fish, you can steam fillets or portions. Paired with a salad, some rice, and a nice veg, this dish is a complete meal that gets on the table fast enough to be a weeknight stalwart or a meteor dish for weekend entertaining. Steaming is an easy technique that allows for keeping a lot of moisture in the fish as well as delivering maximum flavor by using the wine and aromatics in the liquid base that you bring to a boil.

*Andrew*

2 whole black bass, 2 to 3 pounds each, cleaned and scaled, head-on

Salt

One 4-inch knob fresh ginger, half very thinly sliced, half cut into very fine threads

3 garlic cloves, thinly sliced

2 cups Shaoxing cooking wine or sake

1/4 cup toasted rapeseed oil (available at Asian markets or online) or peanut oil

1 bunch scallions, sliced into fine threads about 4 inches in length

1/4 cup aged natural soy sauce

**Special equipment: bamboo steamer**

Wash and dry the fish very well. Season the fish with salt inside and out and set it aside. You can score it if you like. Place the sliced ginger and garlic inside the fish cavities.

Place 1½ cups of the wine into the base of a steamer and add a quart or so of water, along with any ginger or scallion trimmings you have left. Place the fish on small plates and steam for 12 to 15 minutes, until cooked through. Use an instant-read thermometer to take the temperature along the backbone. It should read 130°F when done.

While the fish is steaming, heat the oil in a small pot over medium heat.

When the fish is done, slide it onto a large platter. Place the ginger threads and scallion over the fish. When the oil is almost smoking, drizzle it over the fish along with the remaining wine and the soy sauce.

# Bluefish Flambé

**SERVES 4**

Bluefish is available in a range of sizes, from the small "snapper" blues, which are milder in flavor than very large fish and whose fillets can be an inch thick or more. Given this range, you'll need to adjust the cooking times according to your fish.

Bluefish has a thick layer of bloodline (dark tissue that runs just under the skin in the middle of the fillet). Though I like the flavor of the bloodline, some people find it too strong. It can easily be removed after cooking by peeling back the skin and using a knife to scrape away the dark tissue; it will flake right off the fillet.

Be careful with the flambé. It's awesomely dramatic as you are creating a burst of flavorful, controlled flame, but it's exactly that: a burst of flame. Pro tip: Keep your eyebrows!

1¼ pounds bluefish fillets, preferably from larger fish with fillets ¾ inch or thicker, skin on
Salt
Freshly cracked Black Pepper–Fennel Blend (page 53) or black pepper
5 tablespoons butter
Zest and juice of 1 lemon (2 to 3 tablespoons juice)
¼ cup Pernod or Herbsaint*
2 tablespoons chopped soft herbs, such as parsley, chives, cilantro, or fennel fronds

* Flambé requires alcohol to flame the dish. If you don't partake, finish the sauce with 2 tablespoons red or white wine vinegar and 2 tablespoons water instead.

Season the fish with salt and let it rest for 15 minutes. Completely coat the flesh side of the fish with pepper-fennel blend, gently pressing to adhere.

Melt the butter in a large sauté pan over medium heat. (Yes, this seems like a lot, but it will become part of the sauce later.) When the butter is foaming and begins to brown, place the fish skin-side down in the pan and cook for 4 to 5 minutes, until it begins to color. Flip and cook until done, 2 to 3 minutes. Add the lemon zest to the pan. Turn off the heat and carefully add the liquor. Turn the heat back on and carefully ignite the liquor by tilting the pan away from you toward the flame of a gas stove or use a match. Cook until the flames subside, then add the lemon juice and herbs. Swirl to incorporate.

# John Dory Marinated in Sweet-Sour Caponata

John Dory is among the most unique
looking fish. (Really, look up a
picture of this fish!) Its flat oval
body is similar to flounder, but it
has an upright swimming habit. It has
a thin and gelatinously rich silver
skin that for this recipe is removed,
though you could keep it on to add
body and texture to the sauce. This
preparation of stewed vegetables,
basically a highly flavored
ratatouille, with the addition of the
sweet-salty kick of vinegar, raisins,
and sugar, provides a perfect
counterpoint to the rich, oily fish.
The cooked fish is nestled into the
just-cooked vegetable mixture and
left to chill and mingle. It can be
served at room temperature or warm.

1¼ pounds John Dory fillets, skin-off

Salt

1 cup plus 1 tablespoon extra-virgin olive oil

2 garlic cloves, sliced

¼ cup slivered almonds (or roughly chopped whole almonds)

2 tablespoons raisins

1 tablespoon fennel seeds

2 tablespoons capers, rinsed and patted dry

1 tablespoon red chile flakes, such as Aleppo or gochugaru

1 red onion, cut into ½-inch pieces (about 1 cup)

1 red bell pepper, cut into ½-inch pieces

1 small eggplant, cut into ½-inch pieces (about 2 cups)

¼ cup red wine vinegar, or more if needed

1½ tablespoons brown sugar, or more if needed

1 cup soft herbs, such as picked and torn basil, cilantro, mint, and/or parsley leaves, for garnish

1 baguette, sliced ½ inch thick, brushed with extra-virgin olive oil, and toasted

Season the fish with salt and let it rest for
10 minutes.

In a large sauté pan, heat 1 tablespoon of the oil
over medium-high heat, add the fish, and sear one
side of the fish until just colored, about 4 minutes.
Turn the heat off and flip the fish. Let it rest for
3 minutes to cook through. Remove the fish to
a baking dish just large enough to hold it.

In the same sauté pan, heat the remaining cup of
oil over medium-high heat. Add the garlic, almonds,
raisins, fennel seeds, and capers. Cook for about
3 minutes, until the raisins plump and the garlic is
lightly colored. Add the chile flakes, onion, and bell
pepper and sauté until the vegetables are beginning
to wilt, 3 to 4 minutes.

Add the eggplant, and stir to combine and soak up
the oil. Cook for an additional 3 to 4 minutes, until
the eggplant begins to soften. Add the vinegar and
brown sugar and stir to combine. Season with salt
and more vinegar or sugar as needed. Continue to
cook until liquid has reduced to a thin glaze. Pour
the still warm vegetables over the fish to bury it.
Let the dish cool to room temperature. Better yet,
chill overnight and gently rewarm in a 200°F oven.
Scatter the herbs over the top and serve with the
toasted baguette slices.

# Blackened Drum, New Orleans Style

**SERVES 4**

This dish, invented by the legendary
New Orleans chef Paul Prudhomme,
is one of the dishes that put Cajun
cuisine on the map. Like so much about
New Orleans, this recipe is over the
top, with a potent and heady spice
mix that is seared until blackened,
coaxing out a bitterness and sweetness
in the spice. To take best advantage
of the delicious leavings in the pan
once the fish is cooked, we create an
accompanying vegetable dish of sweet
red onions, bok choy, and pecans to
act as a perfect foil. Be warned,
this is quite a dramatic dish that
creates a good bit of smoke. So be
sure you've got your ventilation
kicked up.

*Andrew*

This preparation works especially
well for snapper, corvina, barramundi,
cobia, and yellowtail.

1¼ pounds drum fillet, skin off
**Salt**
**1 recipe Blackening Spice Mix (recipe follows)**
**4 tablespoons (½ cup) butter, melted**
**¼ cup vegetable oil**
**1 red onion, sliced into thin wedges (about 1 cup)**
**4 baby bok choys, cut into quarters**
**½ cup pecan pieces**
**1 lemon, cut into wedges**

Lightly season the fish with salt and let it rest for
10 minutes. Spread the Blackening Spice Mix over
a plate.

Heat a large cast-iron skillet or heavy-bottom sauté
pan over high heat until it is screaming hot. Combine
2 tablespoons of the butter with the oil in a small
bowl and brush the fish with the mixture until it
glistens all over. Dredge one side of the fish in the
Blackening Spice Mix, coating it evenly. Place the fish
in the pan spice-side down and drizzle the remaining
butter-and-oil mixture over the top. Reduce the
heat to medium-low and cook without flipping until
a dark crust forms, 4 to 5 minutes, then flip and
cook through, another 1 to 3 minutes. Remove the
fish from the pan. Increase the heat to medium-high
and add the remaining 2 tablespoons butter, the red
onion, bok choy, pecans, and a pinch of salt. Cook
until the vegetables are just softened and the nuts
are toasted, about 5 minutes. Serve the vegetables
alongside the fish with the lemon wedges.

# Blackening Spice Mix

**MAKES 6 TABLESPOONS**

Typically blackening spice mix has salt in it. We don't include it here because we preseason our fish. If you are making it to use on its own, add 2 tablespoons kosher salt.

- 1 tablespoon smoked sweet paprika
- 1 tablespoon dried oregano
- 1 tablespoon garlic powder
- 1 tablespoon onion powder
- 2 teaspoons mustard powder
- 1 teaspoon ground allspice
- 1 tablespoon freshly cracked Black Pepper–Fennel Blend (page 53)

Combine all the ingredients in a small bowl. The spice mix will keep in an airtight container for up to 1 month.

# Branzino with Thai Flavors

SERVES 4

I encourage you to cook and eat whole fish. The flavor is better. Think of a sautéed boneless skinless chicken breast versus the same muscle eaten off a whole roast chicken. There is simply no comparison. Eating whole fish is a more sustainable way to eat, is cheaper than buying filleted fish, replicates the outdoor cooking experience for those of us who fish a little, and, let's face it . . . it's a more visceral and personally authentic way to cook.

Around the world, whole fish, steamed or fried, grilled or sautéed, are ubiquitous. Whole fish is eaten in every home and almost every restaurant as well. If you love to cook and you love Thai food, I think you will cook this dish again and again.

Chef Eric Ripert designed a special pan he calls La Poissonnière from de Buyer that is ideal for cooking small whole fish, but any large sauté pan will do. If you want to buy this pan, I think you will use it all the time. It's made in Vosges, a city famous for crafting pans for centuries. Proceeds from purchases of the pan go to support City Harvest's vital work feeding New Yorkers in need. Buy it at shortorder.com/products/la-poissonniere-pan.

Andrew

2 cleaned branzinos, head on (about 1 pound each)
1 teaspoon salt
1/4 teaspoon ground white pepper
1 cup rice flour
1/2 cup cornstarch
1/4 cup toasted rapeseed oil (available at Asian markets or online)
6 garlic cloves, sliced
1-inch knob fresh ginger, thinly sliced
4 shallots, sliced (about 3/4 cup)
2 red Thai chiles, sliced
4 makrut lime leaves
2 tablespoons Thai red curry paste
2 tablespoons oyster sauce
2 tablespoons palm sugar
1 cup coconut milk
1 tablespoon fish sauce
3 limes
1 large handful Thai basil leaves*
Cooked sticky rice

* Genovese basil leaves make a decent substitute.

Pat dry each fish and make some lateral slices angled toward the head. Season all sides and the cavity with the salt and white pepper and set aside.

Preheat a fish pan, large sauté pan, or large well-seasoned wok over medium heat.

In a wide bowl or plate, combine the rice flour and cornstarch. Lightly dredge the fish in the cornstarch mixture.

Add the oil to the preheated pan, then add the fish and brown both sides, about 2 minutes per side. Remove the fish to a side plate.

Add the garlic, ginger, shallots, chiles, lime leaves, curry paste, oyster sauce, and palm sugar to the pan. Cook briefly, stirring, then add the coconut milk, fish sauce, and the juice of 1 lime. Cut the remaining limes for use at the table. Simmer the sauce for a minute or two, then return the fish to the pan.

Cook for 2 minutes, then flip the fish. Cook on the second side for another 2 minutes. You want to cook the fish for a total of 4 minutes on each side. If you find the sauce reducing too much, add some water.

Place the fish on a platter and stir the basil leaves into the sauce. Pour the sauce over the fish and serve right away, with plenty of sticky rice and lime wedges on the side.

# Risotto with Striped Bass

**SERVES 6 TO 8**

This is one of my favorite spring dishes
to make for a casual party: Lay out some
snacks and pop some rosé for guests, throw
a big salad in a bowl in the refrigerator,
toss some crusty bread in the oven, and
the elegance of this simple rice dish will
floor your friends and family. Nothing
says spring to me like peas and morels. I
spent years working overseas, mastering
the art of risotto. Follow this recipe
closely, make sure your risotto isn't
stiff, that it runs slightly on the plate,
and you will make this dish over and over.

2¹/₂ cups cooked and cooled fresh peas or fava
beans (defrosted frozen peas will work too)

¹/₂ cup parsley leaves

Salt

2 tablespoons extra-virgin olive oil

1 shallot, minced (about 3 tablespoons)

2 cups Arborio rice

2 cups room-temperature light-bodied Italian white
wine (a nice pinot grigio works well)

10 cups Andrew or Barton's Rich Fish stock
(page 86 or 87), brought to a simmer

4 tablespoons (¹/₂ stick) butter

3 cups morel, spring chanterelle, or other
mushrooms, sliced if need be depending on size
and species

1¹/₂ to 2 pounds striped bass fillets, skin off, cut
into 1-inch pieces

Freshly ground white pepper

1 cup grated aged parmesan cheese, plus more to
pass at the table

Combine 2 cups of the peas, the parsley, and a pinch
of salt in a food processor and process until smooth
(add a splash of cold water or extra-virgin olive oil
to help the machine run, if needed). Pass through
a sieve if you want an extra smooth texture,
and reserve.

Heat the oil in a very large sauté pan with straight
sides of at least 3 inches in height over medium
heat. Add the shallot and sauté until glassy, about
4 minutes. Add the rice, stir, and cook for a few
minutes to coat the rice and warm through, but
don't toast the grains.

Add the wine, stir, and cook until the alcohol smell
has dissipated, about 2 minutes. Lower the heat
and cook for a minute or two. Add 3 cups of the
hot stock. Stir every 1¹/₂ minutes or so, making sure
to maintain a simmer. When the stock is almost
fully absorbed, add 3 more cups of the hot stock.
Stir well. Continue to lightly simmer and stir every
1¹/₂ minutes or so.

Meanwhile, heat 2 tablespoons of the butter in
a medium sauté pan over medium-high heat until
it foams. Add the mushrooms and cook for 2 to
3 minutes, searing well until just cooked through.
Season with salt and reserve.

Taste the rice after the last batch of liquid has
been added. You don't want any crunch, but you
don't want mushy rice either. When the rice is
about 5 minutes away from being done (no longer
crunchy), season the fish with salt, add it to the pot,
and stir gently to fold the pieces into the risotto.

Keep adding stock, 1 cup at a time, stirring, and
cook until the rice is tender and the fish is just
about cooked through. Stir in the remaining 1 cup
of stock, the remaining whole peas, and pea puree.
Season with salt and white pepper. Stir again and

remove from heat. Add the cheese and remaining
2 tablespoons butter and stir to combine and melt
the butter.

Taste for seasoning and remember, risotto
shouldn't be dense. It should be served all'onda, as
the Italians say, which means "with waves." You
should see its creaminess and it should spread
across a plate, not in a runny or liquidy way but the
way hot lava creeps across the land. If you need to
stir in some more stock, go ahead—just don't make
soupy rice.

Serve on warm plates with the mushrooms
scattered on top. Pass the cheese at the table and
serve with a crisp salad.

# Grilled Barramundi with Fennel Frond–Almond Pesto

**SERVES 4**

Fennel is normally sold with at least a few inches of its feathery green top and celery-like hollow stalks still attached to the bulb. These cook so differently from the bulb itself that unless you're using it for a salad, this is a really great way to use up what is pretty much a different product.

1 tablespoon salt
1/2 teaspoon onion powder
1/2 teaspoon ground coriander
1/2 teaspoon ground ginger
1 1/4 pounds barramundi fillets, skin on
3 tablespoons extra-virgin olive oil
1 fennel bulb, very thinly sliced, leaves and stalks reserved (about 1 1/2 cups)
Juice of 1/2 lemon (about 1 tablespoon)
1 recipe Fennel Frond–Almond Pesto (recipe follows)

In a small bowl, combine the salt, onion powder, coriander, and ginger. Season the fish with the mix and let it rest for 15 minutes.

Prepare a grill with a medium-hot fire. Brush the fish skin with a scant bit of the oil. Grill skin-side down until it is cooked about 80 percent of the way through, 4 to 6 minutes. Flip and cook for 1 to 2 minutes longer to cook through. (The fish can also be broiled, skin-side up, for 6 to 8 minutes.)

In a medium bowl, toss the sliced fennel with the remaining oil and lemon juice and season with salt.

Serve the fish drizzled with Fennel Frond–Almond Pesto and topped with the fennel slaw.

## Fennel Frond–Almond Pesto

**MAKES ABOUT 2 CUPS**

2 cups roughly chopped fennel leaves and stalks (from 1 fennel bulb)
1/2 cup almonds
2 garlic cloves, smashed
1 cup extra-virgin olive oil
Juice of 1/2 lemon (about 1 tablespoon)
Salt

In a sauté pan, combine the fennel leaves and stalks, almonds, garlic, and 1/2 cup of the oil and heat over medium heat until the almonds just begin to color, 3 to 5 minutes. Remove from the heat and let cool. Transfer to a blender or food processor and blend, drizzling in the remaining 1/2 cup oil, until smooth, or leave chunky as desired. Season with salt.

The pesto will keep in an airtight container in the refrigerator for up to 1 week.

# Sweet and Sour, Sticky and Spicy Hamachi Kama (Broiled Yellowtail Collar)

**SERVES 6**

This is one of those one dish, two ways meals that I love. At home, I serve these collars on separate platters, one for the pile of plain salted and grilled/broiled collars served in a traditional Japanese way with the grated daikon mixture and soy dipping sauce, the other for the tare-glazed collars that I cook and then brush with the sauce to glaze or place the collars in the pan with the glaze. Either way, pure bliss. I consider the collars of fish to hold the most delicately textured and moistest, tastiest bites on the animal. Far better than the cheeks.

You can do the same dish with any large fish collars, from salmon to tuna.

Serve with Japanese short-grain rice cooked with some kombu and shaved dried bonito flakes, along with steamed green vegetables like bok choy, gai lan, or cabbage. I like to serve this dish on pieces of banana leaf, which are available frozen in any Asian market.

6 or 8 pieces yellowtail collar, roughly 10 ounces each
Salt
1 tablespoon vegetable oil
1 cup finely grated daikon radish

2 scallions, thinly sliced (¼ cup)
Shichimi togarashi (Japanese seven-spice) or finely ground red chile flakes, such as Aleppo
Naturally brewed Japanese soy sauce (Yamasa is good brand)
2 lemons, cut into wedges
1 recipe Sweet and Sour Glaze (recipe follows)

Pat the fish collars dry and rub them with about ½ teaspoon salt. Let the collars come to room temperature.

Place a rack 4 to 5 inches from your broiler's heating element and preheat the broiler to high. (You can also grill the collars.)

Line a baking sheet with foil and rub it with the oil. Place the pieces of collar on the foil, skin-side down. Broil for 4 to 6 minutes, until the exterior of the fish is browned in spots and blistered in others. Flip and blister the other side. Char marks are even better. When the fish flakes easily, it is done, 10 to 15 minutes total cooking time.

Gently squeeze the grated daikon to remove some liquid, then place it in a small bowl. Add the scallions and some togarashi. Spoon onto plates or a large platter. Place a small bowl for the soy sauce and a small piece of banana leaf on the plate. Place the fish on the leaf, pour some soy sauce in the bowl, garnish with a lemon, and invite guests to season the soy sauce with the daikon mixture and lemon.

Drizzle some of the glaze over some of the collars or serve alongside it.

Alternately, serve the collars Japanese BBQ style by brushing well with the glaze as they emerge from the broiler. I like to serve some plain and some with the more traditional sauce.

# Sweet and Sour Glaze

**MAKES ABOUT 1 CUP**

1 cup dashi (page 83)

2 cups sake

²/₃ cup soy sauce

¹/₂ cup mirin

¹/₃ cup light brown sugar

¹/₃ cup rice wine vinegar

**Pinch of Japanese red chile flakes or shichimi togarashi (Japanese seven-spice)**

Combine all the ingredients in a small pot. Bring to a simmer over medium-low heat and reduce slowly until its bubbles are getting larger and holding some shape; that means when cooled a bit it will be syrupy. If overcooked it will be bitter. Test the sauce by dipping a spoon in; if the sauce holds its shape on the spoon as it cools, it's done. Serve immediately, or cool and store in an airtight container in the refrigerator. It will keep for months.

# Rockfish Cioppino

My mother went to Mills College in San Francisco and came home an accomplished cook. Her roommate was Vic Bergeron's daughter. Trader Vic, as he was better known, taught them to cook his style of food, but also often took them out. My mother fell in love with cioppino, the Italian-American fish stew of the California wharves. We ate it every week in the summers growing up, and I still make it frequently at home almost year-round. The fish and shellfish here are a delicious combination, but I often use just one type of bivalve and one type of fish. There are no rules here. Just deliciousness.

½ cup extra-virgin olive oil

4 garlic cloves, thinly sliced

1 leek, white and light green parts only, halved lengthwise and thinly sliced crosswise

1 fennel bulb, thinly sliced (about 1½ cups)

1½ tablespoons dried oregano

½ teaspoon red chile flakes, or more to taste

4 cups Basic Fish Stock (page 85)

4 cups Tomato Sauce (page 123)

1 pound littleneck clams

1 pound mussels

1 pound large shrimp, shelled and deveined

4 pieces rockfish fillets (about 4 ounces each)

Salt

½ cup celery leaves (optional)

Coarsely chopped parsley leaves

Toasted or grilled sourdough bread

Heat the oil in a very large heavy pot over medium heat until it shimmers. Add the garlic, leek, fennel, oregano, and chile flakes and cook, stirring frequently, until the vegetables have softened, about 3 minutes. Add the stock, bring to a simmer, and cook for 15 minutes, or until reduced by half. Pour in the tomato sauce, bring to a simmer, then reduce the heat to low and simmer for about 20 minutes, until the flavors develop more complexity and the acid in the tomato mellows out a bit. Add the clams, cover, and cook for 5 minutes, shaking the pot occasionally. Stir in the mussels and cook for 1 to 2 more minutes, until the clams and mussels open. Set the clams and mussels into 4 very large bowls, discarding any that didn't open. Season the shrimp and rockfish with salt. Place the shrimp in the pot first and the fish on top, pressing gently to partially submerge it. Cover and cook until the fish and shrimp are just cooked through, about 5 minutes. Transfer the fish and shrimp to the serving bowls. Compose the seafood as you like. Stir in the celery leaves, if using, and ladle the tomato mixture over the seafood. Garnish with parsley and serve with toasted or grilled bread.

# Spice-Roasted Tilefish with Grapes and Shallots

**SERVES 4**

Tilefish has a sweet, crab-like flavor and a unique buttery-yet-taut texture. The beautiful skin of these fish are mottled with blue and silver and yellow. The skin crisps well, though it requires high heat to do so. In this dish, we don't try to crisp it, but rather use the skin to protect the moisture in the flesh, which is scooped from the skin. This is a one-pan dish with crunchy almonds, savory roasted shallots, clusters of grapes, and bitter radishes that cooks, crisps, crunches, and caramelizes all at once.

1 tablespoon kosher salt

1 teaspoon cumin seeds

1/2 teaspoon ground ginger

1/2 teaspoon ground coriander

Pinch of ground cinnamon

1 1/4 pounds tilefish fillets, skin-on

2 lemons, cut into wedges

1/4 cup plus 1 tablespoon extra-virgin olive oil

2 garlic cloves, grated on a Microplane or minced

1/2 cup slivered or baton-cut almonds

4 shallots, quartered

8 ounces grapes, cut into small clusters*

1 bunch radishes, each cut into quarters

1 cup roughly torn herbs, such as chervil, dill, mint, and/or parsley

Freshly cracked Black Pepper–Fennel Blend (page 53) or black pepper

* I like to leave the grapes in clusters, as it provides interesting architecture to the presentation of this dish.

Preheat the oven to 425°F.

In a small bowl, combine the salt, cumin seeds, ginger, coriander, and cinnamon.

Place the fish skin-side down on a baking dish and season the flesh side with the spice mixture. Place the lemon wedges around the fillets. Drizzle the fish with 1 tablespoon of the oil.

In a large bowl, combine the remaining 1/4 cup oil with the garlic and almonds. Add the shallots, grapes, and radishes. Toss to combine and season with salt. Arrange the grape mixture around the fish. Place in the oven and roast for 10 to 12 minutes, until the almonds are toasted, the grapes are blistered, and the fish is cooked through. Remove from the oven. Squeeze the roasted lemons over the dish and top with a scattering of herbs and pepper-fennel blend.

# Curry-Spiced Tilapia with Almond-Mint Brown Butter

**SERVES 4**

This is a classic dish of pan-seared fish in a brown butter sauce. We've pumped it up by seasoning the fish with curry powder. This adds a welcome point of interest as the spices bloom into the fish after a brief turn in butter. The sauce, made in the same pan after the fish is removed, combines the nuttiness of the butter and toasted almonds with the salty punch of butter-crisped capers. And, of course, we throw some mint in there, because mint! This recipe works especially well with thin fillets such as tilapia, perch, ocean perch, or branzino. The curry is a particularly good pairing with freshwater fish, adding welcome subtlety and nuance.

1¼ pounds tilapia fillets, skin-off

Salt

1 tablespoon curry powder

6 tablespoons butter

2 tablespoons capers, rinsed, patted dry, and chopped

¼ cup sliced almonds

2 garlic cloves, grated on a Microplane or minced

¼ cup mint leaves, roughly chopped

Juice of 1 lemon (2 to 3 tablespoons)

Season one side of the fish with salt and the curry powder and let it rest for 10 minutes.

Heat 2 tablespoons of the butter in a large sauté pan over medium-high heat until it is melted and golden brown. Add the fish to the pan spice-side down. Cook for 3 minutes. Flip the fish, reduce the heat to medium, and cook for another 3 to 4 minutes, until cooked through. Remove the fish from the pan. Add the remaining 4 tablespoons butter and cook until browned and nutty in aroma, about 3 minutes. Add the capers, almonds, and garlic and cook for about 2 minutes, until the nuts are toasted. Add the mint and lemon juice. Turn off the heat and swirl to incorporate and emulsify the sauce. Spoon the sauce over the fillets and serve.

# Grouper Veracruzana

**SERVES 4**

This wonderful dish starts with a
very flavorful base of tomatoes
stewed with all sorts of tasty
things: chiles, capers, olives, and
oregano. Though ours is inspired by
the traditional Mexican dish, it
reads equally like an Italian dish.
Grouper, with its taut texture, is the
very best fish for this dish, though
nearly any other flaky white-fleshed
fish would be a great stand-in. There
is something about the confident
flavor of grouper that pairs so well
with these strong flavors.

1¹/₄ pounds grouper fillets, skin off

**Salt**

¹/₄ cup plus 1 tablespoon extra-virgin olive oil

1 chile, such as jalapeño or serrano, thinly sliced*

1 onion, finely diced (about 1 cup)

4 garlic cloves, sliced, or more if you like

2 tablespoons capers, rinsed and patted dry

¹/₄ cup white or rosé wine or lager beer

¹/₄ cup sliced pitted green olives, such as picholine
or Manzanilla

6 plum tomatoes, cored and cut into ¹/₂-inch pieces

4 bay leaves

1 teaspoon dried oregano

**Cooked rice**

**Corn tortillas**

**Cilantro leaves**

* Make this as spicy as you like. I prefer to make it fiery
by including a couple fruity-flavored habanero chiles
along with the jalapeño.

Season the fish with salt and let it rest for
15 minutes.

Heat ¹/₄ cup of the oil in a large sauté pan over
medium-high heat. Add the chile, onion, garlic, and
capers and cook until the onion is translucent and
the garlic is nutty in aroma, 3 to 5 minutes.

Add the wine, olives, tomatoes, bay leaves, oregano,
and a good pinch of salt. Reduce the heat to medium
and simmer for about 10 minutes, until it has
a chunky, sauce-like consistency. Taste and adjust
the seasoning as needed. Reserve.

Heat the remaining 1 tablespoon oil in a shallow,
wide pan big enough to hold the fish over medium-
high heat. Cook the fish on one side until it begins
to color lightly and is cooked about 60 percent of
the way through as visible on the side of the fillets,
about 3 minutes. Flip the fish and pour the tomato
sauce over the top. Reduce the heat to low and
simmer to cook the fish through completely and
allow the flavors to meld, 5 to 10 minutes (depending
on the thickness of the fish). Remove the bay
leaves and discard. Serve with rice, tortillas, and
a scattering of cilantro leaves over the top.

# Weakfish Couvillion

**SERVES 6 TO 8**

Couvillion typically refers to a thick, tomato-based seafood stew from Louisiana. It is a Cajun or Creole version of the French court bouillon, which is more of a seasoned stock used for poaching seafood.

In Cajun country, the addition of the tomato roux makes this a hard recipe not to fall in love with. Steeping the fish in the sauce makes mealtime a breeze.

Isaac Toups, the James Beard Award-winning chef behind the modern Cajun eatery Toups' Meatery, taught me to make this dish with speckled trout, and it's one of my all-time favorite ways to eat any type of fish fillet. This dish employs two techniques that I love. First, the brick roux, which is luscious with caramelized tomato flavor. Second, the steeping method for cooking the fish, which is how I poach chicken, shrimp, and fish fillets, so they *slowly* cook. The result is moist and tender deliciousness. Simply the best.

*Andrew*

6 tablespoons butter

1/2 cup all-purpose flour

1/4 cup tomato paste

3 cups red cherry tomatoes

1 yellow onion, minced (about 1 cup)

1 red bell pepper, seeded and minced

2 celery stalks, minced (about 1 cup)

3 bay leaves

Salt

4 garlic cloves, grated on a Microplane or minced

1 1/2 tablespoons thyme leaves

2 teaspoons smoked sweet paprika

1 teaspoon red chile flakes

1/2 cup white wine

2 tablespoons Worcestershire sauce, or more to taste

6 cups Basic Fish Stock (page 85) or Andrew or Barton's Rich Fish Stock (page 86 or 87)

Freshly ground white pepper

2 to 3 pounds weakfish fillet, skin off, cut into 4- to 5-ounce pieces

1 bunch scallions (about 8 pieces), sliced

Cooked long-grain rice, for serving

Combine 3 tablespoons of the butter and the flour in a dutch oven. Set over medium heat and cook, stirring, until a golden-brown roux is formed, about 5 minutes. Stir in the tomato paste and cook, stirring, until it begins to caramelize, about 5 minutes. Add the cherry tomatoes and lightly crush them with a wooden spoon, spreading the mixture across the bottom of the pot. Cook, stirring occasionally, until the mixture begins to stick to the bottom of the pot, about 10 minutes.

Add the onion, bell pepper, celery, and bay leaves. Season with salt and cook for 4, minutes, until the vegetables have a shine to them. Sir in the garlic, thyme, paprika, and chile flakes and stir.

Immediately add the wine and Worcestershire sauce and stir well. Add the stock, in thirds, whisking to fully incorporate the liquid before adding more. Bring to a simmer, then reduce the heat to low and simmer uncovered for 45 minutes. Taste and adjust the seasoning with salt and white pepper. Keep tasting and simmering until the liquid is thick enough to coat a spoon.

Add the fish, making sure all the pieces are submerged in the liquid. Return the liquid to a simmer and cover. Cook for 30 seconds, then turn off the heat and let it rest for 15 minutes to cook the fish through.

Garnish with the scallions and serve with rice.

# 4.11
# Shellfish and Cephalopods

# Chilled Shrimp and Celery Salad

**SERVES 4**

Celery is an underappreciated ingredient. Sure, it gets simmered into soups and stocks or dipped into ranch dressing on a veggie platter, but it can be so much more than that. This salad puts it front and center, its cool flavor and crisp texture accentuated by the sweetness of apple. Slice the shrimp as thin as possible in little curls so they can integrate well into the salad.

*[signature]*

I love to briefly smoke the shrimp for this salad. I use a smoking gun, a tool for easily adding just a whiff of smoke flavor and aroma. Place the shrimp in a bowl, use a smoking gun to add smoke. Five minutes is all you need.

8 ounces poached or smoked shrimp (or scallops), shell off

¼ cup extra-virgin olive oil

Juice of 1 lemon (2 to 3 tablespoons)

1 tablespoon dijon mustard

Salt

Freshly cracked Black Pepper–Fennel Blend (page 53) or black pepper

1 celery head, sliced on a slight bias as thinly as possible (about 4 cups), tender leaves reserved

½ cup dill fronds

1 small apple, cored and thinly sliced

Slice the shrimp lengthwise as thinly as you can, perhaps 3 or 4 slices each, and reserve.

In a large bowl, whisk together the oil, lemon juice, and mustard and season with salt and pepper-fennel blend. Add the celery, dill, and apple and toss to coat in the dressing. Place the salad on serving dishes and top with the shrimp. Garnish with the reserved celery leaves and more pepper-fennel blend as desired.

# Surimi Carpaccio with Aioli, Pecans, Radish, and Tarragon

SERVES 4

This is not the imitation crab of salad bars in days gone by. Surimi, made from Alaska pollock, can be fantastic in quality and flavor, and nowadays there's no reason to shun it. Don't think of it as imitation crab trying to be something it's not. Rather, here it's presented for what it is: deliciously sweet (like crab) with a toothsome bite, paired with mustard-spiked aioli and cool, svelte tarragon. Bitter endive and crunchy pecans round it out for an elegant, easy plate.

**1 pound surimi sticks**

**3/4 cup Aioli (page 96)**

**1 tablespoon dijon mustard**

**Zest and juice of 1 lemon (2 to 3 tablespoons)**

**3 to 4 radishes, cut into very thin matchsticks**

**1/4 cup pecan pieces, toasted**

**2 tablespoons chopped tarragon**

**Red chile flakes, such as Aleppo or Urfa**

**1 to 2 Belgian endive heads***

*If you can find it, a mix of red and white endive would be beautiful.

Slice the surimi sticks as thin as you can on an extreme bias.

In a small bowl, combine the aioli, mustard, and lemon zest and spread it evenly on the bottom of a large platter or divided among plates if serving individually. Overlay the surimi slices in a nice pattern. Scatter the radishes, pecans, tarragon, and some chile flakes over the top. Drizzle with lemon juice. Cut the very base of the head of the endive to release the leaves and continue to cut as you get deeper into the head. Place the endive in a bowl alongside the surimi. To serve, scoop the carpaccio onto the endive leaves.

# Boiled Octopus

## SERVES 4

This is the base recipe from which other octopus recipes begin. Once completed, the octopus is entirely ready to eat and delicious just as it is. Toss with a scant bit of sherry vinegar and olive oil and you have a wonderful appetizer.

Make sure to leave the colorful and flavorful purple skin as intact as possible. To achieve this, it's best to let the octopus cool completely in the cooking liquid before handling.

There are many traditional/regional methods for tenderizing octopus. Each is defended by its practitioners as being as sacred as Grandma's honor, a relevant metaphor, as these colloquial techniques are often passed from generation to generation, venerated as a "only-we-know-the-secrets-of-the-universe" truism. From a lashing against the rocks (Greek), to rubbing with radishes (Japanese), to plunging thrice into boiling water (Spanish), these old ways are built upon a grain of truth. The method here invariably yields great results. If it doesn't, blame Bart's grandma, for she never once cooked an octopus.

One 3- to 4-pound octopus, cleaned
Salt
4 bay leaves
2 cups red wine, a fruity style like a grenache
2 rosemary or thyme sprigs

Raw octopus is almost exclusively sold frozen and precleaned and often requires a full day to thaw, so plan ahead. Frozen cooked octopus tentacles can be terrific and save time.

Rinse the octopus well and season generously with salt.

Place the octopus, bay leaves, wine, and rosemary in a large pot. Add enough cold water to cover the octopus and bring to a simmer over medium-high heat. Skim away any foam that rises to the surface. Weigh down the octopus with a plate or two. Add more water to cover if necessary. Cover the pot with a well-fitting lid and return to a simmer. Lower the heat to medium-low and cook for about 45 minutes. Check for tenderness with the tip of a knife in the thickest part of the tentacle. Once it's tender enough to pierce with a knife, remove from the heat and let it cool in the liquid.

To serve, remove the octopus from the liquid and pat dry. Slice and serve as is, or continue with additional preparations.

# Chile-Maple Glazed Octopus

**SERVES 4**

Cooked octopus tentacles are available frozen and are usually a great product. This glaze, a wonderful combo of sweet-salty-spicy, is made for the grill, as it reduces and chars on the outside surface, lending bitterness to counteract the sweet and providing a nice textural contrast.

*[signature]*

¼ cup extra-virgin olive oil

1 tablespoon fennel seeds

1 tablespoon smoked sweet paprika

2 teaspoons onion powder

1 teaspoon garlic powder

½ teaspoon red chile flakes, such as Aleppo or gochugaru

Freshly cracked Black Pepper–Fennel Blend (page 53) or black pepper

½ cup maple syrup

¼ cup lemon juice (about 2 lemons)

¼ cup red wine vinegar

Salt

1¼ pounds octopus tentacles, cooked (page 332)*

1 cup picked soft herb leaves, such as mint, cilantro, or chives

Lemon wedges

*You can also use cooked octopus purchased from the store.

You can always add more chile flakes, so go easy with the initial measure here. Or sprinkle extra chile flakes on once cooked.

Combine the oil, fennel seeds, paprika, onion powder, garlic powder, chile flakes, and pepper-fennel blend to taste in a sauté pan and heat over medium-high heat for 30 seconds. Reduce the heat to low, add the maple syrup, lemon juice, and vinegar, and season with salt. Slowly reduce by one-third (to about ⅔ cup total). Cool to room temperature.

Place the tentacles in a large bowl or zip-top bag with enough glaze to generously coat. Handle the octopus gently to avoid sloughing off the purple skin. Allow to marinate for at least 1 hour or, better, overnight in the refrigerator. Remove from the marinade and grill or broil over/under high heat, as close to the flame as possible. As it sears and warms through, baste with the remaining marinade.

Serve with tufts of herbs and lemon wedges.

From left to right: Pulpo a la Gallega (Spanish-Style Ocotpus) (page 336),
Boiled Octopus (page 332), and Chile-Maple Glazed Octopus (page 333)

# Pulpo a la Gallega
# (Spanish-Style Octopus)

**SERVES 4**

Pulpo a la gallega is a simple and traditional dish from the north of Spain in which cooked octopus is dressed with paprika and served over boiled potatoes. This version is a little untraditional in that I sear the octopus and add an ajo y perejil (garlic and parsley sauce) with the paprika, combining elements of my favorite Spanish flavors. I serve this dish at room temperature.

The octopus is already cooked. You're not trying to cook it again— just searing to give it color and textural contrast.

Look for precooked frozen tentacles to save time, though you can skip this step and serve as is.

Salt
1 pound new potatoes, skin on, boiled in heavily salted water until knife tender
1¼ pounds octopus tentacles, cooked (page 352)
½ cup extra-virgin olive oil
4 garlic cloves, grated on a Microplane or minced
1½ teaspoons smoked sweet paprika
1 teaspoon red chile flakes, such as Espelette, Aleppo, or Urfa
¼ cup chopped parsley
1 tablespoon sherry vinegar
Freshly cracked Black Pepper–Fennel Blend (page 53) or black pepper

Boil the potatoes in heavily salted water until knife tender. Drain and reserve.

Preheat a grill with a hot fire. (Alternatively, you can use the broiler.) Cut the octopus into large pieces. Place the octopus in a large bowl and toss with 2 tablespoons of the oil. Grill or broil, turning periodically, to lightly char all over. Remove from the heat and reserve.

Heat the remaining 6 tablespoons oil in a small saucepan over medium heat. Add the garlic and cook until it barely begins to brown and smells nutty, about 4 minutes. Turn off the heat. Add the paprika and chile flakes and stir to combine. Add the parsley and vinegar and season with salt.

Slice the potatoes into ¼-inch rounds and lay them on a platter or individual plates. Top with the octopus, drizzle with the sauce, and finish with a few cracks of pepper-fennel blend. Serve at room temperature.

# Shrimp Toast

**SERVES 6 TO 8 AS AN APPETIZER**

I make this all the time for friends and family. According to my parents, shrimp toast was my introduction to Chinese food. It was the first thing I ate when they took me to my first Chinese restaurant in 1963, when I was two. The contrast of crispy and soft is what may have sold me then, but it for sure sells me on this dish now.

These days, I like serving shrimp toast with good Chinese soy sauce, black vinegar, chile crisp, sweet Thai chile sauce, and Chinese hot mustard and letting guests do their own thing. It's a choose-your-own-adventure way to enjoy one of my favorite snacks or first courses, although shrimp toast and a big salad with a soy, lemon, and peanut dressing is a superb dinner any day of the week.

6 to 8 slices supermarket white bread

1 pound wild-caught brown shrimp or high-quality farmed shrimp, peeled and deveined, chopped coarsely

4 ounces skinless fresh pork belly, chopped*

1 egg white

2 garlic cloves, grated on a Microplane or minced

3-inch knob fresh ginger, grated on a Microplane or minced (about 1 tablespoon)

1 teaspoon toasted sesame oil

2 teaspoons soy sauce

4 scallions, thinly sliced

2 teaspoons cornstarch

1/2 teaspoon salt

Pinch or two ground white pepper

4 cups peanut oil

1/3 cup sesame seeds

* I use side pork too, which is often available in conventional supermarkets.

Preheat the oven to 225°F.

Place the bread on a baking sheet and bake for 15 to 20 minutes. This will dry the bread, help to prevent oil absorption, and firm it up to make spreading your shrimp mixture easier.

Meanwhile, combine the shrimp, pork, egg white, garlic, ginger, sesame oil, soy sauce, three-quarters of the scallions, the cornstarch, salt, and white pepper in a food processor and pulse, scraping down the sides as necessary, until a paste forms.

Spread about 1/4 cup shrimp paste on the top of each piece of bread from edge to edge, maybe a smidge more, enough to reach a height of about 1/4 inch in the middle of the bread. Cut the bread into quarters, either straight across or diagonally.

Heat the peanut oil in a wok or heavy-bottom pot to 375°F.

Sprinkle the toast generously with sesame seeds. Place 6 to 8 quarters of shrimp toast into the oil, shrimp-side down. They will float and begin bubbling immediately. Cook for a minute or two, then turn them over and cook for another minute, or until they are golden brown and cooked through. Remove the toasts to paper towels to drain.

Garnish with the remaining scallions and serve.

# Crab and Tomato Salad with Cilantro and Sumac Vinaigrette

**SERVES 4**

This salad depends on two things: quality crab and perfect tomatoes. Any type of crab will do, so pick whatever inspires with quality, be it frozen king or snow crab legs, fresh Dungeness or blue. The sweet-salty crab combines with creamy avocado for a decadent texture. Sumac is an herb used primarily in Mediterranean cuisine, though sumac plants grow all over. (But be wary of harvesting your own, as there is a poisonous variety.) It has a brilliant ruddy red color with a piercing lemony tang. This dish is a great heavy appetizer or light entree and sings of summer.

8 ounces crab meat, picked through for cartilage

2 ripe avocados, cut into ½-inch chunks

1 red onion, very thinly sliced (about 1 cup)

1 jalapeño or serrano chile, very thinly sliced

2 tablespoons chopped cilantro

1 recipe Sumac Vinaigrette (recipe follows)

Salt

1½ pounds heirloom tomatoes, cored and cut into thick slices

In a medium bowl, combine the crabmeat, avocados, red onion, chile, and cilantro. Toss with half of the vinaigrette and a pinch of salt. Gently toss to combine.

Arrange the tomatoes on a plate, drizzle with a few tablespoons of vinaigrette, and season with salt. Arrange the crab mixture over the top and drizzle with the remaining vinaigrette.

## Sumac Vinaigrette

**MAKES ¾ CUP**

This vinaigrette makes for an awesome sauce drizzled over roasted or grilled seafood of any kind.

¼ cup lime juice (about 2 limes)

½ cup extra-virgin olive oil

1 tablespoon ground sumac

1 teaspoon dijon mustard

1 teaspoon onion powder

1 teaspoon garlic powder

Freshly cracked Black Pepper–Fennel Blend (page 53) or black pepper to taste

Salt to taste

In a small bowl, whisk together all the ingredients. The vinaigrette will keep in an airtight container in the refrigerator for up to 1 week.

# Thai-Inspired Grilled Squid Salad

**SERVES 4**

Grilled seafood salads are such a ubiquitous part of global seafood cookery, and here in America, it's rare that we bump into them. I see them in the form of bad room service Caesar salad with a shrimp add-on for $18. Yikes! I think this elegant salad comes together quickly and is inexpensive to make. It banks on the complexity of Thai cuisine flavor profiles for its rampant popularity: sour, salty, bitter, sweet, and spicy. It also features two ingredients that you should have in your pantry: palm sugar, which is my favorite sweetener for many savory dishes (and its glycemic index is lower than other sugars), and toasted rice powder, which gives many room temperature and cold Southeast Asian dishes their unique aroma, flavor, and texture.

*Andrew*

1¼ pounds squid, cut into ¼-inch rings, tentacle clusters cut in half

2 tablespoons vegetable oil

Salt

1 serrano chile or 2 Thai bird chiles, minced

2 garlic cloves, grated on a Microplane or minced

2-inch knob fresh ginger, minced (2 teaspoons)

2 tablespoons palm sugar or brown sugar, or more to taste

¼ cup fish sauce

Juice of 2 limes (about ¼ cup)

1 red onion, thinly sliced (about 1 cup)

4 Roma tomatoes, seeded and trimmed, cut into thin strips

3 mint sprigs, leaves picked (⅓ cup)

4 cilantro sprigs, leaves picked (⅓ cup)

Handful of Thai basil leaves, torn

1½ cups sliced European cucumber (about ½ large cucumber)

1 tablespoon toasted rice powder

1 head butter lettuce, chopped, 4 whole outer large leaves reserved

4 scallions, chopped

Let the squid rest for a few minutes to come to room temperature.

Set up a natural hardwood charcoal fire with a grill surface right over the coals. The idea here is that you need a high coal bed right under the grill to get any char on the squid without overcooking because they are done really quickly. I also use a mesh grate so the squid doesn't fall into the fire. Brush the squid with the oil, season with salt, and grill for just a minute or 2. If you don't have a passion for outdoor cooking or access to a grill, you can quickly sear the squid in batches in a large pan preheated over very high heat.

In a small bowl, combine the chile, garlic, ginger, palm sugar, fish sauce, and lime juice to make a dressing. Reserve.

In a large bowl, combine the onion, tomatoes, mint, cilantro, basil, cucumber, and toasted rice powder.

Lay a large lettuce leaf on each of 4 plates.

Thinly slice the squid, quarter the tentacles, and toss with the dressing.

Combine the chopped lettuce and the vegetable and squid mixtures. Immediately divide the salad onto the lettuce leaves, garnish with the scallions, and serve.

# Lobster Waldorf Salad

SERVES 4

This borrows from the classic chicken Waldorf salad of the famed Waldorf Astoria hotel in New York City. The creamy mix, made rich with aioli, features a perfect trio of tarragon, grapes, and almonds, a slight change from the original recipe, which features walnuts.

*[signature]*

Though I am quite the purist when it comes to lobster rolls (two ingredients: lobster and butter or lobster and mayo), I do like using this salad as a nontraditional take on the classic shore-side dish. You can make this into a roll by putting it in a top-split buttered and toasted hot dog bun.

½ cup Aioli (page 96) or mayonnaise

Juice of 1 lemon (2 to 3 tablespoons), or more to taste

2 tablespoons chopped tarragon

Freshly cracked Black Pepper–Fennel Blend (page 53) or black pepper

1 pound lobster meat (4 cooked 1¼-pound lobsters, see page 371, shelled), meat cut into ½- to ¾-inch pieces

1 cup quartered red grapes (about 20 grapes)

½ cup slivered almonds, toasted

Salt

Bibb or butter lettuce or butter-toasted hot dog buns

In a large bowl, whisk together the aioli, lemon juice, and tarragon and season with pepper-fennel blend. Add the lobster, grapes, and almonds and gently stir to combine. Adjust the seasoning with salt and/or lemon juice. Serve over lettuce or in buns.

# Seared Squid with Mint, Tomatoes, and Radish

**SERVES 4**

Fresh squid, with its beautiful purplish skin intact, takes on a seriously sensual tone when seared. This helps to develop a deep and savory flavor that will be an epiphany to those who have only experienced squid as marinara-drenched, breaded, and fried rings. This preparation is meant to be enjoyed at room temperature. So don't stress about putting it all together à la minute. In fact, if left to marinate in the vinaigrette for at least 15 minutes, it only improves in flavor and texture.

1¼ pounds whole squid, cleaned, skin left intact if present*

1½ pounds heirloom tomatoes, cored and sliced

Salt

½ cup extra-virgin olive oil

1 shallot, diced (about 3 tablespoons)

2 tablespoons sherry vinegar

1 tablespoon dijon mustard

Freshly cracked Black Pepper–Fennel Blend (page 53)
or black pepper

4 to 6 radishes, thinly sliced

1 bunch mint, leaves picked and torn

½ bunch parsley, leaves picked

* Use cut rings and tentacles if whole is unavailable.

Season the squid and tomatoes separately with salt and let both rest for 10 minutes. Drain off any liquid from the tomatoes and reserve.

Heat 2 tablespoons of the oil in a large sauté pan over high heat. When the oil is shimmering, add the squid and sear until deeply colored, no more than 2 minutes per side. Remove the squid from the pan and let it drain, reserving any liquid they exude. Off the stove, add the captured tomato water and the squid liquid to the pan. Stir to remove any bits from the pan.

In a large bowl, whisk the pan liquid with the shallot, vinegar, the remaining 6 tablespoons oil, and the mustard and season with salt and pepper-fennel blend.

Lay the sliced tomatoes on a platter. Slice the squid as thinly as possible, place in a large bowl, and toss with the radishes, mint, parsley, and half of the vinaigrette. Season with salt. Scatter the squid and radish mixture over the tomatoes and drizzle with the remaining vinaigrette.

# Squid with Red Onion, Aioli, Almonds, and Sumac

**SERVES 4 AS AN APPETIZER**

This is my take on a dish I had at La Cave wine bar in Paris, the sister restaurant to the much-lauded Septime. The cooking here is the epitome of modern French cuisine: authentic, intelligent, soulful, and attentive to quality of product and provenance, all of this dished out in an actually-friendly environment. Of all the dishes I had there (and I went back three times over the course of two days), it was the simple combination of poached squid, aioli, and sumac that stuck with me most. I've added some texture here with the red onions and almonds. And I make this more of a salad by adding greens and, of course, some mint leaves.

*Jet*

1/2 cup white wine

1 bay leaf

**Salt**

1 1/4 pounds fresh squid, tubes sliced as thinly as possible, tentacles cut into 4 pieces each with 2 tentacles per piece

1 cup Aioli (page 96)

1 red onion, very thinly sliced (about 1 cup)

1 head frisée, outer green leaves trimmed and cut into 2-inch pieces

1/2 bunch mint, leaves picked

Zest and juice of 1 lemon (2 to 3 tablespoons juice)

2 tablespoons extra-virgin olive oil

1/4 cup chopped almonds, toasted

2 teaspoons sumac

Freshly cracked Black Pepper–Fennel Blend (page 53) or black pepper

Combine 4 cups water, the wine, bay leaf, and a heavy pinch of salt in a large pan and bring to a boil. Place the squid into the liquid, stir, and immediately turn off the heat. Let it rest for 30 seconds, then drain, pat dry, and chill in the refrigerator.

Spoon a couple tablespoons of aioli onto plates. In a large bowl, combine the squid, red onion, frisée, mint, lemon zest and juice, and oil and season with salt. Place the salad over the aioli. Scatter each plate with the almonds, sumac, and pepper-fennel blend.

# Vietnamese-Style Caramelized Shrimp (Tom Rim)

**SERVES 4 TO 6**

I will gladly bang the same drum as I have throughout this book. Great food is all about contrasts. Here it's sticky sweet/salty, crunchy/soft, sweet/bitter, hot/ room temp . . . it's what makes this dish so delicious. The fish sauce caramel vibe is based on a variation of a true Vietnamese caramel sauce/ technique called thit kho. In that recipe you make a caramel, add lots of sliced shallots, black pepper, and fish sauce, and simmer until syrupy and without sugar lumps. It's a Viet master sauce, and I love the flavors.

I typically marinate the shrimp before I leave the house, and when I come back from work, I can get dinner on the table in a snap. This is also a good gateway dish for family members who may not know about the glories of fish sauce. It will convert them from the merely curious to the addicted.

2 pounds fresh shrimp, head-on

4 garlic cloves, very thinly sliced

2 shallots, very thinly sliced (about ¾ cup)

1 teaspoon salt

1 teaspoon ground white pepper

3 tablespoons sugar

1 tablespoon chicken bouillon powder

3 whole hot dried chiles

2 teaspoons dark soy sauce

5 to 6 tablespoons toasted rapeseed oil*

3 tablespoons fish sauce

3 scallions, cut into 2-inch lengths

Cooked rice

* This is also known as caiziyou in Chinese. The toasted flavor makes all the difference. I get mine at themalamarket.com.

Cut off the top ¾ inch of the shrimp heads using scissors (the sharp bony part). Cut off the legs and remove the tail shell by jiggling the tail feathers until they release. Remove the rest of the shell. Using a sharp knife, lightly score the shrimp along the back side and remove the vein.

Place the shrimp in a bowl and add the garlic, shallots, salt, pepper, sugar, bouillon powder, chiles, and soy sauce and toss to combine. Cover and marinate in the refrigerator for at least 8 hours or overnight.

Heat the oil in a wok set over high heat. When the oil is beginning to smoke, swirl it around and add the shrimp, pouring from the bowl into the wok all at once. DO NOT STIR. Use a rubber spatula to get all the contents of the bowl into the wok and spread the shrimp up the sides of the wok. Cook for 4 to 6 minutes, until the sugar is caramelized and thickened. Toss the contents of the wok and cook for another 2 minutes. Add the fish sauce and cook for 2 more minutes. Add the scallions and cook for another minute, tossing well. Serve with plenty of hot rice.

# Shrimp al Ajillo-Style with Almonds and Tarragon

**SERVES 4 TO 6**

Having lived and cooked in Spain as well as running a restaurant for Spanish Chef José Andrés, I have deep appreciation for the traditions of Spanish cuisine. That is why I call this al ajillo-style, in that with the addition of almonds and tarragon it is not traditional. My version is an intensely flavored and textured take, equally good served with a baguette or over pasta. As with all cooking, it's best to have your ingredients set up ahead of time. With this dish in particular, given the cooking time is short and demands your attention, it's best to have everything organized and at hand before you start.

1¼ pounds medium shrimp, peeled and deveined
Salt
1 cup extra-virgin olive oil
8 garlic cloves, sliced
4 dried chiles, such as de arbol or Calabrian
2 bay leaves
½ cup roughly chopped almonds
½ cup white wine
¼ cup brandy
Juice of ½ lemon (1 to 1½ tablespoons)
2 tablespoons chopped tarragon
Crusty bread, for serving

Season the shrimp with salt and let rest for 10 minutes.

Heat the oil in a large sauté pan over high heat. Add the garlic, chiles, bay leaves, and almonds and cook until the garlic begins to color, 2 to 3 minutes. Carefully add the shrimp and toss to coat with the oil. Spread evenly in the pan and cook, without stirring, until the shrimp begin to color, 2 to 3 minutes. Flip the shrimp, remove from the heat, and carefully add the wine and brandy, then return the pan to the heat and bring to a boil. Beware: It will catch on fire. This is okay. Reduce the heat to maintain a simmer and cook for about 2 minutes. Remove the shrimp from the pan onto a serving platter. Return the pan to the heat and reduce the sauce until the alcohol aroma dissipates, about 2 minutes. Remove from the heat, add the lemon juice and tarragon, and season with salt. Serve with plenty of crusty bread.

# Cumin-Butter Grilled Lobster

**SERVES 4**

There is something hauntingly elegant about cumin and lobster, and the simplicity of the pairing is perfect. It's worth it to take your time cooking this dish. Lobster takes up a lot of surface area on your grill, and overcrowding the grill will lead to inconsistent results. One or two at a time is a lot easier to handle. Once all the lobster has been seared, place all of them back on the grill for 30 seconds to warm through.

It is particularly important to get great-quality, fresh cumin. Burlap & Barrel has an incredible mountain cumin that I love. Or try our friends' Skordo brand cumin.

**Salt**
**Four 1¼- to 1½-pound lobsters**
**1 cup (2 sticks) salted butter, at room temperature**
**2 garlic cloves, grated on a Microplane or minced**
**1 tablespoon cumin seeds, toasted then lightly ground or chopped**
**Zest and juice of 1 lemon (2 to 3 tablespoons juice)**
**½ bunch parsley, leaves picked and finely chopped**

Bring a large pot of heavily salted water to a boil over high heat. Place the lobsters headfirst into the water. Cover and cook for 2 minutes. Turn off the heat. Remove the lobsters from the water.

Rip off the claws/knuckles at the body, return them to the water, and let rest uncovered with the heat off for another 3 minutes. Slice the lobsters in half lengthwise by placing the tip of a large knife just below the face and rotating 90 degrees down. Turn the lobster and repeat the cut to separate the two halves. There may be a small amount of shell fragments just behind the face on the inside of the lobster. Remove these as well as any of the green tomalley and discard. Remove the claws and knuckles from the water, shuck the meat, and reserve.

Melt 4 tablespoons of the butter with the garlic and cumin in a small pan over medium heat. Cook for 2 minutes, or until the garlic is softened and no longer smells raw. Remove from the heat and add the lemon zest and juice and the remaining 1½ sticks butter and whisk to incorporate.

Prepare a grill with very high heat.

Toss the claw and knuckle meat with some of the cumin butter.

Slather the cut side of the lobsters with a small amount of the cumin butter. Grill the lobsters, cut-side down, directly over the coals for 1 minute. Flip and add a bit more of the cumin butter, nestling the claw and knuckle meat into the head cavity. Cook until the butter begins to simmer in the shell, about 3 minutes. Remove the lobster to a plate and keep warm. Repeat until all the lobsters are cooked. To serve, drizzle any remaining cumin butter over the plates and scatter with the parsley.

Left to right: Andrew's Crab Cakes (page 354)
and Barton's Crab Cakes (page 355)

# Andrew's Crab Cakes

**SERVES 4**

These are what has commonly been referred to as Baltimore-style crab cakes, which are made with an egg and mayo base that's absorbed by the cracker crumbs to serve as a binder around the lumps of crab. There is no onion, bell pepper, or other ingredients to interfere with the pure joy of exquisite high-quality fresh jumbo lump crabmeat—those are the pieces from the largest pocket of the "shoulder" of the blue crab's largest legs.

I am not a big fan of the term *signature*, but this is one of those dishes that has become one for me. I am so indebted to my friend Judy, who taught it to her daughter Carol, who passed it on to me over three decades ago. If you stick to this list of ingredients and don't skimp on the technique of letting the mixture set and then resting the pucks, crab cake heaven is in your future.

I make a great mayo-mustard sauce to go with these cakes. Combine 1:1 dijon mustard to mayo and season with lemon juice to taste.

1 large egg, beaten
½ cup Hellmann's or Duke's mayonnaise
1 tablespoon dijon mustard
1 tablespoon Worcestershire sauce
½ teaspoon Crystal Hot Sauce
1 pound jumbo lump crabmeat, picked over for any shell pieces
20 saltine crackers, finely crushed
¼ cup canola oil
Lemon wedges

In a small bowl, whisk the egg, mayonnaise, mustard, Worcestershire sauce, and hot sauce until smooth.

Place the crabmeat in a medium bowl and add the cracker crumbs. Gently fold in the mayonnaise mixture. Try not to break any of those beautiful lumps as you work to combine the ingredients. Cover and refrigerate for at least 1 hour but not more than 4 or 5 hours or the crumbs get gummy.

Scoop the crab mixture into eight ⅓-cup mounds and lightly pack each mound into a patty 1 to 1½ inches thick. Refrigerate uncovered for 2 hours.

Heat the oil in a very large skillet over medium-high heat until it shimmers. Add the crab cakes and cook until deep golden on both sides and heated through, 3 to 4 minutes per side. Transfer the crab cakes to plates and serve with lemon wedges and the mustard sauce. If desired, serve with my favorite Coleslaw recipe on page 296, but this dish works well with your favorite slaw too.

# Barton's Crab Cakes

SERVES 4

I keep my crab cakes very simple. As a child of the Chesapeake region, I've had every type of crab cake you can imagine. Many are adulterated with unnecessary ingredients. Were they tasty? Of course. But simplicity really allows the crab to shine. I prefer brioche breadcrumbs for the sweetness they impart and for how they virtually melt into the mixture. Panko breadcrumbs work just fine too. A flattering sauce made of sour cream and mustard adds a point of visual interest as well as a bit of piquant punctuation.

*Bart*

1 pound jumbo lump crabmeat, picked over for any shell pieces

½ cup brioche breadcrumbs or panko

½ cup mayonnaise

Juice of 1½ lemons (about 3 tablespoons)

1 tablespoon Old Bay Seasoning

Dash of Tabasco or other hot sauce

3 tablespoons butter

½ cup sour cream

¼ cup whole grain mustard

Salt

In a large bowl, gently mix the crab with the breadcrumbs and let it rest for 10 minutes to allow the breadcrumbs to absorb any liquid from the crab.

In a separate bowl, combine the mayonnaise, 2 tablespoons of the lemon juice, the Old Bay, and hot sauce. Add to the crab and very gently mix to combine, trying not to break up the pieces of crab. Place the mixture in the refrigerator and let it rest for at least 1 hour and up to overnight.

Form the mixture into 4 cakes.

Melt 2 tablespoons of the butter in a wide nonstick sauté pan over medium-high heat. When the butter begins to foam, place the cakes in the pan and cook until golden brown on the bottom, 4 to 6 minutes. Add the remaining 1 tablespoon butter, flip the cakes, and cook them for another 2 to 3 minutes.

In a small bowl, whisk together the remaining 1 tablespoon lemon juice, the sour cream, mustard, and a pinch of salt.

Serve with a swoosh of the sauce and the crab cake over the top. This is especially good served with spicy greens such as arugula or an Asian mix.

# Salt and Pepper Soft-Shell Crab

**SERVES 4**

These crabs are addictive. Be careful. I also make the same dish with shrimp-just butterfly and devein the shrimp, cutting through the shell but otherwise leaving it intact and attached.

I serve these with the cucumber salad below and plenty of rice. If you like, include the Bangalore-Style Roadside Dipping Sauce for Fried Seafood (page 358) as well. That sauce is superb for fried anything, if I am being honest.

For years I was very catholic about only sautéing soft crabs, but over the years I have found that frying seals in their flavors so well that they are almost crabbier than their sautéed cousins.

8 soft-shell crabs

4 cups peanut oil

1 cup cornstarch

3 egg whites

12 scallions, cut into 2-inch lengths

5 dried red chiles

1 tablespoon coarse-grind sea salt

1 teaspoon ground white pepper

2 tablespoons sugar

White rice

Cucumber Salad (recipe follows)

Bangalore-Style Roadside Dipping Sauce for Fried Seafood (recipe follows), optional

Using sharp kitchen scissors to quickly dispatch the crabs, cut just behind the eyes and mouth of the crabs to remove the face. Gently flip up the shell on both sides and cut away the lungs. Peel back and cut away the apron, the small flap on the belly side of the crabs. Place the crabs on a plate lined with paper towels. Refrigerate for a few hours to dry them.

In a large wok, heat the oil over high heat to 375°F.

Spread the cornstarch in a shallow bowl. In a large bowl, whip the egg whites well until foamy. Working in batches, dip the crabs in the egg whites, then dredge them in the cornstarch. Shake them free of cornstarch and fry until crisp. Remove from the oil to paper towels to drain.

Carefully pour out most of the oil, leaving about 2 tablespoons in the wok. When smoking, add the scallions and chiles. Toss quickly to mix, then return the crab to the wok. Toss to coat, adding the sea salt, pepper, and sugar by sprinkling as you rotate the food across the wok surface. Don't dump the seasoning!

Serve with white rice and cucumber salad, with dipping sauce if you like.

# Cucumber Salad

2 European cucumbers, halved and seeds removed

1 teaspoon salt

1 tablespoon toasted sesame oil

2 tablespoons rice vinegar

1 tablespoon sugar

1 tablespoon toban djan (fermented chile bean paste)

1 Fresno chile, sliced into thin rings

3 tablespoons peanut oil

1 teaspoon Sichuan peppercorns, crushed

3 dried red chiles (arbol chiles work well)

Slice the cucumbers into ⅓-inch-wide pieces. Place in a colander and toss with the salt. Allow to drain in the colander for 20 minutes. Remove the cucumbers to paper towels.

In a small bowl, combine the sesame oil, vinegar, sugar, toban djan, and Fresno chile and reserve.

Preheat a wok over medium-high heat. Add the peanut oil, Sichuan peppercorns, and dried chiles and cook just for 15 to 30 seconds, until fragrant. Add the cucumbers and cook, tossing, for 15 to 20 seconds max, and then spill the entire contents of the wok into a large shallow bowl. Pour the liquid seasonings over the cucumbers and cool in the refrigerator for 30 minutes before serving.

# Bangalore-Style Roadside Dipping Sauce for Fried Seafood

MAKES ABOUT 1 CUP

About twenty years ago, I cooked a private event for a hundred or so diners to raise money for a charity in New York City. One of my courses was a fried seafood appetizer, and I served a bright lemon sauce for dipping along with family-style platters of the seafood. After the meal, an Indian gentleman approached me, and after a short conversation, he told me he worked in the seafood export business and that we had friends in common in Southern India and Maryland. He gave me a version of this recipe on a card, declaring it to be the best dipping sauce for fried seafood. Well, I tried it and he was more than right. In fact, fried fingers of fish, pork, chicken, venison, just about anything dipped into this sauce is a game changer.

½ cup thinly sliced shallots (about 2 large shallots)

2 hot chiles, thinly sliced, about ¼ cup (I like to use serrano chiles)

⅓ cup naturally brewed soy sauce

¼ cup Chicken Stock (page 90)

3 tablespoons Chinese rice wine or Japanese sake, optional

3 tablespoons sugar

1 tablespoon grated fresh ginger

3 garlic cloves, thinly sliced

In a small bowl, whisk all the ingredients to combine and serve. This recipe goes pretty flat after a day. I store in an airtight container in the refrigerator, and if there's any left after about 24 hours, I turn it into a salad dressing or a marinade for chicken.

# Shrimp and Butternut Squash Linguine with Raisins, Walnuts, and Parsley

**SERVES 4**

We are fans of the sweet-sour combination, and how the lemon and raisins (also the squash) carry the nuttiness of the walnuts and brininess of the shrimp. Preparing the squash with a peeler allows the very thin strips to cook quickly and integrate into the architecture of the pasta. Cubed squash would simply sit on top. As confetti-like strips, it blends into the dish, its flavor and texture coupled with the other ingredients.

**Salt**

**8 ounces linguine**

**¼ cup extra-virgin olive oil**

**1 red onion, thinly sliced (about 1 cup)**

**4 garlic cloves, sliced**

**¼ cup walnuts, chopped**

**2 tablespoons raisins**

**12 ounces shrimp, peeled and deveined, sliced in half lengthwise**

**Zest and juice of 1 lemon (2 to 3 tablespoons juice)**

**½ small butternut squash, cut into ribbons using a peeler or on a spiralizer, loosely packed (about 4 cups)**

**¼ cup chopped parsley**

Bring a pot of well-salted water to a boil. Add the linguine and cook to al dente according to the package instructions. Drain and reserve 1 cup of the pasta water.

While the pasta cooks, in a large sauté pan, heat the oil over medium heat until it shimmers. Add the onion, garlic, walnuts, and raisins and cook until aromatic and just softened, about 3 minutes. Add the shrimp, lemon zest, and butternut squash and cook, tossing, for about 2 minutes more. Add the cooked pasta and ½ cup of the reserved cooking water and bring to a simmer. Add more pasta water if needed so the sauce is loose enough to coat the pasta with a slight pool at the bottom of the pan. Add the lemon juice and parsley and toss well to combine. Season with salt as needed.

# Pasta with Crab, Shrimp, and Lobster Sauce

**SERVES 4**

Slice me thin and call me prosciutto, but seafood sauce is always a killer formula for me. I love the rich briny intensity of this dish's sauce, and the pasta can be scaled up or down by weight depending on how soigné you want to be. Use a lot of pasta and extend some expensive seafood a long way. Use less pasta to make the shellfish the star and this is a Saturday night splurge for the home cook.

A word about the tarragon: Barton and I love fennel and all the flavors in that realm. Well, tarragon is the herb that carries that same flavor and is indispensable here unless you don't like that flavor at all (sad). Feel free to substitute fresh basil or oregano.

8 ounces U-15 wild-caught brown shrimp or high-quality farm-raised shrimp, peeled and deveined

Salt

8 ounces pasta*

3 tablespoons butter

1 garlic clove, thinly sliced

3 tablespoons minced tarragon

Lobster Sauce (recipe follows)

8 ounces jumbo lump crabmeat, picked over for any shell pieces

Freshly cracked black pepper

Zest and juice of 1 lemon (2 to 3 tablespoons juice)

2 tablespoons thinly sliced chives

*I love serving this with medium-sized shells, conchiglie, mezzi rigatoni, nested fettuccine, bigoli, bucatini, or calamarata.

Slice the shrimp in half lengthwise and set aside.

Bring a large pot of heavily salted water to a boil. Add the pasta and cook until al dente according to the package directions. Drain and reserve ⅓ cup of the starchy pasta water.

While the pasta is cooking, melt the butter in a large sauté pan over medium heat. When the butter is foaming, add the garlic, tarragon, and shrimp and cook until the shrimp are just coiling up, a sign that they are almost done.

Add about 3 cups of the Lobster Sauce and the crabmeat to the pan with the shrimp and season with pepper. Add the pasta, lemon zest, and lemon juice to the pan and toss well. Cook for another 2 to 3 minutes, adding some of the pasta water as needed to form a rich, coating sauce.

Divide the pasta into bowls and garnish with the chives.

# Lobster Sauce

**MAKES ABOUT 4¹/₂ CUPS**

1 large lobster (1¹/₂ to 2 pounds)

¹/₄ cup extra-virgin olive oil

1 dried arbol chile, stem removed

Bouquet garni of 3 sprigs each fresh oregano, basil, and parsley

1 shallot, minced (about 3 tablespoons)

4 garlic cloves, sliced

1 cup white wine

2 cups Andrew's or Barton's Shellfish Stock (page 88 or 89)

¹/₄ cup long-grain rice

One 24-ounce can San Marzano tomatoes, pureed with the juice

2 tablespoons tomato paste

1¹/₂ cups heavy cream

Cut the lobster into pieces, including the head and body, crack the claws, and reserve.

Heat the oil in a large wide pot over medium heat. When the oil is shimmering, add the chile, bouquet garni, shallot, and garlic. Cook for 1 minute, then add the wine and cook for 2 minutes, or until the alcohol aroma has dissipated. Add the shellfish stock, bring to a simmer, and simmer for 8 minutes. Add the lobster pieces, cover, bring back to a simmer, and cook for 7 minutes.

Pull out the lobster claws and tail pieces. Remove the lobster meat and reserve it in the refrigerator for lobster salad or some other glorious use. I make it my lunch while I am cooking. Return the lobster body without its shell to the pot. Discard the shells.

Add the rice. Cover and simmer for 20 minutes. Add the tomatoes and tomato paste, return to a simmer, and simmer uncovered for 15 minutes. Season with salt, add the cream, and simmer for an additional 10 minutes.

Turn off the heat and let the dish rest for 30 minutes.

Working in batches, pulse/puree in a blender. Strain, pressing down on the solids to extract as much liquid as possible. The sauce will keep in the refrigerator for up to 1 week and in the freezer for several months. It rarely makes it into my freezer; we use it as a sauce for fish, or in soups or simply with more pasta.

# Squid with Angel Hair

**SERVES 4**

I like tender small squid, tubes of
4 to 6 inches, and yes, I love the
tentacles. For squid ink, you can
buy it or use the ink sacs that come
from whole squid if your fishmonger
has them.

This dish is the one that I have
loved to make since my father's
version first graced my lips as a
young man. About thirty-five years
ago, when I went to Sardinia for
the first time and had a version of
it with breadcrumbs, my food life
changed, literally.

I now keep several types and sizes
of breadcrumbs in my freezer, and I
almost always serve pastas and salads
with sturdy seasoned breadcrumbs
because, well, once you try this it
will change your life too.

*Andrew*

To clean fresh, whole squid, remove
the skin, then the interior "pen"
(the long quill-shaped clear plastic-
looking bone on the inside of the
tubes). Remove the mouth and pull
the tentacle cluster from the tube,
discarding the viscera. Rinse and pat
dry. Slice the tubes into 1/4-inch rings
and cut the tentacle clusters in half.

1 cup vegetable oil

1/4 cup brined capers, patted dry and at room temperature

6 tablespoons butter

Salt

4 garlic cloves, grated on a Microplane or minced

Several pinches of red chile flakes

2 high-quality anchovy fillets, mashed with a fork

1 cup Andrew's or Barton's Rich Fish Stock (page 86 or 87)

2 teaspoons squid ink

8 ounces angel hair pasta

1 1/4 pounds Rhode Island or California squid, cut into 1/4-inch rings, tentacle cluster cut in half

Zest and juice of 1 lemon (2 to 3 tablespoons juice)

1/4 cup extra-virgin olive oil

1/4 cup coarsely chopped parsley

1 cup or more breadcrumbs (recipe follows)

1/4 cup thinly sliced chives (1/2 bunch)

In a small pot over medium heat, heat the vegetable oil to 350°F. Add the capers and fry for 3 minutes or so, until crispy. Remove with a slotted spoon to drain the oil and transfer to paper towels. Reserve the oil.

Heat the butter in a small pot over medium heat until melted and golden brown, stirring well to make sure you loosen any solids stuck to the bottom of the pan. Reserve.

Bring a large pot of well-salted water to a boil.

Transfer some of the oil you fried the capers into a large sauté pan. Add the garlic and heat over medium heat for 45 seconds or less. Don't let it turn color; you just want to soften it. Stir in the chile flakes, anchovies, and fish stock. Reduce by about a third. Remove from the heat and stir in the squid ink. Transfer the contents of the pan to a bowl.

In a fresh sauté pan, heat 2 to 3 tablespoons of the caper oil over medium heat.

Drop the pasta in the water and stir after 30 seconds. You will only be cooking the pasta in the water for 4 minutes or so, until very al dente. After 2 to 3 minutes of the pasta cooking, add the squid to the preheated sauté pan and sear it hard and fast. Toss quickly and add the brown butter, lemon zest and juice, and the squid ink mixture. Drain the pasta, reserving 1 cup of the pasta water.

By now the squid ink mixture will be simmering. Add the almost-cooked pasta to the pan with the squid ink, olive oil, and parsley. Season lightly with salt. Toss together well.

Continue tossing and cooking for another minute or so, until the pasta is perfectly cooked (it should be tender but maintain a bit of chewiness. It should not get stuck in your teeth!). Add a few tablespoons of pasta water if you need to cook longer or to adjust the consistency of the sauce. You want the sauce to cling to the pasta and squid, but you don't want it pasty or too thick. Plate the pasta into 4 bowls.

Garnish with the breadcrumbs, crispy capers, and chives.

# Breadcrumbs

**MAKES ABOUT 3 CUPS**

$^1/_2$ loaf day-old Italian bread, cut into small pieces (4 to 6 cups worth)
$^1/_2$ cup coarsely chopped parsley ($^1/_4$ bunch)
$^1/_4$ cup extra-virgin olive oil
Zest of 2 lemons
1 large shallot, minced (about $^1/_4$ cup)
2 garlic cloves, grated on a Microplane or minced
Salt

Preheat the oven to 375°F.

In a food processor, combine the bread, parsley, oil, lemon zest, shallot, and garlic in a food processor until medium-sized crumbs form. Spread on a large rimmed baking sheet, season with salt, and bake, stirring occasionally, for 15 to 20 minutes, until golden and crisp. Let cool and store in a clean dry airtight container in the freezer.

# Sea Urchin Pasta

**SERVES 4**

Sea urchins are spiny, round animals, technically echinoderms without internal bone structure. Sea urchin lobes are sweet and from a flavor standpoint remind me of foie gras with just a hint of a coppery finish. Each urchin, when cracked open, has six bright orange lobes of its roe/gonads (the animals are both male and female) hanging on to the interior of its shell.

I love sea urchin pasta, a modern izakaya offering that in Japan is made with fresh but lower-grade urchin. It is not a luxe dish. In our country, if you have a resource for fresh frozen broken urchin lobes, jump on it. All the flavor at a third the price.

I had been making this for years by blending sake and sea urchin with an immersion wand and using thin Japanese wheat noodles. I loved it. Then my friend Kenji López-Alt turned me on to the idea of using crème fraîche in the mix, and I think it provides the extra creaminess and acidity that makes the dish just that much better.

8 ounces fresh sea urchins*
1/3 cup crème fraîche
Zest and juice of 1/2 lemon (about 1 tablespoon juice)
2 tablespoons toasted rapeseed oil**
8 ounces spaghettini
1/2 shallot, minced (about 2 tablespoons)
Red chile flakes

Freshly ground black pepper
1/2 cup sake (get a good one that's as bone dry as you can find)
Lemon zest
2 scallions, green parts only, thinly sliced
Kizami (shredded) nori***
Salt

* I order mine from e-fish.com, yamaseafood.com, or brownetrading.com. If you have access to fresh whole Santa Barbara urchins, you can crack them open yourself to harvest the "tongues" of urchin.

** This is also known as caiziyou in Chinese. The toasted flavor makes all the difference. It is available at themalamarket.com.

*** Available at Asian markets or at thejapanesepantry.com.

Bring a large pot of well-salted water to a boil over high heat.

Puree 6 ounces of the urchins (reserving the rest for garnish) with crème fraîche and lemon juice. Set aside.

Heat the oil in a large sauté pan over medium heat and sweat the shallots for 2 to 3 minutes. Add the chile flakes and pepper and cook for 30 seconds. Add the sake and bring to a simmer. Cook for about 30 seconds, until the alcohol aroma dissipates. Remove from the heat and reserve.

Cook the pasta in boiling water until al dente. Drain, reserving 1 cup of pasta water.

Return the pan of sake to high heat, add the pasta, the sea urchin mixture, and the lemon zest and toss for 1 minute. Add a few tablespoons of the reserved pasta water and cook for 30 seconds. If you need the sauce a tad looser, add a tablespoon or two of pasta water. Season with salt and divide among 4 plates. Garnish with the scallions, the 2 ounces reserved sea urchins, and some kizami nori.

# Lobster with Brown Butter and Zucchini

Zoodles! Zoodles are zucchini that has been cut into long thin strips, linguine shaped, either by hand, a mandoline, or a spiralizer. This culinary trend that's worth making permanent is a great way to incorporate a serious portion of veggies into a meal, adding color and flavor, too. You can bulk it up further by tossing in some cooked pasta.

This recipe has a couple details that need attention to make this simple dish reach its potential. First is to save any liquid that comes from the lobsters while cleaning them. You could also save a cup of the lobster cooking water. The other important step is to NOT salt the zoodles until the very end of the preparation when you will spoon the sauce over the top. Salt draws out moisture, and adding it early will overly wilt the thin zucchini strips. Keep the moisture-and flavor-in the zucchini.

**8 tablespoons butter**
**2 garlic cloves, grated on a Microplane or minced**
**1 shallot, finely diced (about 3 tablespoons)**
**2 zucchinis, cut into noodles (see headnote)**
**1 tablespoon fennel seeds**
**Pinch of ground mace or freshly grated nutmeg**
**1/2 cup white wine**

**1 pound lobster meat (4 cooked 1 1/4-pound lobsters, shelled), meat cut into 1/2- to 3/4-inch pieces, reserve any liquids**
**1/4 cup chopped tarragon**
**Salt**

Heat 1 tablespoon of the butter in a large sauté pan over medium-high heat. Add the garlic and shallot and cook until translucent, about 3 minutes. Add the zucchini noodles and toss to combine. Cook for 1 to 2 minutes, until the zucchini noodles barely begin to soften. Remove the zucchini to a colander set over a bowl to collect the juice. Scrape any bits of garlic and shallot from the pan and add to the zucchini. Cover the colander to keep the zucchini warm.

In the same pan, heat 5 tablespoons of the remaining butter and the fennel seeds over medium-high heat until the butter is nutty-brown and toasty-fragrant and the bubbling/foaming subsides, 3 to 4 minutes. Add the mace and cook for another 15 seconds. Add the wine, bring to a simmer, and cook until the alcohol aroma dissipates. Add the reserved lobster liquid and collected zucchini juice. You should have 1 cup total liquid between them. Add more water if needed to make 1 cup. Bring the combined liquids to a vigorous simmer and reduce slightly, 1 to 2 minutes. Add the lobster meat, the remaining 2 tablespoons butter, cut into pieces, and the tarragon. Swirl to incorporate the butter and emulsify the sauce. Season generously with salt. Arrange the zucchini noodles in piles on a platter or plates and spoon the lobster meat and sauce over the whole plate.

Seafood Paella
(page 368)

# Seafood Paella

**SERVES 6 TO 8**

Paella, the storied dish of eastern Spain, is inherently celebratory. Even if made unceremoniously on a Tuesday night, when the broad, shallow pan is presented, the saffron-tinted steamy rice never fails to impress. The quality (and freshness) of rice matters, but not as much as the deliciousness of the stock used. It's absolutely worth taking the time and expense of making my Rich Fish Stock (page 89), as this provides the foundation for a "wow" result.

A paella pan is not expensive and not only adds to the proper preparation of the dish but provides a handsome serving dish upon the table. (I use my paella pan as a cocktail tray when not employed as a cooking vessel.)

This recipe calls for Arborio rice, the Italian kind for risotto. Other more traditional varieties of rice, such as Valencia or Calasparra, require more liquid. Be mindful of this if swapping one of these in.

6 cups Barton's Rich Fish Stock (page 89)
12 littleneck clams
10 saffron threads
Salt
4 ounces bacon, chopped
1/4 cup extra-virgin olive oil
1 shallot, finely diced (about 3 tablespoons)
1 red bell pepper, seeded and finely diced
3 garlic cloves, very thinly sliced

3 cups Arborio rice
8 ounces squid, cut into small rings
1 cup fresh or frozen green peas
8 ounces shrimp, head on if possible
1 pound meaty white fish, such as Pacific rockfish, cobia, or sturgeon, cut into 1-inch cubes
2 tablespoons chopped chives or parsley
2 lemons, cut into wedges
2 cups Aioli (page 96)

Special equipment: 17-inch paella pan (or large ovenproof sauté pan)

In a stockpot, bring the stock to a simmer over medium-high heat. Add the clams, cover, and cook, shaking the pot occasionally, until they open, 7 to 9 minutes. Remove the clams, discard any that do not open, and reserve. Strain the stock through a fine-mesh strainer and discard any grit. Add the saffron to the liquid. Season with salt. Reserve off the heat.

Preheat the oven to 400°F.

In a 17-inch paella pan, cook the bacon in the oil over medium heat until crisp, about 8 minutes. Add the shallot, bell pepper, and garlic to the pan and sauté until softened, 2 to 3 minutes. Add the rice and squid. Stir to coat and toast for 1 minute.

Add the peas and reserved stock to the rice. Bring to a simmer over medium heat and cook for 10 minutes. Nestle the shrimp and fish pieces into the rice. Place the pan in the oven and cook for 10 to 15 minutes. Remove from the oven and arrange the clams on top of the rice. Cover with aluminum foil and let rest for 10 minutes.

Serve as is, or return the pan to the stovetop over medium heat for about 5 minutes to crisp the bottom layer of rice. Sprinkle with the chives and serve with lemon wedges and aioli.

# Surf and Turf

On one hand it evokes the look of a dish I despise. A steakhouse menu offering that typically involves a luxury item from the sea perched atop an 8-ounce portion of a mushy overpriced piece of grilled beef tenderloin. We all eat that dish pulled apart on the plate, not together on the fork.

On the other hand, I adore oysters cooked in rendered beef or poultry fat. I can't get enough of paella with clams, squid, and Ibérico pork riblets. I long for pasta with clams, oregano, and a spicy sausage. I crave shrimp étouffée studded with smoky, spicy andouille sausage. Add some rockweed (easily collected from along the coast) or a few sheets of dried kelp to the heavily salted water to further accentuate the fresh, tidal aroma.

I think the world of good food is made up of contrasts. Hot and cold, salty and sweet, crunchy and soft, and on and on. The more contrasts, the better the dish. The elements help focus each other. When it comes to surf and turf, the devil is in the details. Sautéed lobster with a sauce made with Calabrian 'nduja sausage is as good as food gets, in my opinion. The two main ingredients must make each other better, and if they don't, abandon ship.

# Lobster Boil New England Shore Dinner

**PER PERSON**

Growing up in D.C., I was a guest (or child of the hosts) at many a crab boil. Such hours-long feasts were fueled by plenty of ice-cold beer to keep the guests patient, slowly picking their way through a pile of Old Bay—caked crabs. More often than not, these crabs were the result of my (and my brother's) labor, hunting docks along the Chesapeake, netting crabs from the pilings. Now that I'm a seasoned resident of New England, I've grown into the various traditions of the lobster boil.

Though crabs and lobster are so different, the same general idea applies: a one-pot meal for many, meant to be eaten slowly and with participation required! This is no "lazy-man's lobster" pre-picked to be consumed quickly. No. You gotta get in there, get your hands dirty, and earn your delicious reward.

Among the most essential steps in this recipe is to present it with flare. Upending a giant pot onto a table thickly lined with newspaper, revealing the heap of steaming delight within, the steam made all the more scene-setting by its contrast to the cool of a New England coastal evening. Perhaps the tide has just shifted and the pine-perfumed air is suddenly seasoned with the salt-fragrant glory of a cool sea breeze rolling in, steam spectral as it dances about the colorful boiled bounty.

*[signature]*

*Ever had sausage boiled with lobster and then dipped in butter? It's as tasty as it sounds.*

**Salt or seawater**
**1 ear corn**
**4 ounces small new potatoes**
**½ red onion cut in wedges, with the stem intact for structure**
**One 4-ounce sausage link (I prefer spicy Italian, but you really can't go wrong)**
**1 lemon, cut in half**
**Several bay leaves for the whole pot**
**1 lobster**
**Drawn butter (it just means melted) or aioli\***

\* I serve both.

In a very large pot, bring a couple gallons of highly salted water to a raging boil. Depending on how many people you are cooking for, you might need to cook in batches. Generally, I'm cooking 4 at a time. I cook mine outside on a turkey fryer propane jet engine.

Add the corn, potatoes, onions, sausage, lemon halves, bay leaves, and rockweed/kelp (if using) and cover. Bring the water back to a full boil.

Add the lobsters headfirst and be sure to nestle them into the water. Cover and cook over high heat according to the cook time chart. When the time is up, turn off the heat and let them rest, covered, for 5 minutes (just as you would for a roast turkey or steak).

To serve, place everything in the middle of a table lined with newspaper and let your guests have at it. Or if you're feeling fancy, divide up and plate everything individually with ramekins of drawn butter and aioli.

## Lobster Cook Time

| Lobster Weight | Time |
|---|---|
| 1 pound | 5 minutes |
| 1¼ pounds | 6 minutes |
| 1½ pounds | 7 to 8 minutes |
| 1¾ pounds | 8 to 9 minutes |

Note: These times are shorter than most recommendations, but they take into account that the lobster will rest, covered, after the heat is turned off.

## Salted Butter with Lobster

Throughout this book we call for unsalted butter universally. Nothing against salted butter, it's just that we like to have control over the seasoning that goes into our meals and prefer to use salt strategically for flavor enhancement, moisture retention, and bridging flavors among ingredients. To do so requires the application of salt at different times throughout the process. So, if the butter, often the first ingredient used in a recipe, brings all the salt, you lose some of the benefits that you can accrue by a more intentional seasoning. Sometimes the seasoning process isn't straight salt, sometimes it's a salty component, such as anchovies or parmesan. These all play into the overall seasoning strategy.

An exception to this is drawn butter, a fancy term for melted butter when served with steamed lobster or clams. When butter is a stand-alone ingredient, salted butter rocks. When salt is added as part of the churning process, there's just something about the flavor that adds a delightful pep and liveliness to the butter that can't be achieved by adding salt to melted unsalted butter. Outside of seafood, the other exception we make is salted butter on toast, always.

Lobster Boil New England
Shore Dinner (page 370)

# Barton's Crawfish Boil

SERVES 4

Hot damn! Ain't nothin' like a steamy,
slow meal, gathering friends and family
for hours to leisurely pick apart and
savor this wonderful Southern delicacy.
There are a few online sources for
crawfish coming out of Southern states
that do a very nice job of delivering
vigorously alive little creatures.
In keeping with tradition, I like my
crawfish to be make-me-sweat sweltering
spicy, so I'll add ten or so jalapeños
to the boil broth along with the
potatoes and sausage. If it's your
thing, make sure not to skimp on the
ice-cold beer to accompany, maybe even
going so far as to pour a can or two
into the boil broth.

*Jet*

To eat crawfish, grab the head with one
hand and the tail with the other hand
and gently twist the tail away from
the body while pulling to separate
the two. Pinch from the bottom of
the underside of the crawfish tail
and pop the tail meat out by simply
pressing up along it and squeezing it.
Don't forget to suck the head!

Why stop at four people? A meal like
this begs for a crowd. The ratio of
ingredients per person makes this
recipe very easy to increase as needed.

Two 4-ounce jars Cajun Seasoning and/or Seafood
Seasoning blend of your choice

2 lemons, halved

1½ pounds red potatoes, cut into quarters

12 to 16 pounds live crawfish (3 to 4 pounds per
person)

1 pound smoked sausage, such as andouille, cooked
or raw

2 red onions, cut into 8 wedges each, leaving the
root intact

4 jalapeño chiles (or more)

4 sweet corn ears, shucked and halved

Spicy Garlic Butter (recipe follows)

Pour 5 to 6 quarts of water into a large stockpot, add
the seasoning and lemons, and bring to a boil. Add the
potatoes and cook for 5 minutes. Add the crawfish,
sausage, onions, chiles, and corn. Bring back to a boil
over high heat, then reduce the heat to maintain
a simmer, cover the pot, and simmer for 5 minutes. Pull
out 2 of the lemons and use them to make the Spicy
Garlic Butter. Turn off the heat and allow to rest in the
cooking liquid for 20 to 30 minutes. Drain off the liquid.
Line the table with several layers of newspaper and
spread out the feast. Serve with Spicy Garlic Butter.

## Spicy Garlic Butter

MAKES ABOUT 3/4 CUP

1½ cup (1½ sticks) butter

10 garlic cloves, grated on a Microplane or minced

1 lemon reserved from Barton's Crawfish Boil

1 tablespoon red chile flakes, such as Urfa,
gochugaru, or Aleppo

In a small pot over, heat the butter with the garlic over
medium heat until aromatic, about 5 minutes. Turn off
the heat and squeeze in the juice of 2 lemon halves
from the Crawfish Boil cooking pot. Add the chile flakes.
Stir until the ingredients are combined. Serve warm.

# Acknowledgments

We are deeply grateful to the many individuals and organizations that have supported and guided us throughout this journey.

With apologies for any omissions, the authors would like to thank:

Jennifer Bushman, who literally made this book happen by sheer force of will, an insane work ethic, and buckets of grit. The Fed by Blue advisory board and cofounders, especially Jill Kauffman Johnson and Katherine Bryar. Multiplier, for their fiscal support. Our broadcasts partners at PBS. Builders Vision, especially Peter Bryant and Laura Rodriguez. Alison Attenborough and her food styling team, Olivia Annacone Cisic, José Andrés, Josh Bider, Rebecca Brooks, Sarahjane Coolahan, Linda Cornish and Seafood Nutrition Partnership, Scott Feldman, Jeff Googel, Madeleine Hill, The Harry Walker Agency, Gavin Kaysen, Dusti Kugler, Intuitive Content, David E. Kelley, Fiona Lewis, Rod Mitchell, Heather Morse, Paul Nathanson, Willie Norkin, Diego Oka, Jacques Pépin, JP Samuelson, Martha Stewart, Adam St. Gelais, Matt Tinker, Tom Wiese, Patrick Weiland, and Claudette Zapeda.

Andrew would especially like to acknowledge Noah Zimmern who inspires me every day to be the best I can be and Lisa Visser for whom a lifetime of thanks would never be enough.

Barton would especially like to acknowledge Ladyfish and the kid squids for all the tasting of recipes and feedback.

Finally, our deepest gratitude to the many hands, hearts, and minds that helped us along the way, we thank you for your tireless effort and belief in the power of blue foods to inspire change and build community.

# Universal Conversion Chart

| OVEN TEMPERATURE EQUIVALENTS |
|:---:|
| 250°F = 120°C |
| 275°F = 135°C |
| 300°F = 150°C |
| 325°F = 160°C |
| 350°F = 180°C |
| 375°F = 190°C |
| 400°F = 200°C |
| 425°F = 220°C |
| 450°F = 230°C |
| 475°F = 240°C |
| 500°F = 260°C |

**MEASUREMENT EQUIVALENTS**

Measurements should always be level unless directed otherwise.

| |
|:---:|
| $\frac{1}{8}$ teaspoon = 0.5 mL |
| $\frac{1}{4}$ teaspoon = 1 mL |
| $\frac{1}{2}$ teaspoon = 2 mL |
| 1 teaspoon = 5 mL |
| 1 tablespoon = 3 teaspoons = $\frac{1}{2}$ fluid ounce = 15 mL |
| 2 tablespoons = $\frac{1}{8}$ cup = 1 fluid ounce = 30 mL |
| 4 tablespoons = $\frac{1}{4}$ cup = 2 fluid ounces = 60 mL |
| $5\frac{1}{3}$ tablespoons = $\frac{1}{3}$ cup = 3 fluid ounces = 80 mL |
| 8 tablespoons = $\frac{1}{2}$ cup = 4 fluid ounces = 120 mL |
| $10\frac{2}{3}$ tablespoons = $\frac{2}{3}$ cup = 5 fluid ounces = 160 mL |
| 12 tablespoons = $\frac{3}{4}$ cup = 6 fluid ounces = 180 mL |
| 16 tablespoons = 1 cup = 8 fluid ounces = 240 mL |

# Index

Note: Page references in *italics* indicate photographs.